Fire AT MY Feet

A LIFETIME FIGHTING WILDFIRE IN OREGON FORESTS

CLAY DICKERSON

FIRE AT MY FEET
A LIFETIME FIGHTING WILDFIRE IN OREGON FORESTS

iUniverse books may be ordered through booksellers or by contacting:

iUniverse
1663 Liberty Drive
Bloomington, IN 47403
www.iuniverse.com
1-800-Authors (1-800-288-4677)

The views expressed in this work are solely those of the author and do not necessarily reflect the views of the publisher, and the publisher hereby disclaims any responsibility for them.

Because of the dynamic nature of the Internet, any web addresses or links contained in this book may have changed since publication and may no longer be valid. The views expressed in this work are solely those of the author and do not necessarily reflect the views of the publisher, and the publisher hereby disclaims any responsibility for them.

Any people depicted in stock imagery provided by Getty Images are models, and such images are being used for illustrative purposes only.
Certain stock imagery © Getty Images.

ISBN: 978-1-5320-6335-0 (sc)
ISBN: 978-1-5320-6336-7 (e)

Library of Congress Control Number: 2018914692

Print information available on the last page.

iUniverse rev. date: 12/28/2018

Fire

Feet

PART ONE

Learning Years in the Southwest

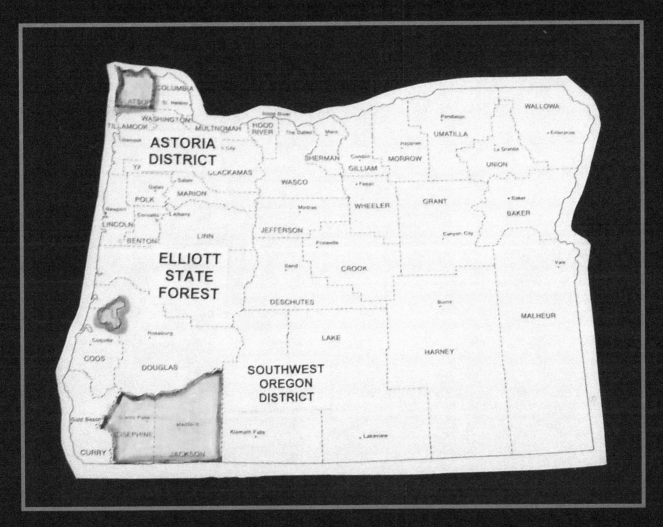

This map of Oregon shows the Department of Forestry Southwestern District located primarily in Jackson and Josephine Counties on the southern border of the state.

The Astoria Unit with responsibility for Clatsop State Forest, is located in Clatsop County at the mouth of the Columbia River at the upper left. The Elliott State Forest, mostly located in the Coos Bay Unit in Coos and western Douglas Counties is immediately below the center-left on the Pacific Coastline.

Map by CC Dickerson

CHAPTER 1

*I*n the rim of mountains and foothills that define the northern edge of the Rogue Valley, there is a promontory that can't be easily missed. Mount Sexton, named for an old pioneer family, seemed to stand guard over my childhood home in Hugo.

Known by local residents as just "Sexton", it stands separate and proud.

The mountain overlooks the rolling hills, canyons and random flat spaces spread at its base. Little did I know that this mountain would one day provide a vital guiding suggestion at a time when I couldn't find an answer. That gentle nudge it gave me would influence my entire life.

Mount Sexton as seen from the author's family hay-field. Barn is barely visible and house is behind trees on hill in center.

Photo courtesy of CC Dickerson

BEFORE THERE WAS A STORY

An idyllic childhood was spent playing, working at all kinds of farm type-chores, and generally enjoying my young life in a wide-open way. My family lived on a modest sized farm where an ever-watchful mountain rose up behind our house. Mt. Sexton was akin to the big brother that I didn't have, seeming to watch over me as I worked and played. It was kind of comforting that it was always there.

Ours wasn't a large farm, but my parents managed to squeeze a living from the ground for many years. I was barely a year old when we moved into the modest house with thick porch columns. It sat on a knoll, giving a mistaken look of wealth. At the base of the driveway, a hard-used barn partially blocked the wide view of a lush hay-field over twenty acres in size. The flatland was a well-watered alluvial space, created when two seasonal creeks ran nearly parallel; one on the eastside and the second to the west.

Altogether, we owned somewhere around ninety-five acres. Except for the hay-field, most of the property was less productive grassland, a couple of deteriorating orchards and overgrown brushy woods. With my younger brother and sister, I spent a lot of time learning every secret about that property.

When I was old enough to be of use, I became my dad's side-kick. We built and repaired fences, planted and harvested hay, worked and milked cows, cleaned the barn, cared for and trained horses, gardened, and took on just about every other supporting job to keep our family housed and fed.

In the spring of 1962, my June graduation from Grants Pass High School was beginning to loom over my future. Only a few months of summer would follow the graduation ceremony. Then I would be forced to enter and stay forever in the world of adults – a place I really wasn't quite ready to be. A slower transition to being a grown-up was beginning to really appeal to me.

My mom was pushing hard for more schooling. She was just finishing her own education, so figured I should go too. I thought that by going to college, I might be able to postpone for a while, my fate of growing up. The catch was that I would have to scrape together enough cash to pay for tuition.

I had a rather casual attitude toward school. To keep at it for another four years wasn't really appealing. High school was nearly done and I tried to ignore the approach of college in the fall. My thoughts were more inclined toward the seductive desire for car ownership, as with it, would come a level of freedom that I did not yet enjoy. The funding for either a car or school was dependent upon my finding a well-paying summer job.

I'd suffered though some less than satisfactory job situations before. Although no official employment was involved, since the tender age of five or six years I'd worked for my dad doing just about every kind of farm work known to man. At one time I loved being at my dad's side. Over the years I came to realize my efforts there mostly involved a lot of sweat and blisters, and usually included the smelly tang of manure. Also, notable lack of money was attached, making such work even less attractive.

As I grew older, I'd found dubious alternative work away from my dad's farm chores. I'd spent the last few weeks of the two previous summers working the harvest in the hop fields near Grants Pass. This was not your Mickey Mouse kind of work either. Like work at home, it was also very physical and also produced a lot of sweat. There was a paycheck, but I thought it pretty small compared to the total effort I put into earning it. I was a little wary.

Since I didn't really like to think too much about the collegiate possibility, I concentrated on my other goal – a car. To acquire such ownership, I was willing to temporarily sacrifice a level of personal comfort with physically demanding work. Still, I had hopes for a sedate kind of a summer job. Whatever I found would have to pay well. To be blunt, my interest in work was mostly how much money was involved, not so much the kind of job to earn it.

I was a fairly quiet kid who enjoyed a good book or maybe just daydreaming in a comfy chair on a shady porch - my dog at my feet or on my lap. I liked the peace found in the woods, where I enjoyed hunting and being in the company of my own thoughts. That spring I spent a whole lot of time just thinking of a summer job away from my parent's farm, away from my dad's directions, and not too physically hard. The dream job would pay well, of course.

I was not totally dense – around Grants Pass there simply were very few high paying, low effort jobs for a tall skinny farm kid like me. Still, I sought a solution by analyzing every job I could think of, just in case.

I grudgingly went through my daily farm chores on our place near Hugo, enjoying the always-spectacular Oregon springtime under the watchful eye of the big mountain, and thinking deeply all the while.

Since the fields of our family farm lay at the foot of Mount Sexton where an Oregon Department of Forestry (ODF) fire Lookout tower - of sorts - was partly in view, it eventually dawned on me that maybe the best job fulfilling my ideal just might be that of summer Fire Lookout.

This idea brought a halt to my musings.

Perhaps I'd stumbled onto an answer! Lookouts lived in or near the tower. Such a job would take me away from home and from farm chores – at least most of the time. It seemed, in my inexperienced musing, that a Fire Lookout job was important but didn't require any specialized skills. Jobs of importance always paid well - so I thought. I could take my dog and my books, maybe even my rifle!

My imagination had me sitting in a comfortable well-furnished tower with the valley spread below. (Nothing like the little shack that I knew was atop Sexton.) I would read a chapter in my book at my leisure, pause to mark the page, then take a few moments to carefully scan the skyline for distant telltale smoke. I would efficiently man the radio with vital information.

Isn't fantasy a wonderful thing. I would earn hundreds of dollars and never break a sweat all at the same time. It would be perfect.

The dreamy prospect in my mind looked so positive that I immediately began to track down what was necessary to pursue my vision. Soon I was off to the Employment Office to pick-up an ODF employment application. I completed the form on the spot and turned it in. Just a few days later I received a phone call from ODF asking me to come into town for a job interview. Remarkably all was going according to my plan. I was overwhelmed with wonder and excitement!

With great anticipation I borrowed my dad's car, traveling into Grants Pass for the job interview. I stepped onto the old ODF Compound on 12th Street for the very first time.

ODF Grants Pass Unit office in the 1950's with Lookout Tower.
Courtesy of ODF Fire History Museum

Overall the meeting went very well, but not exactly as I had imagined. The interviewer, who was the Grants Pass Unit Forester, had a hearty persuasive way about him. Sometime during our twenty-minute conversation I suggested that the ideal job for me might be that of Fire Lookout.

He didn't even blink. He glibly stated that ODF hired mostly college girls as Lookouts. Strong and able young guys with a lifetime background of hard farm work - like me - were desperately needed to work on hand line crews or as crewmen on engines patrolling rural sections of the district. Despite my small error, his whole attitude made me feel vaguely heroic just for filling out the application. Then he offered me a full-time summer job at remarkable pay for kids in those days, $198 per month! The norm was around $1 per hour – about 20% less.

Maybe I was taken with his broad compliments and warm smile. His uniform with sleeve patch and brass badge was impressive. I sure didn't have a clear idea exactly what his brief description of the work really meant. He didn't hide anything, but I had completely overlooked the 24/7 work week without any days off, and how the pay was by salary with no overtime (surely a factor when fighting fire), ever earned or paid out. I probably would have figured it all out if I thought it through at length, but the sudden job-offer, with a very good income attached, was kind of a distraction.

On the spot I accepted the proposed three-month job as a woodland firefighter. We shook hands.

Driving home to Hugo, I was exhilarated with a wonderful feeling of achievement. The positive excitement continued for sometime. Okay, the job was going to take some hard work, but I guess I could handle that. I'd been doing hard work long enough. Just one summer of sweat would be well worth it when I brought home my car. Everything else was just what I wanted.

Right?

As I have aged, I have come to grudgingly concede that Fate (or is it Destiny), has a really warped sense of humor when dabbling in people's lives. Or maybe this was just ironic? Whatever was in the works that day, the kid that was me at that time was sucked right in …

…because there is a little bit more to be told about this whole wonderful job opportunity.

My dad was an extraordinarily hard worker. He always worked long hours on our farm every day, and was constantly looking for extra short-term work to supplement the skinny budget that sustained our family. For example, besides the farm, Dad drove a school bus from September until June for many years, adding enough extra income to keep the home fires lit.

In my enthusiasm before and after my job interview, I blabbed too much. Dad was so impressed with the potential and the income I'd bragged about attached to my ODF summer work, that without my knowing, he also applied for a position.

My dad was hired by ODF within days as a Fire Warden. He was assigned to a patrol engine for the rural Merlin/Hugo area. His away-from-town base station was our farm.

Guess who was assigned as the crewman on that engine?

This is how the stage was set for the beginning of my life's journey; a path that continued for nearly four more decades. Time has told the story that this new summer job was about to become a very important and positive turning point in my life. My Dad's role in this foundation was important.

Oh yeah. I did earn enough to buy a car. In the fall I sold my last motorcycle, a 1954 Harley twin that was a piece of junk. I took a 1950 Olds sedan in trade, which I also sold soon after. Then I bought a '55 Plymouth Savoy. As teen cars go, it wasn't great, but at least I had nowhere to go but up.

CHAPTER 2

My professional career for most of the next forty years, was nearly all as an employee of the **Oregon Department of Forestry.** I began my lifework at age seventeen as crew on a fire patrol rig north of Grants Pass, Oregon, assigned to the rural Merlin/Hugo area where I grew up.

I retired in 1999 from ODF as the Southwest Oregon District Management Unit Forester. As such I was responsible for all forest management actions on state-controlled lands in the district. I'd held that position for almost twenty-five years.

To successfully perform the work required in that role, both a formal education plus extensive experience in all facets of the job were necessary. I met these requirements by earning a degree in Forestry (OSU '67), and spending nine years directing reforestation and other forest management activities for the Clatsop and the Elliott State Forests in ODF districts located in the Oregon Coastal Range.

Summertime wildland fire fighting was always a big part of my job throughout those many years. I worked in-district, and was also sent all over the state of Oregon, plus making several excursions into northern California and southeastern Washington.

DRESSING THE PART

I began what became a lifetime career with the Oregon Department of Forestry (ODF) in June of 1962. I was assigned as a crewman on a fire patrol engine, and my dad was the newly hired Merlin/Hugo Fire Warden (AKA Fire Officer) driving that engine and acting as my immediate supervisor.

Before that initial ODF job, I'd spent my entire youth until then doing essentially farm work, mostly for my dad. Over fifty years have passed since, and I still find it hugely ironic that I put so much effort that first spring, trying to find some way to avoid working for my dad any more. It came to be, that it was my great good fortune to have Dad at my side that first summer.

I was seventeen, with about four weeks to go until my 18th birthday. My dad was a healthy sixty-one, still very strong and vigorous. Our workdays when on fire patrol, usually were out on the road, but our base away from the in-town ODF Headquarters (HQ) was our farm near Hugo.

So much for my escape.

Dad and I entered into employment with ODF as relative equals, both being novices to the wildfire experience. Almost everything was new to me, but Dad had things from his lifetime that had brushed against some of the common needs of the firefighter job.

Our first task was to learn as much as possible about how to fight wildland fire. ODF conveniently provided a very structured two-week Fire School that began our first day when reporting for the season. Similar required annual training is extremely important for all fire personnel, even today. Back then the instructors might be local people or out-of-district staff, all with a lot of fire experience. Sharing that personal knowledge was invaluable, as the written materials were few and mostly of local origin. The subject matter of the training mostly involved use of the equipment and an emphasis on safety procedures. Physical fitness was checked, but not to the standard and completeness of the present.

Today's Fire Schooling is really just basic training, either by private contractor or public agency. Now the written materials are more universal, and have been somewhat standardized by the US Forest Service (USFS). Necessary certification for employment on any private contract or agency crew is often included with the training. The certification is required, and can also be acquired through other educational avenues.

ODF Grants Pass office in 1961 with new main building completed and Lookout Tower removed.
Courtesy of ODF Grants Pass Unit

Fifty some years ago, it was our own responsibility to arrive at work properly outfitted. Firefighting outfits logically had more of a lean toward function than to style. Back then we pretty much copied what loggers wore with some differences. Clothing when fighting fire was and still is very important, as serious injury and even lives can depend on having the proper gear. Uniforms weren't worn much then except for those in supervisory jobs, so differences in dress could be found from one person to another.

There were some basic dress codes for all crew personnel, such as hard hats and high top boots. Crewmen mostly wore loose fitting black Frisco pants held up by suspenders or belt. At our choice, the legs were often pegged (cut off) at boot top to keep flammable cuffs up and away from burning debris. Favored shirts were long sleeved black and white pinstriped - known as Hickories - that buttoned or zipped up the front. The cloth of both pants and shirt were tightly woven heavy cotton, resistant to tears and unlikely to ignite at the touch of a live ember. Hardhat, bandana, canteen and gloves completed the ensemble. The supervising Wardens wore suntan shirt and pants, with the old ODF emblem on the sleeve, a nametag, and if qualified, the badge of a Forest Officer.

When Dad and I began, outfits and uniforms were purchased by the individual firefighter mostly from Penney's and the local logger's supply store. At that time, the familiar treated fire-resistant yellow shirts and green cargo pants of today were not yet available. Now line crews carry additional safety equipment and a few personal items in a backpack also designed to attach various tools. We had no pack and most tools were simply carried in our hands. Everything else, plus our lunches, was stowed in our vehicle. Sometimes a snack, like an apple, was stuffed into a pocket.

Wildland firefighters literally walk through flames, so foot protection was and still is most important. Heavy leather boots that lace to at least an eight-inch top encase every foot. Boot soles were usually of treated rough tread for traction and durability. Thick woolen sox gave padding and insulation, plus the added bonus of absorbing a lot of sweat. Many guys wore two pair at a time. I preferred a longer over-the-calf style to discourage crawling bugs.

Quality hard-hats have been part of the costume for all of my years on fire lines. My first hard hat was issued by ODF and returned at the end of summer. The aluminum hat was painted fire-engine red with a full brim all the way around. I see this style still in use nowadays.

I was required to have my own hard hat when I later enrolled in the OSU School of Forestry, so bought one from the Corvallis Logging Supply in the fall of 1964. It was very heavy-duty aluminum, but with just a front bill, a more common modern style. With use, our hard-hats tended to become kind of personal. Once I owned my hat, I painted it a deep candy-apple red and used that hat through school and at work for many years. ODF issued a new, rigid plastic hard hat to me about twenty years later. It's an improved model for more safety. That newest hard hat has one of the revised versions of the ODF emblem on the front, and my name and personal call number on the back. It is white in color, indicating Overhead staff. My older, once flashy, now dinged up and scratched billed hard hat is safely stored in my closet alongside my last official, now retired ODF issued white hard hat. I still grab one or the other when I do heavier outdoor work where head protection is needed.

In 1962 all the new clothing we bought was pretty expensive, especially the boots. I knew kids who may have otherwise quit after the discomforts of their first fire, but then decided to stick out the whole fire season to simply justify and make up the initial cost of the outfit.

Dressing for my first day of Fire School, I discovered that I liked the way I looked in my new fire clothes. The raised heels of my boots lifted my height to well over 6 '4" (several inches taller than my dad), and the bulky clothing filled out my bony frame. The image reflected in the full-length mirror hanging in the hall at home looked a lot like a man.

The new job promised an unfolding chapter of my life that seemed exciting in my mind. I never dreamed the adventure would be my life!

My initial Fire School seemed pretty dry and dull for the first several days. As if sensing my disappointment, about half way through the closing second week, almost everyone in attendance was startled when the big electronic fire bell attached to the ODF Unit Main Office-building loudly rang out. It was a real fire!

This first fire incident was somewhere around the City of Rogue River – a perennial hot spot. We newbies had only general training at that point, but we were put on the line. We got to learn the finer points of digging hand trail through doing the real thing. Flames were nearby. It was exciting but I didn't feel it was very dangerous, as a good share of those working with us (probably a full third), were returning personnel from previous summers. For sure, the hands-on lessons on that day were not boring and also well learned.

The presence of all that experience on the line was very important, steadying the workers. Pointers were quietly given by the fellows calmly working close-by, as the kind of scary flames were just a few feet away.

CHAPTER 3

*T*ools in use for wildland firefighting in western Oregon are mostly specific to the job. For those who work on the fire line, pretty much the simplest hand tools haven't changed much for about seventy to eighty years. Larger, mechanized equipment is continually modernized and improved.

Patrol engines with slide-in or built-in tanks, specialized aircraft, and bulldozers are all very important. But crews of young people using smaller power saws and only hand tools, along with a huge expenditure in human effort, do most of the work.

A SLOW START

In the summer of 1962 the two-week ODF Fire School was finished well before July arrived. The on-going daily engine patrols then began in the district, with a regular workday for the fire crews being 9 AM to about 6 PM.

Dad and I usually carried a large lunch with us on patrol every day even if we intended to arrive home at about mealtime. We never knew when we would be called to back-up an adjoining patrol area or be kept out past the end of our shift. When mealtimes came while we were away from home but not actively assigned, we'd find a shady spot on a back road, break out the sandwiches my mom packed each morning and enjoy a leisurely picnic. If we were at home we couldn't get too involved in any project because we were required to be ready for a call at a moment's notice.

My dad, the Merlin Area Fire Warden testing the patrol engine pumping equipment at our Hugo farm in 1962.
Photo courtesy of CC Dickerson

My anticipation of an exciting summer began to fade as the beginning days of the season were filled with checking burn barrels and writing permits. The routine grew to be boring and sometimes led to a little extra work, at least for me. There were times when an inspection of a barrel site would find a situation that was not safe. The most common example was dry grass or other vegetation too close to the barrel. Normally Dad would tell applicants that they must clear the ground back ten feet down to bare mineral soil, before a permit could be issued.

There were times when the people would do the work immediately as we waited. Others would postpone the work until later and would call to have us come back again for a final inspection.

A third situation also occurred more frequently than I liked. The applicant would be a frail elderly neighbor, unable to do the necessary work. They might ask who might be hired to clear the space. Although we weren't supposed to do this, my dad would instruct me to spend several minutes in practicing the use of a Hazel hoe or Pulaski to clear the area of any vegetation.

Unless the day was warm I didn't mind this chore too much. Soon enough though, the summer heat rose. That meant I'd quickly work up a good sweat clearing the space. My dad would remain clean and cool while I got to spend an entire tour sitting around in dirty, sweaty clothes. From far in the future I look back and recognize what my dad was doing, using these opportunities to build strength and stamina in his crewman/son. At the time it seemed kind of unfair to me.

At the start of the fire season there was so much free time on patrol that I almost felt embarrassed. On the other hand, for the first time in my life I was given a lot of empty time to share man-to-man conversation with my dad. These unexpected discussions were a surprise that I've come to appreciate more as the years have passed.

The author and his dad with 1954 Dodge Power Wagon equipped with a 240-gallon slip-in tank, gas powered pump and hand-controlled hose reel.
Photo courtesy of CC Dickerson

However, our job was to fight fire – and we did. A couple of small escaped debris burns gave us important familiarity with the tools and equipment for when it would be urgent. A lifetime of experience working at my dad's side let me almost read his mind before he barked out procedural orders. We were a pretty good team.

Then, a fire incident early in the summer occurred near Hugo almost in our back yard. My Dad and I were on patrol a few miles from home when we got a fire call on our radio. The fire was reported on the north side of Three Pines Road where we lived. The address was about ¾ mile from our farm.

As we drove the familiar route toward home, the stated location worried us considerably. A chilling clutch of fear grabbed at us as we drove the familiar quiet roads toward home. The smear of smoke in the sky was ominous.

No one in our neighborhood had more than very small grassy green spaces around our homes. The natural fuels on hillsides around the whole valley were beginning to be very dangerous, approaching tinder dry. In our neighborhood, there were big patches of explosive buck brush, large and small fields of uncut dry native grasses, and too many places where thick, dry leaves and other natural debris lay beneath oak, madrone, and pine trees.

Within minutes we arrived at the scene to find a small grass fire racing up a modest hill, moving north away from the paved road. We could see immediately that this speedy grass fire was beyond the ability of just one engine crew to corral it. Dad called HQ Dispatch about the need for more help.

Meanwhile the fire was moving very fast. Fortunately, it was between houses and passing by every structure. From the first, it was a scramble trying to protect the houses each with a different access point from the road. We were contending with gates and fences and working around patches of manzanita and buck brush too thick to easily get through while on foot with the hose from our engine.

At my dad's instruction, I left the truck taking a shovel in a "run and fight" operation. He drove ahead from house to house, warning occupants as I struggled through or over fences and around brushy spots, heading the flames as I could. Despite my efforts, I only slightly slowed the fire.

The grass/brush fire continued moving up over the top of the low hill. It was heading toward a small vineyard with more scattered houses beyond. Templin Avenue was one of two dead-end access roads to a large wild area to the northwest of our farm.

The fire was nearing the end of Templin Avenue and showing impressive flame length. Then it entered into a tangled stand of dense madrone and pine. The heavier fuels immediately slowed it down. The sound of it changed from a snapping hiss to louder and scarier pops and crackles as it climbed the sap filled ladder fuels.

It seemed longer but in only about fifteen minutes, additional help began to arrive. Our reinforcements included a couple of ODF engines, the Hotshot hand trail crew from HQ and a dozer. Dad had rustled up several local residents who were now armed with shovels, soaking-wet gunnysacks or whatever else they could lay hands to.

Attack came from every side. In the midst of all this activity we even got an assist from a retardant bomber out of Medford. The airplane made a pass over the main body of the blaze, dropping bright pinkish-orange slimy retardant, slowing the fire's spread. The GP Rural Fire Department (RFD) also was notified because of the houses, and sent out an ancient tanker truck with no muffler. We could hear its approach five minutes before arrival.

As the combined forces began to contain the bigger section of the fire, there was a radio call to watch for smaller spot fires starting in the grassy vineyard on the northeast side at the very end of Templin. Dad and I had rejoined one another and moved our engine ahead of the fire in that direction.

A good family friend owned the vineyard, and my Mom with my younger brother (age 14) and sister (age 12) were there to help as they could. A very brief impromptu family reunion took place near the neighbor's fence. Together we witnessed the GP RFD vehicle with roaring engine come up Templin. The red lights blinked and the siren blared as the RFD rig arrived, acting ready to face the fire menace.

Just as the RFD volunteers burst from their truck looking every direction for any flare-up, my younger brother, his wet gunnysack in hand, strolled to the single three-foot diameter spot fire. He casually dropped his wet sack and with a couple of healthy stomps, put out the flames.

There were no structures nearby and no other evidence of fire anywhere. The poor RFD guys just stood there unsure what they should be doing. In a way, I felt a little sorry for them.

The final size on the Three Pines Fire was about seventy-five acres, but not much damage was done. No homes or other buildings were lost.

An investigation revealed later that the cause of the fire was the fault of a neighbor lady. She had cleaned out her woodstove or fireplace that morning, then carried the warm ashes in a metal bucket down to the end of her driveway. She dumped the still warm stove debris in the dry runoff ditch next to a wooden driveway culvert. It was clearly an invitation for the fire debris to ignite the poorly designed culvert into burning.

Now that the fire was pretty well out, Dad and I had a regular, twice a shift job for several days. After initial containment and mop up of the fire was done, it was our job to make twice daily trips through the burned over area looking for and extinguishing any smokes that cropped up. There were several. Our diligence with the standard post-fire mop-up continued until no more smokes were found for two full days.

CHAPTER 4

Today, residents of Josephine County are familiar with the ODF Grants Pass Unit Headquarters location near the I-5 Exit 61 on the old Highway 99. The road has been renamed Monument Drive – a main artery in the North Valley area.

The original ODF compound was on a hillside overlooking Grants Pass. It was moved from town during the winter of 1979. The office was reopened to the public in early January, 1980. I know because I was working there when the staff first helped design and construct all the new buildings, then hauled everything from Grants Pass ourselves.

When I first began as a summer employee in 1962, the original compound was still located on 12th Street in Grants Pass. It was in an inappropriate residential neighborhood that had grown up around the compound on the mostly empty hillside. Many of the old buildings are still there, but re-purposed as single-family homes. Several very large conifer trees are still there to mark the spot.

LIFE AT HEADQUARTERS

That first summer the Merlin/Hugo patrol engine was a state-owned 1954 Dodge Power Wagon. It was four-wheel drive, painted red with black fenders and had a slide-in water tank. This was a lot of truck and out-shined the clunkers we had on our farm. It was kind of slow but would go most anywhere my dad pointed the front end. During fire season this rig was kept at our place in Hugo at night. Some of our workdays began at the 12th Street HQ Compound in Grants Pass. On those days we drove the ten miles into town.

There was a two-way radio built into the dashboard of the truck, plus a portable, or peanut radio that could be hand-carried or attached on a belt over the shoulder when we left the truck. At first Dad and I were intent on listening to all the radio calls. Required roll call from HQ Dispatch was periodically done and helped us practice correct radio protocol. Soon we were used to the speaker traffic and were able to pick out our engine call number - 224, or 424 for the hand-held - even with the volume turned low and while in conversation.

Usually patrol was a quiet time in the truck. We planned long loops out country roads that took us into the district, then brought us back home a couple of times during the day. If something came up where we made use of the equipment, we would take a few extra minutes to be sure our engine's water tank was full and everything back to readiness before leaving again.

That was the last summer the nine-man Hotshot Crew plus two additional engine crews bunked out at HQ. They lived and took meals at the Compound Crew House. With no days off, the place was always lively.

There were two cooks on the payroll also living at the HQ in a small cabin next to the Crew House. They produced three very nourishing and delicious meals a day for those people based there. When there were crews coming in from late fires or held on standby at HQ, they were also given meals along with the approximately 14 regular Crew House residents. I always enjoyed the chance to eat at the Crew House because the food was great and there was always plenty of it. Later when the Crew House kitchen was closed down, crews out late received vouchers to eat at various restaurants around town. My favorite was the Rogue Food Shop on H Street next door to the Rogue Theater.

*Crew House at GP HQ 1962 housed and fed two patrol engine crews and the 9-man
Hotshot crew during summer months. This practice was discontinued in 1963.*
Courtesy of ODF Grants Pass Unit

With any group of young men predominantly in their late teens and early 20's there will be a lot of competitiveness and even more horseplay. Work schedules were usually 8 hours per day (unless there was an incident which could stretch the day until the following morning) and 7 days per week. The long hours could become really dull waiting at the compound for a fire call out, as some engines did. Any change of pace was welcomed. With our base away from the HQ, I missed some of the camaraderie and shenanigans that happened once in awhile at the main office.

Downtime at HQ did not include any lying around - ever. There were chores and a lot of them. The most common work for crews around the compound involved keeping machines and equipment in complete readiness. Sharpening and repairing tools were always an assigned downtime activity.

Newer light engine with power hose reel about 1968. Similar engines provided the primary initial attack on fires.
Courtesy of ODF Grants Pass Unit

The compound buildings always needed care and maintenance both inside and out. All the remote out-lying ODF buildings and Lookout towers also needed regular paint and repair. A really basic thing like delivery of 5-gallon jugs of drinking water to a dry lookout was eagerly embraced when it showed up on the assignment list. It provided a welcome distraction of a trip out of town for one crew or another.

Early that season and the next two years following, fire personnel went into the woods and cut cedar shake bolts, hauled them back to HQ, split shakes and re-roofed the warehouse, the pump house and a few out-laying guard stations. Another common job was simple firewood production. There were several buildings used year-round that made use of a wood-burning furnace during the winter months. Truckloads of firewood were cut, delivered and stacked at out-laying sites to heat these buildings. Most of this work was done by hand, as power tool use had summer restrictions. Very few ODF jobs would be considered as anything but physically challenging.

There was a basketball backboard and hoop mounted on one of the shop buildings, but it suffered a lonely life during working hours. Crews worked, they didn't play games. Besides, the heavy boots everybody was wearing really messed up basketball footwork.

As the fire season progressed, crews were called out to fires more and more often, infringing on chores and maintenance activities. I recall the painting of HQ buildings that was abruptly interrupted several times at the sound of the fire bell. Painting tools were left as they lay when engines were immediately manned. Brushes were left filled with paint, as no one could take the time for cleaning when the bell rang out.

The Fire Bell was electrically operated and mounted on the side of the HQ building. Like the hard hats, it was also painted bright red. When it was activated for a call, everyone including, I'm sure, many nearby residents living several blocks away could not miss it. That bell was loud enough to wake the dead!

The least popular of all chores at HQ was keeping the 12th St. compound grounds neat and tidy. I cannot think of any of the younger guys that enjoyed the compound gardening tasks. With the crews feeling about the landscaping jobs the way they did, when discipline was needed, yard maintenance and painting chores became the very top priority to the boss-man in charge. He seemed to know that the landscape work was the most despised by the young crewmen. Excellent insight by that man.

ODF Grants Pass Unit Forester 1962 – John Langrell
Courtesy of ODF Grants Pass Unit

Try as they did, those in supervisory jobs weren't always on top of finding useful tasks to keep all that concentrated youthful energy under control. Sometimes the never-ending washing of trucks and filling of water tanks turned into spectacular unplanned water fights. The soapy tank water, intended to better smother flames - especially on oily fuels like manzanita and scotch broom - compounded water fight fun. The soap added an interesting dimension beyond simply wetting down one's foe. The more vigorous the water-fight, the more suds created. I recall mountains of soapy foam engulfing strapping young fellows…sometimes swallowing whole trucks as well. The Assistant Unit Forester in charge was not pleased when these accidents happened. He knew how to deal with the unwieldy participants.

If Dad and I happened to be in town when a water fight broke out, my dad would not permit me to become much involved in such frivolous activities. A mixed blessing – on hot days I missed out on being cooled to the skin, but I also avoided the dreaded punishment of "tidy the compound".

When that hated command came from the headman to those in trouble, the young crewmen learned that it meant removing every bit of wayward grass or trash from the landscaped and graveled areas—no matter how minute the offending individual piece. Lawns came to resemble putting greens, at times with edges trimmed with scissors. Every square inch of space was thoroughly raked until sufficiently pleasing to the headman's taste—even the graveled driveways. A few misplaced bits of gravel could lead to an entire area being groomed a second time. Everything was raked, inspected and re-raked until there were times the compound grounds closely resembled a classic Japanese garden, with carefully tended grass and gravel in neatly even grooves throughout. Even so, the water fights still broke out when the weather was hot.

My lack of participation in the horseplay (albeit at my dad's command) seemed to earn a reputation for me as a serious young man and worker that I probably didn't deserve at that point. Another positive check for Dad.

All personnel were paid only once per month. July 1st was the first payday each summer. On that day all the seasonal crewmen on the local ODF payroll learned of a wage increase up to $222 per month. With my limited farm-boy experience the amount was a small fortune.

The big boss allowed all the crewmen to take staggered times away from HQ to go down town to their bank and cash paychecks. For many of the younger guys this was their first paycheck - ever. I recall that one of the Hotshot crewmen asked the bank teller for all of his pay in $1 bills. It made an impressive bankroll as big as my fist!

As for myself, being under the watchful eyes of my dad, most of my pay went straight into a savings account. Oh well. In Hugo opportunities to spend money were limited to a couple of tiny gas stations that also sold an occasional stale candy bar. My job sure didn't include any extra days off to travel into Grants Pass for a spending spree, so every pay-day my savings balance grew. Withdrawals were few and far between.

CHAPTER 5

*F*ire behavior is based on science. By theory it should be fairly predictable. Science has been able to replicate structure fires with some accuracy, but wildland fires defy similar attempts. Even the most knowledgeable and experienced wildland fire veteran is occasionally startled by the varied ways of wildland fires.

The best way to approach wildland fire fighting, is to always expect the worst, but stay observant and be ever-ready so advantage can be taken if a positive opportunity shows up. On the fire line, diligent monitoring is vital. In addition, both caution and aggression are good traits to possess, along with the experience, the ability and the intelligence to choose the right emphasis at the right time.

The reason it is so hard to out-guess what a particular wildland fire will do is because of the huge list of variables that are in the mix with every situation. The three basic elements that sustain any fire are Air, Heat, and Fuel. In the natural, outdoor environment, each of these can fluctuate between positive and negative on a very broad scale. They also each interact with the other two elements to create other long lists. The combinations are almost endless.

This is especially true with fires in southwestern Oregon. Diversity in all things is the norm in that area — especially with fuels and weather. In SWO the multitude of different geographies and really unique atmospheric weather twists caused by odd mountain placement, plus a huge array of plant types (fuel), give every fire unique and very dangerous possibilities,

FROM NOVICE TO VETERAN

The weather in 1962 got hotter and fuels got dryer. It was inevitable that a bigger fire would hit the district eventually. It finally came mid-afternoon on a hot day, I think in late July (though maybe early August).

Dad and I were out patrolling our assigned district. At first, the radio call we received seemed to be another stand-by and back-up directive. Dad began to move the engine to the indicated location, a turnout on Highland Avenue immediately next to the I-5 overpass on Merlin Hill. We'd had a few smaller fires and except for the Three Pines Fire, as yet there had been nothing of much consequence.

Before we arrived at the stand-by location another radio call came. Our engine went to active status. We were coming up the north side of Merlin Hill on Highland Avenue when we heard the change. Over the hilltop to Morgan Lane at the far north end of town, then turn left to access the wilder section of Granite Hill Road. From there we had to refer to a map to find our way to the place directed by Dispatch.

There wasn't too much smoke yet. Later in the day it billowed above our heads, turning the bright clear sky to an ugly color of jaundice. We were now traveling on the southside of the hill, and our engine was notified by the radio to turn left off Granite Hill Road onto a narrow, graveled road with no name. This rough track became thinner and more overgrown the farther uphill we drove. It was gouged with ruts and potholes making for a bumpy ride. It had been dug out of the steep east by southeast face of Merlin Hill, on the side away from town.

Our instructions said find a certain ravine, secure the engine if necessary, and to use water from our tank to stop any fire from moving uphill in the indicated gully. We found the designated place and began following the orders.

As we worked, a Grants Pass Rural Fire Department (GP RFD) tank truck came wheezing up the road and stopped a bit behind us on a curve. The hillside was very abrupt at that site. There would be no passing the RFD truck until its driver moved it.

The RFD people were supposed to respond only to rural subscribers' structure fires, so we were a bit confused as to why one of their rigs appeared. At first Dad and I thought maybe the RFD had picked up our radio instructions, as they sometimes did, and had come to offer help.

As we went about our required preparations, the people in the RFD tanker didn't really seem interested in us at all. The two occupants of the tanker didn't approach or even wave at us. Maybe they were looking for high ground to check out the fire, or to find a place to turn-around their lumbering tanker? We noticed when the two men left their truck parked. They began to climb the steep bank above, toward what looked to be maybe a house or other structure far up the hillside almost hidden in the tangled brush. Dad told me it was their business and we had ours.

Going about our directed work, soon we had the ravine pretty well soaked down. We thought the completely soggy ground and brush would be a sufficient barrier to an approaching fire, or at least would slow it down.

We were wrong.

There was no warning. We were at the ready, but in spite of our best efforts to stop it, an astonishing wall of fast-moving flames swept up that gully with a loud and deep-throated WHOOSH! I felt a blast of heat as the fire arched over our heads and continued on its destructive path up the hill.

I was stunned by how fast the fire passed over us...and I was sure glad to be with my dad, because the experience scared the holy horse-feathers out of me!

An explosive wildfire crossing a roadway in southwestern Oregon.
Courtesy of ODF Grants Pass Unit

This may have been the most dangerous event in my life up to that time. I was embarrassed to find a bit of a tremble in my hands and my breathing ramped up to almost gasping. My Dad was all business. He took a quick assessment of my condition and of his own. Although both of us were a little singed around the edges, mostly we were just fine.

Our rig also appeared untouched. Then my dad, true to form, calmly directed me to continue to wet down the still warm and smoking embers on the blackened ground that now surrounded our tiny island of safety. He called in our status and the current status of the fire to Dispatch.

The distant RFD tanker was still parked out beyond the blackened path of the fire. The two crewmen returned from their wanderings sometime around then. They climbed into their truck without so much as a glance, whoop or holler in our direction. The noisy rig backed out of sight around the curve—it was as if they had never been there. How strange?

The RFD tank truck leaving was a help because the immediate dispatch instructions responding to Dad's call directed us to quickly go to a new location. There was a small delay, as in our inexperience we had used the hard hose from the reel for our job and had to take a few extra minutes to wind it all back in. (Cloth hose can be wadded up and shoved into the truck bed or even dropped off in an emergency. Hand–reel hose was attached.) The simple chore gave me a few minutes to calm down too.

Once the reel-in was complete, and since the RFD was no longer blocking the road, we jumped into our engine and took a hurried drive back out toward Highland Avenue as told.

The increasing radio traffic we were now hearing indicated that many other patrol engine crews were being called to work on this fire. It was spreading fast toward the out-laying residential parts of northwest Grants Pass. Our next responsibility was near the intersection of Highland and Vine Street west of the I-5 freeway. Burning debris carried on the afternoon breeze had ignited spot fires on the narrow land strip between the two roadways, but I-5 remained open. It was feared that the small blazes of grass and scattered brush on the west side of the freeway would burn together and become big enough to also cross Highland Avenue. That would threaten the few houses then in that neighborhood.

An arm of the main fire had already crossed Highland Avenue farther up the hill. It had burned about 1/10th acre on the west side of I-5 before being smothered by another engine crew. We worked for some time in our newly assigned area, dousing the mini-fires. It was nearly dark when we were able to report our success back to headquarters.

No crews were released in spite of the late hour. Our engine was moved once more, back across the freeway to the east. We were in the vicinity where we had been over-run by the fire earlier. A long night had just begun for us.

The rest of that extended shift was spent working on the very steep ground on the backside of Merlin Hill. Mostly we were near the fire, in direct attack with hand tools in tow, away from our engine. The Merlin Hill fire eventually grew to 400 +/- acres. It was my first large, over-night fire.

For most of the rest of that night we were assigned as hand support for a TD 14 dozer that was building trail on the fire's eastern flank until dawn.

Hours passed. As fatigue set in, my ability to track what was happening with the fire faded away. Many years of fire experience since then brings certain memories to mind, all running together, similar but different. There is always the fatigue – arms and shoulders that tire and become muscle sore. Heavy and clumsy feeling, somehow things keep moving. Legs that go numb, except when cramps clamp up the back of calves and thighs—bringing groaning pain. The soles of your feet burn, less from the heat, more from the weariness. To be permitted to just sit down for a few minutes is a genuine treat.

There always seems to be climbing, first up and down and then across an endless hillside. There is a rank stink of smoke and the sting of hot ash on sweaty forehead and cheeks. I recall the complete deliciousness of gulping water running down from my mouth, wetting my neck, soaking my shirtfront, soothing my dry smoky throat. Teeth feel gritty, as if chewing sand. The most wonderful sensation is pulling off boots and sox, feeling cool air and wiggling toes. This small comfort is best left until after being released from the line, as feet swell quickly and don't easily fit back into boots.

Sometimes fighting fire in the very early hours of a coming day brings an odd mix of sensations. Sweat from hard work would run down my face at the same time that a bit of a night-time breeze would chill the sweat running down my back, causing a shiver of cold at the same moment. Another strong memory was feeling so hungry that I felt close to throwing up, then realizing hours later with no breaks and still working, that I didn't feel hungry anymore.

I think on that night of the Merlin Hill fire, once in a while there were short rest periods when we just sat or lay in the dirt on the freshly built cat-trail, maybe five minutes here and there. The newly turned dirt usually feels cool at night and sometimes even soft. I could have gladly slept if allowed. Instead slowly I would have stood and returned to swinging shovels full of dirt to reinforce the line, over and over and over and over.

05/02/2006 7:05 pm

ODF dozer building line as it attacks a fire. Dozers are effective wildfire equipment on moderate slopes. Many parts of the SWO landscape is too steep for safe dozer use building fire line.

Courtesy of ODF Grants Pass Unit

The rhythm was important. It was a distraction from the sore back muscles and stiff legs, shoulders and arms. Sometimes I'd recite poems or the lyrics to some song in sync. It helped make the hours pass.

I recall the dozer we were assigned to, at one point having to carve a full road out of a very steep hillside to lay that trail. It was a slow and very dangerous process, putting the dozer at a precarious angle on the hillside. After much work, the attempt was successful.

My dad and I acted as support crew for the cat-skinner for several hours. This is called swamping. We cleared brush and smaller trees from the dozer blade again and again. It was our first experience at this, so we learned new techniques and safety practices when on the ground working at the dozer operator's bidding. After the line was complete, Dad and I watched over it. We hiked back and forth again and again as the flames on that flank of the fire moved to the edge of the exposed soil. Our line held. Many things with that big fire were new to me and sunk into my sub-conscious mixing with later experiences. A lot of that first fire is pretty hazy to me.

When our truck was released near dawn the next morning and we got back home to Hugo, my mom took a photograph of me with filthy clothes and eyes startling white in a blackened face. Just above my eyebrows and under my matted blond hair, my forehead was clean. The band of my hardhat crossed my forehead just there, black below and mostly white above.

Author, just past his 18th birthday after arriving home the morning after his first over-night fire in 1962. Photo courtesy of CC Dickerson

Maybe I don't really remember any of this – maybe I just have that photograph from the first time, and the detailed description from my dad. Maybe all the rest is bits and pieces from many hundreds of other fires over the years all jumbled in my mind together.

I do recall when my head finally rested on my own pillow around 9 AM that morning. I was completely exhausted from untold hours of hard physical labor, no food and no sleep. To lay down felt so wonderful. My mom had insisted I take a quick bath before sleeping. I could have skipped the washing, but the clean sheets would have suffered. Within seconds after the climb into my bed I fell into a dreamless, coma-like sleep of complete weariness.

CHAPTER 6

*R*ecruiting the necessary workforce for summer firefighting is a growing problem. It's hard, dirty work. Many young people seem to be afraid to challenge themselves with physically exacting employment. For those that will, newcomers should only be used on fire-lines when under direct supervision of those with experience. Wildland fire fighting is not a game. Lives can be saved when veterans work side-by-side with rookies.

Killing fires when they are small is, without doubt, the best philosophy of suppression. Quick reaction time and aggressive response to the potential seriousness of every incident is common sense.

Catastrophic fires are too destructive and powerful to knowingly permit them to prevail. Anyone who wants to argue this by trying to justify how a big burn is "historically natural" needs to think in terms of other tragedies of the past, like polio or maybe flu epidemics – all "historically natural". Are fires good for the forest? The answer is "Sometimes". The problem is control. I defy anyone to accurately predict destruction or benefits before a large summer fire occurs. Temperatures at ground-level are at least 600 degrees. Tree sap boils at much cooler levels. Damage will occur. Any wildland fire is predictable only to a certain point. They can grow at an astonishing rate.

Wildland fire, much like time and tides, bow to no man.

INTEREST BECOMES FIXATION

The Merlin/Hugo engine was released from my first big fire not too long after sunrise the second day. Dad drove us straight home. We both took a few minutes to clean up, then we went immediately to bed.

I awoke very late in the hot afternoon groggy, muscle weary and ravenously hungry. While I wolfed down a delayed lunch my mom shared that Dad and I didn't have to report to HQ until the next morning.

I was pretty wiped out, but still realized that this day was somehow different for me. My outlook about fire and my job had changed. There was some kind of emotion inside me that wasn't there before.

First off, I was more than a little disquieted by the total fear that had filled me as that fire arched over Dad and me the previous afternoon. I felt very humbled by having been so thankful for my dad's presence when in danger. I would do better the next time.

Also, I resolved to do my best to never again have another fire catch me by surprise. This wasn't exactly a vow, but not far from it. This affected (positively I think) my personal fire assessment style for the rest of my career.

There was also something else—something strong pushing me. It was a little like anger—or maybe a very cold rage. It was tight, grim and with purpose. It traveled to work with me the next morning, and remained there in the back of my mind for the rest of the summer, the next and every year after. The remaining six to eight weeks of that fire season had the feeling expanding to become almost obsessive.

I had heard the other crewmen talk about Wildland Fire as a kind of monster. I had dismissed this as something childish, but was hard-put to find a better description.

A few of the crewmen I hung around with were openly hesitant and fearful about wildfire, especially when working near the open flames. I discovered this didn't bother me too much. In fact, I was most comfortable when any fire was visible not too far from me.

Many of the guys went on in some length about the many discomforts of the job. Although I was aware of the dirt, the heat and the fatigue, when actively working a fire, these annoyances were easy for me to ignore. The fire held all my attention. Even revisiting in my memories, I have to really concentrate to identify the long list of physical distractions and discomforts.

Within the assortment of young crewmen, there was a very small group, only two or maybe three of us new guys, who were different—who were like me. We found many more like us in the ranks of the older veterans and the supervisors. Maybe we were all just a little bit crazy. This unique group saw the fires differently than all the others. I began to purposely hang around with this older group when our engine was at the HQ Compound.

As that fire season progressed, some small but significant accomplishments on the job brought more self-confidence to me. A word of praise or a slap on the back, by anyone of the older fire vets, while on the job was remembered and even cherished.

Sometimes the fear I'd felt that day of the burn-over returned, but never again so strong and with it always came the cold resolve. The focus on the fire filled my mind and was pushing me hard. The fear was there but evolved into sizable respect. Wildland fire was a foe of note.

With more experience combined with the new clarity, I developed a knack for knowing the fires; the direction they would take and where best to stop them. As I worked the line, my mind was busy comparing and analyzing. The need to defeat each blaze was compellingly strong and growing. The internal push to learn more about fires was something I'd never experienced from any type of work I'd ever done or any school subject I'd ever studied.

*A B-17 WWII vintage bomber drops retardant on a fire. Air attack can be
very effective in slowing fires, but cost is a big negative factor.*
Courtesy of ODF Grants Pass Unit

The district suffered a second larger fire also around 400 acres, that burned late that summer in the hills surrounding the City of Rogue River. By that time, I was infatuated with whatever it took to kill fires. It wasn't just a craving for the thrill of doing something important, though that was part of it. I very much liked being part of a team that was on a mission. But there was so much more. Respecting the potential danger that every fire represented brought a challenge that was very personal. The challenge kindled what had now become a passion.

Boy Oh Boy— was I ever hooked!

I am still very hard pressed to describe what I was experiencing. It was FUN -- but I knew that was not the right word. I ENJOYED solving the problems that killing fires required – but that wasn't the right description either. Excitement, satisfaction, pride in a significant job completed. All the words I tried to explain my feelings didn't fit. All these years later, words still fail to tell it well. Firefighting filled me with something – a purpose - that wasn't there before.

It was not necessary anymore for my dad to insist I avoid the HQ water fights. From the time of the burn-over forward I listened and watched and learned, paying special attention to the words and actions of the veterans of the trade. I sought out their company, picking up insights and bits of wisdom. I listened to their fire stories, asking questions and storing away bits of information for reference and use when on the line. I copied the way they stood and how they worked. I even copied how they laced their boots. I was aware of the extra effort I was making, but not really understanding the motivation.

Sometimes I'd ask questions during mop-up chores following a fire, but much of my gathering of fire lore happened during lunch breaks at the main office. Pinochle games were wedged into the short daily break at lunch. I acquired another skill, playing strategic card games like Pinochle and Cribbage with the older guys … and I was good at that too.

One day the group of the veteran wildland firefighters shared and explained it to me…

They said I had the BUG.

To use a cliché', firefighters who have this obsessive experience like mine know it's something that gets into every cell in your body and becomes a part of who you are. It doesn't afflict everyone on the job, but those that have it know they are a little different. They recognize the trait in others who are also affected. It doesn't mean those who have it are the best or the brightest, but those that are the most skilled, is the group most often affected. They share a fascination for wildland fire that is unique to them.

For many years, the summer call of firefighting came to me, and I eagerly followed that call. It prompted me to keep my body in top condition. It kept me alert when exhaustion tried to shut-down my critical thinking. I suspect the obsession with wildland fire that was now inside me, was a bit like the yearning of some physical addictions. As I aged the intensity of the feeling faded, but it has never really disappeared.

This fixation with wildland fire fighting was the entrance for me into the study of Forest Sciences. My decision to choose a career path in professional Forest Management came out of several discussions I had with the Grants Pass Unit Forester during those beginning summers.

He noted that firefighting is a part of the larger job of a Professional Forester—a stewardship not to be taken lightly. He said forestry would be a career with great personal satisfaction, as it is an honorable vocation of vast responsibility. It would not be a means to acquire wealth, but there would be an opportunity to help create a legacy (a healthy growing forest) of real value, both esthetically and monetarily, for future generations. The work would mostly be physical and out of doors, with mental acuity with flexibility and great patience required just about every day.

Now that I am retired and looking backward, my career gave me all those things he mentioned and much more. Wildland fire fighting was the start. It strongly influenced my career choice and still touches my life and the lives of those around me in some ways almost daily.

I stumbled into Professional Forestry as a career, though it took awhile before I came to realize it actually has been more of a "calling". There are a lot of trees that are growing today in Oregon because my hands put them into the dirt, or held the Pulaski that built the fire line that protected them. I've personally planned and directed successful rehab and reforestation of thousands of Oregon acres. I've taught bits and pieces of Forestry and related subjects to kids and adults. And more. All of it tracks back to that summer job in 1962.

All I had wanted was to get some freedom from what I thought was my dad's control over my life and some extra cash to buy a car. Instead, I hit the Jack Pot. I sincerely believe that fighting wildland fires changed the direction of my life's path. I know that bit-by-bit the job most certainly changed me as a person.

CHAPTER 7

*D*uring my first summer fire season with ODF I developed a fascination with fire behaviors. I tried to learn as much as possible from my more experienced co-workers.

I think I became something of a pest by asking a barrage of questions of anyone I thought might have the knowledge I was seeking. The patrol engine Wardens/Fire Officers and older veteran firefighters, the mid-level supervisors, the District Foresters, and even the dozer operators (a very skookum bunch) all were approached. Near the end of the season it felt good when I was asked if I wanted to return the following June. My answer, of course, was "Yes".

One summer's experience gave me a taste of wildland fire fighting. The work suited me - I wanted more. After two seasons, I began to try out some of the info I'd gathered up. I came to thoroughly live the rule to expect the unexpected.

By my fifth fire summer, others considered me a knowledgeable veteran. At the end of those five years I moved into year-round forestry work that was of a scope that was much wider than just fire suppression. Comprehensive and balanced multiple-use forest management was the new, bigger subject for me. Yet, a part of me knew there remained a huge amount of fire lore I still hadn't mastered. My thirst for more remained.

A LUCKY WINTER - A SECOND SUMMER

Over the winter months a couple of unexpected things developed that were really helpful in my mom's college plans for her eldest child. At the end of the summer, with no action by me, my daily schedule at ODF was altered so I could continue work at the HQ office until the fall rains began.

When the other school-aged crewmen were released, I was moved to a different job — from patrol engine crewman to temporary night Dispatcher. I was only eighteen. The new schedule and duties allowed me to commute to Ashland for college classes on weekdays. My nights were spent at the Grants Pass HQ, sleeping on a relief cot near to the dispatch equipment, with an ear tuned to the two-way radio and telephone.

I reported to work in the afternoon as soon as I could arrive after classes. The dispatcher would relieve me early enough in the morning so I could get to my first class. My evenings were spent manning the office and dispatch upstairs, where I could eat dinner and study while on the job.

The October 1962 Columbus Day Storm shut down the Fire Season, so after the storm, I was unemployed for a few weeks. Then, one of the mid-level supervisors called me around Thanksgiving with another short-term job cutting Christmas trees for the California market. That extra income and with cash from my savings, I paid for another college term.

A month or so later when winter tree planting season began, some of the older fire guys were organized into a tree planting crew and asked me to participate over Christmas Break. Our work was planting a harvested area on state owned land in Upper Windy Creek. (Before I retired that area was commercially thinned, producing smaller mill logs and chips for paper.) This third short-term job again was in the nick of time to pay my bills.

When June 1963 rolled around, I had a year of college paid off and completed. I also had carried around a head full of fire lore all winter and was eager to get back to ODF patrol. Wildland fire still was my fixation.

June of 1963 arrived right on schedule. Much like the year before, I was eager and looking forward to the first day of Fire School. This year, though, I arrived with a more purposeful attitude. Within minutes of the opening I morphed from mostly bored college freshman to rapt attentive student of fire. The desire to know everything I could about wildland firefighting was renewed with intensity!

Most of the information covered at Fire School was review, but seemed fresh and intriguing to me. My understanding from personal experiences the summer before, plus the answers to all my questions stuffed into my brain made just about everything fascinating to me.

Fire School that year was different from the year before. My dad had agreed to the use of about a half-acre of open woodland on our Hugo farm to be used as part of the curriculum. The previous year a fortunately timed actual fire had provided on-the-job training during Fire School. This year space in our middle pasture was well prepared. Surrounded by watchful patrol engines with full water tanks, a practice fire was lit. Crews built hand line to surround the flames with help from and under the direction of veteran fire fighters. Engine crews had opportunity to practice their fire-hose techniques. Methods of mop-up were practiced, both that using water and dry mop as well. It was a kind of homey event, as my mom sent down several cut watermelons as refreshments, delivered from our house by my two younger sibs.

With that essential training done, time seemed to fly backward. It felt like just overnight from the year before. Dad and I were together again in the big Dodge Power Wagon. The second summer was different though, because several work-filled weeks passed before we went into the routine of daily patrol.

The district was a mess. The 1962-63 winter that had started off with the brutal Columbus Day Storm in October, then pretty much followed through with deep snow and lots of Oregon rain. Many of the outlaying ODF buildings necessary to fire protection and some of the permanent communication equipment, especially at higher elevations, had to be put back into working order ASAP.

Fire School filled the first two weeks of the season, but when finished, the strong young muscles that usually maintained the headquarters compound were reassigned. Everybody was spread across the district to get things back into ship-shape condition. There were several roofs that had suffered injury during the winter, with downed trees taking their toll. Some of the Guard Stations had damage that couldn't be postponed even for a short time. The condition of other facilities was a mystery, with access roads blocked. Road clearing was necessary. Everyone had some sort of maintenance job unless a call came from dispatch stating otherwise.

The repeater radio relay tower on King Mountain had somehow suffered a blow about halfway between ground level and the antenna at the top. This vital part of our communication system was located on the high elevation divide between the Rogue / Umpqua river drainages. The tower construction was in several

10-foot lengths that bolted together. Each section was a three- sided welded framework designed to bolt onto similar pieces above and below until the right height was reached. When Fire Season opened instead of a tall straight figure topped with antennas, now the upper half was laying on the ground and completely useless.

Probably because the access road took off in our patrol area from Jump-Off Joe Creek Road, one of the first maintenance chores assigned to our Merlin/Hugo engine was to deliver replacement parts, apply some TLC to the framework and get that vital radio tower into working condition.

It was good that we drove into the HQ compound early, because it took awhile to get all the replacement pieces strapped to our truck. Eventually we set out for the isolated tower site. The access road was a mess, but another smaller rig had gone ahead to make sure the trek was clear. In protected spots there was still some snow across the road, and periodic washouts and potholes made forward progress challenging and rough. Using the truck's front bumper winch to bolster the 4-wheel drive, we overcame the mangled roadway. Progress was slow. We finally arrived at the barren clearing on the headland where the communication tower was situated. There was a strong cold wind to remind us we were at the top of a rather tall mountain and it still wasn't quite summer.

I should admit that I have always been subject to the heebie-jeebies when in high places. Now a mountaintop isn't so much a problem in itself, unless I find myself on the edge of a sheer face. But tall structures, especially those built on TOP of lofty peaks, fit my phobia problem. When assessing that flimsy radio tower, I began to get very uncomfortable. Dismally I concluded that if there was going to be any tower climbing needed, it was probably going to be my job. My 60+ year-old Dad had no business going up a structure like that.

Fortunately, the supervisor for the north side of the unit had driven the other rig to the mountain top. He took matters in hand, with a well-thought-out plan that involved very little climbing. The remaining erect portion of the tower was lowered gently to the ground, one damaged 10-foot section was removed, and then the remaining top piece was reconnected to the bottom section. Almost magically the tower was again raised into place ready to temporarily handle communications again - albeit 10 feet shorter than it had been.

When patrols were renewed, we quickly fell into the old routines. Still the maintenance chores occasionally cropped up, interrupting the rhythm of the ODF patrols. Small early fires were more frequent than the year before too.

We were called to one of these smaller fires near the beginning of the summer that was the result of a lightning bust. The storm had run through the edge of our patrol area generally to the northwest the previous evening. Last night's stand-by designation progressed to a back-up call almost as soon as we came on duty that morning.

The truck was ready, so with no real reason for delay, we were off toward Galice to assist that crew. In route the radio direction was amended to active-assist.

We turned off the Galice Road at Stratton Creek just short of the old Hellgate Bridge over the Rogue. That bridge was badly damaged during the infamous 1964 flood the next winter and later rebuilt a short way upstream.

Stratton Creek Road was unpaved then and always in terrible condition. A very short way downstream from the bridge it allowed access to an undeveloped sandy beach on the river's north bank. This space was popular with adults and older teens for use as a midnight site for beer parties. The roadway's ruts and ditches also led a few more miles to access a handful of summer cabins before it disappeared entirely in the brush and rocks.

The fire we were looking for was across the Rogue River from the Galice Store. Dad and I both knew exactly where we were going; the riverbank at the spot facing the Galice boat ramp rises directly from the river waters for at least fifty feet almost straight up then slightly angling the rest of the way to the top of the canyon's ridge.

The soils there are half exposed rocks with some bare earth between, with fuels that have always been highly flammable - scrub brush and poison oak, a few straggly oaks and the odd hardy but gaunt conifer. From the store it looks more succulent than the reality. Then farther up and away from the river waters the hotter and more barren the landscape gets to be. The south, shadier riverbank is green and moist with big-leaf maples and healthy pines and firs.

We couldn't quite drive all the way into the blaze, as the roadway disappeared. Instead we had to park behind the Galice truck and hike about a quarter mile or so carrying our hand tools. It was mostly flat and not a rough trek above the cut of the canyon to our left. Hand trail wasn't our primary attack method, so a hard-working afternoon was laid out for us, without the benefit of tapping into the water in our tank.

The fire was about a tenth of an acre when we arrived, burning slowly as there wasn't much wind. Being right off the river, the wind would grow stronger as the canyon warmed. It was important to contain the blaze before the wind became an issue. With just Dad and me plus the Galice Warden and his crew boy, it wasn't too big a job. The fire put up a good tussle, but after several hours of hard work, we got it contained.

Like many Josephine County residents, I'd spent my share of hot summer days bucking the riffles on the Rogue. My friends and I had splashed our way through the waters just a stone's throw below using inner tubes to stay afloat. At that time rafts and inflatable canoes weren't too common.

Fire in explosive mixed brush and trees common to lower elevation lands in Southwestern Oregon.
Courtesy of ODF Grants Pass Unit

It was a little weird to stand opposite the store on the edge of that steep hillside looking down and across the river at a place I knew so well. It was so close, but not easily reached from where I stood. There were river-goers about their fun times, cars driving on the opposite road, and customers for the store coming and going. The back deck had not yet been expanded, so unless they'd noticed the smoke, mostly all the folks across the water seemed unaware of the drama on our side of the river.

The death of the fire was a small victory in the larger scheme of things. Galice was a place that I personally valued, with many good memories. Other people likely felt the same. From what I experienced that summer and the one before, that fire had the potential to have grown and to destroy everything up and down that canyon on both sides of the river.

That little fire was brought down and now was gone. The small danger wasn't given a chance to become any larger. My dad and I and the Galice patrol crew were unsung heroes just out doing our jobs. It felt good knowing we'd done well. No other reward was necessary.

That day comes to mind when I happen to be in the Galice area. The little Galice fire was like a quick blink of bright light in the early quiet days of the season. We returned to our regular somewhat boring routine the following morning.

CHAPTER 8

There were eight ODF Lookout towers in the Southwest Oregon District during those years. Some were very old and in need of replacement. Some weren't actual towers at all, sitting firmly on the ground. The goofy Mt. Sexton set-up was unique.

The north part of our Unit included and supervised two of the towers, and the south part covered the remaining two. The individuals assigned to the towers worked on a two-week rotation (ten days on and four days off) using two groups of people to cover all the towers. There may have been a married couple that pulled a shift too. This arrangement gave 24/7 oversight.

The Forest Service also had a few towers scattered about in the ODF protection area. These were also in contact with our unit Dispatch, but the ODF patrol engines only had the ability to use direct radio contact with those Lookouts on state lands.

LOOKOUT TOWERS

A few days after the King Mountain maintenance adventure, I was forced to face my inner vertigo demon again. Another maintenance task was given to the Merlin/Hugo engine. This time nothing occurred and no one arrived at the last minute to save me from my fear of heights.

District plans called for replacement of the old lookout on Mt. Sexton with new construction. Other ODF lookout towers across the district were also being remodeled or repaired, but the Sexton situation had a long and desperate need for a total upgrade.

Being a life-long resident of the Hugo area, I'd been around and atop the mountain many times. There was a terrific view from the top of our fields on the old family farm down at the base. I knew this from personal experience, knowing that particular panorama from both sides – above and below. From the ODF point of view, Mt. Sexton was a natural site for a fire lookout because the rounded top and semi-barren south face gives a nearly clear and really wide scope of the valley in all directions.

There had been only a small house and a few outbuildings atop Mt. Sexton for several years, mostly belonging to the National Weather Service. The old fire lookout arrangement up there wasn't a tower at all until the new construction that spring. Instead there was a kind of a crow's nest about six or eight foot-square with small windows on each side. It had been cobbled atop the roof of a floorless shed that stood next to the old house. The flimsy contraption looked very much like an over-sized decorative cupola pulled off from some dairy-farmer's barn. There was a fire-finder (called an azimuth table) placed dead center in the space below the eaves, which left little room for anything else. To look out the high-placed windows, it was necessary to climb onto a rickety platform that put the window-sills at about chin height for a person of average height. The table could be slid on a tubular track one way or the other to gain a few inches, to help sight past the blind corners. All things considered, the old Sexton setup was a lot less than ideal.

Sexton Mountain Lookout Tower, about thirty feet from the ground level, with live-in cabin and catwalk.
Courtesy of ODF Grants Pass Unit

Dad and I drove to the top of Sexton as instructed on our list of assigned maintenance duties. We were duly impressed with the spanking new tower now in place. It was of the modern classic style as seen on Smokey Bear posters with the long legs made of several sections of heavy timbers. It was at least three stories tall, maybe more. It also was not yet finished.

Stairs angled up the support timbers to a catwalk that surrounded a single large room at the top. Visibility from this airy space was terrific, with large windows on all four sides. Even the top half of the door was made of glass panes. The bright and sunny cabin on top was large enough to provide comfortable living space; at least twelve feet square. The roof had a wide eave that over-hung the catwalk, providing some shade inside all day. The azimuth table was built on a swivel in the center of the floor, and sat on a lightning proof platform.

Most towers had a kind of security built in for anyone assigned who might feel nervous about the remote locale. The Peavine and Manzanita structures had a section of the catwalk on hinges so that it could be folded back or locked down to prevent access from the stairs. Other towers had stairs that could be drawn up. The Mt. Sexton tower enjoyed almost daily company from the weather service people, and had the luxury of both telephone service and running water. There was only a gate with a bar across the catwalk access. I knew of some towers with only a simple locked door. Some towers depended on only their remote locale for safety, with merely a long footpath to the site.

The job that Dad and I were to finish on Sexton would once more test my inner fear of heights. This time, for me, there was no way out. We'd been sent to dismantle the old cupola, bringing the pieces back to HQ, plus putting a strong roof on the top of the new cabin in the sky – and the necessary climb was my responsibility. My dad was ground-support only.

Just looking up at the tower turned my stomach. The construction crew before us had jerry-rigged a plank platform that hung out beyond the catwalk handrail a long way above the ground. Looking very much like a cheap diving platform for a stupid circus trick, that flimsy construction was jutting out several feet outside of the safety railing. The sight sent chills up my back.

With no other reason for delay, up I went. First up the stairs. I paused briefly several times to let myself adjust to the height sensation. The butterflies in my stomach turned into dive-bombers the higher I went. I made a longer stop on the catwalk. The stopover here was necessary so I could attach a safety belt around my middle, taking great care to securely buckle the belt, making sure it was correctly worn and not too loose.

Something not visible from the ground came into play now; a dangling rope hanging down and over the edge of the eave. I silently thanked whoever had left this thin cord for my use. I gave it a trial yank to ensure its strength, then I hooked the loop at the end to my safety belt. The rope now attached me to a stout eyebolt embedded at the center roof peak.

Feeling just a tad safer, I took a deep breath, then went over the rail, onto the scaffold and clamored to the roof. As if being 40 to 50 feet off the ground wasn't bad enough, the whole vista of the valley below made it seem like I was up twice or three times as high. I had managed to scramble my way far enough to lie belly-down with my toes and fingers seeking something to brace against. For a moment I stayed put, almost afraid to move any farther.

Once more the wind blew – not as cold as on King Mountain, but still chilly. The human brain must block out horrible experiences, because I don't remember a lot about the work on that roof, although I recall the material was aluminum sheeting. That first overwhelming memory of fear is the only thing I can remember clearly. It should be obvious that several times I somehow returned safely to good old Mother Earth, then again climbed the tower to get the job done. Total blank on that part for me. For that I am thankful.

I must have done a good job on that roof too, because it held out for many years. Twenty-five fire seasons later the roof even sheltered my oldest daughter when she manned the Sexton Lookout – complete with her own scary Sexton rattlesnake tale.

Many years later vandals burned the tower almost to the ground when it wasn't occupied one winter. One can only marvel at such stupid acts.

That year of 1963, it was still early in the fire season when an urgent report regarding one of the towers came across our radio one morning. It came directly from the Medford Unit Dispatch as a blanket message to all receivers. A female Lookout on one of their towers was attacked while sleeping the night before. Either the tower she was assigned didn't have a secure catwalk feature, or she hadn't barred the access as was advised. I think it was the tower named Tallowbox, and I honestly cannot recall if I've ever even seen that tower.

A man had driven his vehicle near to her tower late at night, parked and walked quietly to and up the stairway. He beat-up the girl pretty bad and raped her.

The attacker disabled the tower radio and made the young woman walk barefoot out of the tower and down the road to near where his car was parked, but not close enough for her to see it. He left her there on the dirt road in the middle of the woods in the dark, and then drove away. I don't think authorities ever tracked the guy down.

The girl made her way back to the lookout in the dark. Without the radio she was unable to contact anyone to ask for help or report what had happened. All she could do was wait. It must have been a terrifying night for her.

It was the following morning before it was first known that something was wrong. The Medford HQ Dispatch was unable to get a response from the tower at the AM roll-call/check-in. A patrol unit was rapidly dispatched to the tower to check on the Lookout. It was likely mid to late morning before medical help was requested and the Sheriff's Department notified.

Everybody attached to both of the units' headquarters was greatly shook-up about this incident, most especially the other female Lookouts. Patrol engines were immediately sent to visit every tower that day, checking access roads everywhere, advising strangers found that they were not welcome near the towers. Road gates that often were left open, now were firmly closed and locked.

For a while there, no one was looking very hard for smokes or burn barrel violations. Still many roads had no gates and the patrol engines had other duties. A couple of very tense days passed.

In the fading light one evening the young lady on the Peavine Mountain Lookout, above Galice in the Grants Pass Unit, called into Dispatch with a 10-24 report (Unwanted Visitors Present). She saw a man walking on one of the many access roads near her tower, less than a mile away.

She told Dispatch she had barred her catwalk access at the top of the stair. Like many of the tower workers she had acquired a weapon, and now had her .22 rifle out and felt ready to defend herself. Dispatch advised her that help was on the way, and, "Please do not shoot unless directly threatened."

A compelling and immediate message was made to patrol engines nearest Peavine. It was after hours, but four of the closest engine crews manned their rigs and headed to the lookout PDQ. The HQ Dispatch assigned different routes to each crew to prevent escape of the unknown person on the mountain.

The Merlin/Hugo engine with Dad and me on board were included in the call-out. Our rig was responding from the farthest location – over fifteen miles away. Considering the grim report from Medford a few days before, I am sure all units on this call proceeded at the utmost speed.

My dad took the call seriously enough to travel faster than normal, but still within safety limits. Mainly because the big Dodge enjoyed wrestling with its driver and was giving Dad a fair tussle as usual. After about 20 minutes of a wild and rough ride, we were driving a narrow logging road up Peavine Mountain.

An engine-to-engine call came from the Galice truck, the first rig to meet up with the stranger in the woods. They reported they'd found the man camping alone about a mile from the Lookout.

He was a BLM (Bureau of Land Management) timber cruiser who was on the job in a planned timber sale in that area. He'd chosen to camp in the woods rather than drive the long distance back and forth daily from his Medford office.

His story was that after cooking and eating his dinner after a day's work, he had gone for an evening walk before hitting his sleeping bag for the night. He said he was unaware of his nearness to the tower; didn't know anything about the previous incident in the Medford district, and was totally unprepared for how upset everyone was about his presence.

After all this was reported back and verified, all the ODF rigs in-route were released back to station by HQ Dispatch. Following radio protocol, I called back to Dispatch, reporting that the Merlin/Hugo unit was returning to our assigned station.

Dad turned the engine around and we were going down Galice Creek Road to turn back toward Merlin at the river, when one of the other returning trucks called rig-to-rig to our radio. Sometimes in the more broken up topography of the district, radio calls were lost in the mountains and canyons. The moving patrol engines often only heard pieces of radio communications and sometimes missed complete messages. Our fellow responder asked, "Has anyone heard the other (forth) engine give a 'Returning to Station' reply?" was the quarry. "Dispatch says they didn't receive their call."

The responding remaining three rigs in turn each replied with the same message. "No", was the universal response.

This was not good. All engines immediately pulled to the roadside. A short radio discussion had each crew giving their approximate current location to Dispatch, either directly or through another rig. The engine that now was closest set out to retrace the first route the missing crew had been originally assigned.

The rest of us waited in the darkness. It seemed like forever, but finally the returning engine crew reported that they had found the missing rig.

More trouble.

It seems that the now located engine was first driving up to the Peavine Lookout on their assigned route, they rounded a curve and a tire pulled off the rim of a front wheel. Maybe they were going a little too fast, because this is not a real common thing to have happen.

It was good luck that the hillside at that location was somewhat mild. The missing tire caused the vehicle to roll over twice before coming back to rest upright. In some places it could have tumbled several hundred feet before coming to a standstill.

The engine even avoided whamming into any trees on the wooded slope. But it was badly crunched. The attached hose reel on top of the truck's tank had held up under the load on the first roll, but then collapsed and came off on the second toss. The cab was mashed to about half its normal height.

The rig was a newer 1963 Studebaker 4x4 pickup. It sustained major damage, but both the crew were seat-belted in and fortunately wearing their hard hats while in-route as per safety protocol. Their hard hats had broken bands and the support webbing was torn loose, but provided enough protection for both guys on board to avoid serious injuries.

It had been drilled into us that small, seemingly insignificant actions can save (or cost) lives. After the damaged patrol engine was hauled in and put on display at the GP Compound, everybody took extra care about safety rules, like wearing hard hats when in route to an incident and checking air pressure in tires.

Today surveillance cameras have replaced the human presence on all Southwest Oregon ODF Lookout towers. Several of the USFS towers have become remote over-night rentals for city-folk looking for a Wilderness Experience. Across Oregon, only a handful of the Lookout towers from any agency are still in active duty during fire season. Another tradition gone.

(While compiling this book seeking information, I contacted the ODF Historical Museum section at the state capital HQ. I was informed that the wrecked patrol engine from the above incident reappeared around 2005. The Studebaker pick-up was repaired and restored by a private party. It was in use on an eastside ranch in the state of Washington, many years after the above described accident.)

CHAPTER 9

Kids between sixteen and twenty years of age did most of the hard, physical work on fire lines when I started. The majority of the supervisors were around thirty and up. Only one or two were around twenty-five, and few over forty. The Hotshot headman, and that crew's two straw bosses, weren't much older than the youngsters on the line. This select group of very young guys in the lowest tier of leadership roles were burdened with big responsibilities.

They were expected to act appropriately. Sometimes they forgot.

SHORTER THAN A SEVEN-DAY WEEK

So far, this new 1963 Fire Season had been kind of strange, with many unexpected happenings. Not long after the Lookout attack in Jackson County, something completely unforeseen and unrelated to me set up a terrific career opportunity. Again, marveling as I look back over time, the tricky fingers of Fate were busy mixing things up in my life.

It was just after the 4th of July holiday and within days of my 19th birthday. I had been very pleased when all seasonal employees had received a raise on July 1st. My monthly pay was now just under $235 per month. The pay increase was called Comp Pay, which was supposed to take care of any over-time worked above 40 hours per week. Since summer fires tend to blow up in late afternoon near the end of a day's shift, many times evening hours and over-night duty made a week of only 40 hours work somewhat unusual.

Attached to this change, was the initiation of a single day per week of standby time (not to be confused with a day off). That change replaced our 24/7 workweeks. Crews were given 24 hours every week, when they did not have to report at HQ, and no actual work was required - unless, of course, there was a fire and a call was sent out. Technically that was a stand-by day.

A direct outcome of these changes, was that the couple of young fellows that held the two straw boss positions on the Hotshot hand trail crew went out partying. On their first and only night off, they made a series of really bad decisions while under the influence. They must have gotten pretty well smashed that night, as I'm sure neither of them was notably stupid.

Anyway, their evening of good times somehow led them to go to the quiet ODF HQ compound. Here they borrowed some equipment – a couple of Pulaskis (a specialized hand tool that has a sharpened iron head, half axe and half hoe). The daring duo then wandered off hunting for something to dig up or chop down, as per the designated purpose of the tools.

The circumstances of the evening somehow brought the pickled pair and their chosen hand tools to 4th Street about where it turns into Washington Blvd. – one of the most high-profile, historic neighborhoods in Grants Pass. It was another really bad choice.

For no particular reason known, the guys decided to show off their hand trail skills by proceeding down Washington Blvd. in the middle of the night taking out many of the decorative flowering cherry saplings planted in the grassy center course-way. While hard at work, they were caught in the act.

In my advanced years I've witnessed throngs of kids become adults. It is a painful fact that youth and dumb-doings go hand in hand.

ODF had some tolerance for harmless goofing-off, but it never has been an outfit to mollycoddle those who screwed up beyond a certain point. A very obvious line was not to be crossed. The drinking and partying of these tipsy two might have been frowned upon, but seen as youthful lapse outside of work time if no other harm had been done.

When these guys chose to make use of ODF tools in a delinquent act where true damage was the result, AND doing so reflected badly on the department ... well it simply was not forgivable. They were canned.

Dawn came bright and clear, common to July in our part of Oregon. My dad and I took off for the GP HQ a bit early, as was our custom. We arrived with time to spare at the compound ready for the new workday.

We noticed that those few who had come in ahead of us were a-buzz with dramatic news. Hearing a quick rundown of the nighttime caper of the Hotshot straw bosses, we also learned that those responsible no longer worked for ODF.

I pondered this situation for only a few minutes. As a patrol engine crewman, I held the lowest position possible with the seasonal ODF employees. I realized immediately there were now two openings on the Hotshots needing to be filled immediately– both spots that represented a promotion to any engine crewman.

I hardly took a deep breath. I found myself walking with my heart in my mouth to the Unit's main office. No thought was given about how I would phrase my proposal.

The Assistant District Forester's office door stood open. Seated at his desk he beckoned me in. Words came out of my mouth. I think I simply stated that I heard he might need a straw boss for the Hotshot crew. He indicated that was true.

I asked, "How about me?" That was all I said.

It was a very brief interview. Maybe the reputation that I'd accidentally acquired the year before – mostly thanks to my dad - came into play; that as a serious and mature young man I tended to avoid any goofing off. There had also been that extra month in the office the previous fall as the fire season wound down. So maybe my face was a little familiar. Maybe the Unit Forester had noticed my tendency to hang around with the older more experienced guys during breaks and lunchtime with a long list of fire questions.

A hand-trail crew building fire trail. Hotshot type crews can attack fires as quickly as engines, but have the added advantage of being able to access ground where engines and sometimes dozers cannot safely go.
Courtesy of Forest History Center; ODF Archives, Salem, Oregon

I'll never know exactly why I was given this promotion, especially with so little effort on my part. I never asked. Whatever it was, within minutes of my arrival at work that fateful morning, my future summer employment became more focused. Actually, my whole life became more distinct – I just didn't know that part yet. It was another watershed moment.

The headman's answer was "Okay", I think with a nod of the head. He seemed very casual about it all. On the other-hand, I was jubilant!

I was re-assigned from the Merlin/Hugo patrol engine to a straw boss position on the proud Hotshots. I was amazed at the ease with which I acquired the job-change.

I went looking for my dad who was somewhere around the compound. I had big news to share. As I went searching, it came to me that the advancement would bring another raise in pay.

I would be earning well over $250 per month.

CHAPTER 10

*H*otshot crews are hand-trail specialists. They are the elite ground troops of wildland firefighters, trained for working in the roughest of terrain and having great stamina. If conditions are right, a good crew can build up to five miles of fire trail by hand in one twelve-hour shift.

The landscape and the type of fire will dictate suppression methods used. At the end, most every fire makes use of people on the ground with simple tools in their hands. Anchored by smaller chainsaws equipped with brush bars, the most common hand tools in my time were cruisers' axes, machete's, shovels, Pulaskis, Hazel hoes, and McLeods. The cutting edges on every tool were kept well oiled and knife sharp, then sheathed for safety when out of use.

During the historic outbreak of catastrophic larger forest fires in the early 1900s (and they were many in number), USFS hand crews themselves developed some of those specific fire-fighting gadgets still used now. Other tools have been adapted and included in the arsenal of fire tools, as needed.

Fire on different terrain requires tools most appropriate to the site. Today, eighty some years later, Hotshot crewmembers effectively use the same kinds of hand tools and a few power saws, plus human muscle and a whole lot of sweat, to get a really tough job done.

HOTSHOTS AND FIRE TYPES

After about a month into the 1963 Fire Season, I was reassigned from the Merlin/Hugo patrol engine to the SWO GP Unit Hotshot Crew. The job was a low-level leadership position as straw boss. I had no experience with supervision at all. Well, except maybe bossing around my brother and sister.

Coming to the Hotshots in mid-season from a patrol engine was like being tagged to play in the big varsity game when you've always been on the JV bench. I was a little bit overwhelmed. For me, also skipping up from crewman to the straw boss job was the cherry on the cake.

There are several different crew types and machines common to wildland fire fighting. Even today, all the ODF crewmen and officers, even office staff both men and women, are trained in hand tool use and fire trail construction. In times of great need this extra trained workforce has been called out. Their only real limitation is physical conditioning. The main duties of this group are in support areas, but they are there in an emergency.

The actual jobs of hand trail crews and engine crews were both very important. The pay was the same, but the jobs were not.

The engine crews handled initial attack where fires could be accessed by trucks. Engine crews also did a lot of the time-consuming mop-up after a fire, using their large water supply to help with a tedious and dirty job. Engines could be teamed with dozers during a fire if the terrain wasn't too bad, again using their water supply to cool hot spots and quickly tag flames that jumped a cat line. The two-man engine crews were sometimes separated from their vehicles but still assigned as dozer support. Working on foot, they would clean up the cat trail and watch for spot fires that jumped the line, using just hand tools. The Warden on my patrol engine, my dad, had done a very thorough job with training. I knew how to properly make use of all the fire-fighting gadgets and tools. This included everything on the patrol truck, pumps, hand tools and all.

There are only three basic kinds of fires. A Surface Fire is one where fuels are lower level, burning grass and other low-lying vegetation. Aircraft may be called to drop water or retardant to cool especially intense Surface Fires, but the most effective control of a less vigorous Surface Fire is building line and letting the fuel contained be consumed.

Some people may think that aircraft would be safest and most effective for wildland firework. Fixed-wing planes and helicopters are extremely expensive, though. They require highly trained pilots and special support services. In SWO, the up - down mountainous terrain really limits safe aircraft use, in particular on smaller fires.

It might seem that bulldozers would be favored as most productive for building fire line (or trail). The weakness of dozers for initial attack was/is their size. Hauled on a low-boy trailer by a semi-tractor rig, dozers must be moved to within a reasonable distance to first access a fire. This means a very extensive pre-existing road system has to be in place. Even if roads are present, the drive from base location to remote places takes time. Once there, dozers require a large space for their transport to maneuver, plus more precious time to off-load.

Dozers are also expensive machines. The SWO ODF unit in the 1960s owned only two dozers (one in Grants Pass, one in Medford) available for use on almost 1.8 million acres of land under protection. A good share of that land was too steep for a dozer to safely go, and using human effort was more cost effective.

In place of the dozers, Hotshots used for initial attack on any fire is good strategy. First, they can be transported in any multi-passenger vehicle. They can begin building hand line almost as soon as they arrive at a fire, or members can hike over trackless ground to fires in less accessible locations. Since almost every wildland fire begins as a Surface Fire, the smaller scale hand- built trail is sufficient to limit the spread almost every time.

My experience had our Hotshots building fire line starting on a fire's flank, hoping for an opportunity to attack the head if the fire behavior was not too extreme. By building on the flank it meant that when the fire's head met the raw turned earth of the fire line, it would be at an oblique angle, so the effective width of the line was multiplied.

Our hand trail crew was wonderfully versatile. Being nimble enough to switch attack strategy at a moment's notice, another unique advantage was usability on most rough terrain where engines and even dozers could not safely operate.

There is a lot of landscape in SWO that is too steep for even a dozer. This landscape is hand trail terrain. In the 1960s on fires that defied initial attack or out-ran the reach of the engine hoses, the hand crew was the only truly mobile organized trail building "machine" available.

Another plus about the Hotshot crew was their major role in "dry mop-up" operations. Dry mop had to be the dirtiest, most disagreeable work any fire fighter faced. It was also extremely important. Dry mop involved digging out burning material and using dirt to smother embers. Scraping stumps, logs and limbs with sharpened tools to put out hidden hot spots and smokes has always been vital. If left undone, a fire thought to be out, hides like an evil ghost, then can rise from the dead to attack again.

Without thorough mop-up, fires have been known to smolder over several days, weeks, even months, to live again and cause mischief. A creeper fire like that, hidden in stumps or snags either underground or buried in deep duff is called a Ground Fire. It is the second most common type of fire. Many Ground Fires begin as lightning strikes.

As specialists, a point of pride for our Hotshot crew was not only making a quick initial response to fire calls and being usable in multiple ways, we were also able to stick with a fire for the long haul. We had to be in tip-top physical condition to be able to work unbelievably long hours in hot summer weather on the most difficult landscape. Hotshot crews trained to build stamina in the early season, with lots of calisthenics, hiking, and hard practice.

Watching a fully trained Hotshot crew perform while on assignment is almost awe-inspiring. I have seen such teams in action, working systematically and effectively on a side hill that would defeat a mountain goat, producing miles of trail. Hotshots could and still do go almost anywhere to kill fires.

There is a chronological sequence to wildland fire attack. First is to contain it, that is encircle with line (AKA trail). This is a ditch dug down to mineral earth. Nothing that can burn is left on the trail to act as fuel.

Ground and ladder fuels feed a wildland fire.
Courtesy of ODF Grants Pass Unit

After containment, crews monitor the trail to make sure the active spread of flames doesn't slop over or cross anywhere along the line. Eventually all fuels are consumed and the flames lose intensity and heat. If the fire can be approached, crews may be able to knock them down with dirt or water – often both. The last step is mop-up. This step is thoroughly completed inside the burned area. mop up, or digging out stumps and roots to kill lingering embers, is the last thing done before a fire is considered out. It is a vital step that must be done with great care.

Stump-holes can be created when a dead and rotten tree trunk catches in a fire and burns down into the dead roots underground. This leaves a notable dent where the tree trunk or main stem of a bush once stood. The fire underground can die from lack of oxygen, but just as often it smolders along, sometimes for days or even months.

The third type of wildland fire is called a Crown Fire. Hotshot trail crews can handle the first two types, but fires that intensely burn in the forest crown (treetops) is an uncontrollable, very destructive phenomenon.

Some low fires burn hot enough to catch fuel overhead or are located where ladder fuels permit the flames to climb trees. Once off the ground, a fire cannot be well fought on foot. Short term Crown Fires can develop when a Surface Fire with intensity uses "ladder fuels" – such as mid-height brush or dense young tree growth – to climb into above- ground treetops. A single tree here or there is not an issue, but when a forest fire crowns out over a larger space (or a Surface Fire gets too intense) it creates a Fire Storm. That's when fire creates its own draft or weather conditions. Temperatures at ground level can reach 2000 degrees. It also sucks oxygen creating a windy draft.

Trail containment is used with cooler Surface Fires. Direct Attack and post-containment mop-up are used with Ground Fires. The third type, a Crown Fire or very hot Surface Fire, is too dangerous and too intense to be approached by ground crews, engines or dozers. Only by creating very wide fuel breaks can Crown Fires be stopped from the ground. Even then, Crown Fires are known to simply blow past the barrier. The only other option, aircraft, can be used in proximity when a fire crowns, but only if the terrain is reasonable. Many of the deep and narrow mountain canyons of SWO are not safe places for fixed-wing aircraft or helicopters, fires or not.

One of two outcomes will occur with the fire in the treetops. Either the Crown Fire will consume the fuels, cool-off and return to the surface where it can be fought, or the fire will continue to spread from tree to tree, with temperatures becoming so high that fuels explode into full flame some distance before the head. Once over-head, men on the ground have no options except to retreat and regroup.

Extra-ordinary suppression efforts are necessary with a Fire Storm or fire nearing that behavior. A declaration of a Project or Complex alerts protection agencies to down shift to a different organization configuration to make limited resources stretch farther. A shift in responsibilities is done to free up local crews and bring in manpower from other areas. Because the pre-arranged planning has been done, the change-over usually is smooth, but not always. Strategies change. Suppression crews must sacrifice ground. They have no choice but to back off to defensible ground, redefine plans of attack, then take appropriate action. Mostly they hope like crazy the fire somehow cools down.

CHAPTER 11

Fighting wildfire is an occupation filled with lessons. Fire and its use by humans, is said to be the greatest discovery of mankind. Still, for something that is necessary and very common in our lives, fire on a large scale in the natural environment still is not well understood; more so when out of control.

The history of our nation is something of a catalog of fire uses, also a repeat story of fire escapes. Use of wood burning stoves for meal preparation, burning wood to create steam power for industry, vast forested landscapes burned with the purpose to clear land for agricultural use ... all depended on fire as a tool.

Often the fires in history took off, hopelessly out of control. Sometimes homes and farms were destroyed. Sometimes towns or even large cities disappeared. Huge tracts of land were burned. A fire set in Maine to clear ground for farming in the early 1800s is said to have blackened around 3 million acres. Several modern-day fires in urban areas of California caused the deaths of dozens of people, and wiped out whole communities.

Most Oregon residents are at least aware of the infamous Tillamook Burn, a combination of three very bad fires in the 1930s and 40s that lit up around a quarter- million acres of forest. In just the last few years of this newest century in Oregon, the Douglas Complex, the Chetco Bar and the Eagle fires have filled the news with their incredible size.

Whether historical or modern, uncontrolled fires are powerful agents of merciless destruction.

A LOT TO LEARN

When I began with the Hotshots there were only eight guys on the GP crew, including the supervisor and me, the single straw boss. No second straw boss was named for the last two-thirds of that season. No one ever explained why. I was only a grunt on the line, not really knowing what my job was.

I was both humbled and mighty proud of my job change at ODF – and downright scared to death that I'd somehow screw up the whole thing. The job change created a problem for me, as I was at a loss to know just what I was supposed to do as the Hotshot straw boss.

The regular guys on the Hotshots were actually at the same pay level as the engine crews, but they were special – or at least the guys on the engines, including me, thought they were.

The fellow who supervised the crew wasn't much help for me when trying to learn my new job. The work wasn't the problem; it was the leadership component. Still there were some factors that gave me a little more credibility with the other guys on the line than being just a re-assigned engine crewman.

The Oregon Department of Forestry uniform arm patch prior to 1971.
Photo courtesy of CC Dickerson

Since my time to mingle with the other crewmen at the HQ Compound had been pretty limited before my job re-assignment, I was kind of an unknown to the Hotshot crewmen. At the same time, because of my obsession with wildland fire and my incessant questioning of the older veterans, I was on a first-name basis with many of the mid-tier supervisors. Also, I had some un-official seniority just because it was my second fire season.

My paltry experience and limited HQ contacts weren't much, but they were all I had when I joined the hand trail crew. The Supervisor was a few years older than me. I found he was neither a mentor nor a good teacher. He didn't mix much with anyone on the crew.

I had first worried that I wasn't physically prepared for the Hotshot job when compared to the other crewmen. This never became a problem. The crew boss was downright zealous about training; apparently sure in his own mind that everyone was completely out of shape. The proof was that he would pack our crew into our new van first thing many mornings for more training at every opportunity – even though nearly half the season was over.

I welcomed the extra training because the Foreman knew a whole lot of stuff that I needed to get into my head as quickly as possible. It gave a chance for me to learn while on the job.

The physical training was pretty basic. For everything else, I was determined to do well as a Hotshot member. I consciously decided to keep my eyes open and my mouth shut

We would head out to some closed-in area in the woods, but not too far from town, to train all day with no interruptions. On our training exercises, we would do vigorous calisthenics for maybe an hour. My least favorite exercise was to hold both arms with fists clenched out horizontally to the side and then rotate fists in small circles. The length of time doing this seemed to never end, and my arms felt as if they were about to come loose at the shoulders.

After about an hour of several different exercises, the crew lined up and practiced digging trail using the different systems for about 2 or 3 hours more. A lunch break was next, sitting on the trail we had just built. After the break, more trail building went on for another 2 or 3 hours. The day's end was a quick-time march back along the new trail to our truck. Along the day's final hike, the crew boss could stop anytime he saw trail that was not up to his satisfaction and point out what was wrong. This was not a pleasant time, as the guy was overly thorough in describing how badly he thought the job was done.

If negative feedback wasn't too extensive after a training day, the crew would return to HQ tired, but feeling a sense of accomplishment. More often there was little or no positive feed back or "Atta Boy" comments at all. Almost every day the crew returned to HQ dejected and quiet, pretty well chewed around the edges.

I noticed that the crew was really trying. Obvious improvement in the trail building and physical stamina was there, but it wasn't much noted by the boss. I decided to quietly point out the positive efforts, but only with quiet side comments that were honestly earned. I made a point of never interfering with the supervisor's opinions. Maybe I was just chicken.

I came to realize that my few words of encouragement were a part of my straw boss job. I wanted our group to be the strong team I thought they were when I was on the patrol engine.

The foreman finally backed off on the daily training when the ending hike was maybe 3 to 5 miles. No real praise ever came for the effort involved.

The crew vehicle was a new '63 Chevy panel truck. Today it would be called a van – at ODF it was called a Crummy. It replaced a military-style flatbed truck with side racks that I remembered from 1962. The Crummy had built-in seats along each side in the rear. The padded seats were hinged so that they could be lifted and blocked in the UP position. All hand tools that the crew might need were stored under the seats except for the chainsaws and fuel, which went just inside the back doors. In later years the gas-powered tools went into a rack on the roof.

Wildland fire fighters do not have to make mistakes to get into trouble when on a fire. Things happen even to the most alert, aware and experienced. When small mistakes are made, when people are careless or simply not paying attention, those things turn worse real fast. The kind of job we did, and the conditions where we worked were sometimes very dangerous. Everyone had to depend on everybody else to have his back.

Not too long after I joined the Hotshot crew, there was a fire in the southern part of the district. I think it was somewhere between Applegate and Ruch. The Hotshot crew somehow beat the patrol engines to the location; an unusual situation. The fire was on very flat ground. This kind of terrain was uncommon, but does happen in SWO once in a while. I do not recall how the fire had started.

As the Hotshot Crummy approached the blaze the foreman drove into the blackened burned-over area toward the slow-moving spread on the opposite side. The fire had cleared out maybe four or five acres at that point.

The supervisor parked the rig inside the black and ash-covered ground. It was a little smoky here and there, and the ground was still warm to the touch. The crew quietly off-loaded, gathered tools and waited for additional directions from the boss man.

The active spread of the fire wasn't too far away, but even if the wind suddenly changed there wasn't enough fuel left to make our location dangerous. One thing, though... no one seemed to notice that one of the front tires was in a dip in the ground. Maybe none of us saw the stump-hole.

Whatever – the crew left the van and hiked off to the fire's edge to begin building trail.

It was lucky that a patrol engine arrived not too long after we left, and chose to park next to our rig. They were able to quickly pull their hose and put out the vigorously burning front tire on the Hotshot Crummy. The Ground Fire from a smoldering stump could have destroyed the Hotshot Crew's brand-new transport without the good work of that engine crew. In total, that fire finished up around 20 some acres.

The scorched and bubbled paint on the front fender was kind of embarrassing. I don't recall that we ever heard anything much about it from the Overhead bosses, though. Fire Equipment takes a real beating every summer. Sometimes the damage is from lack of awareness. Our crew boss should have known better.

My first summer with the Hotshot crew was much different than when I'd been on the patrol engine. Even though I was part of that hand crew for only about eight weeks that year, I really learned a lot, but some of my education arrived in a kind of backward way; teaching me what NOT to do. Mostly I just paid attention.

When the GP Hotshots were on back-up for the Medford crew going to calls far beyond the familiar Merlin/Hugo patrol area, I found the change of scenery very interesting. But there was much, much more.

I came to know, understand and make good use of the numbering system that identifies Forest Service and BLM roads. It matches survey markings on maps. Seeking out a fire location by comparing maps to azimuth reports as the straw boss led to knowledge about the totally mingled and confusion of land ownership in SWO. What a mess!

Little clues about who owned what became important – for instance, fifty years ago it was a safe bet that any remote mountain road with a tarred or asphalt surface had been built for use on BLM or USFS timber management to likely access timber sales lands. No other owners required such surfacing.

I learned that loggers were very sharp fellows who hated and respected fire as much as the firefighters. Logging equipment would almost always be offered quickly to help out our crews. Sometimes we would arrive at a fire to find that trail work was already underway by an alert logger's cat skinner, yarder or felling crew. When you consider how vital their expensive equipment was to their livelihood, the open sharing of that machinery in the dangerous act of firefighting was all the more impressive in its generosity. And, yes, they were paid rent. When the time factor for fire crews to respond to calls was considered, it was money well spent paying loggers to keep those fires small and hopefully controllable.

Brushy type fuels produce hot, very intense fires, especially with any wind.
Courtesy of ODF Grants Pass Unit

On the Hotshot crew, I was able to apply the bits and pieces I had learned from the older fire veterans by watching, listening, and asking. Soon I could match hand tools needed with fuel and land conditions. McCleods were best with heavy duff or thick dead grass. Machete's and lightweight power brush saws could handle manzanita and smaller oaks and madrone, but shovels, Pulaski's and Hazel Hoes were best all around once digging tools were in play.

Watching how fires moved over different types of terrain and burned through various fuels was really something. Terrain might create unique drafts that helped or hindered our job. Some fuels almost exploded as the fire approached, others resisted the flames with a dogged stubbornness.

I came to understand how the moisture in the fuels interacted with the relative humidity in the air. I watched how flames burned differently with wind and without, uphill, downhill and sometimes across a slope. While working the line, I began to imagine attack strategies I might try if I was making the decisions.

When our crew truck approached a fire, I would note the color of the smoke as a clue to what was going on with the fire even before we arrived. The smell of the smoke also told a story about what was ablaze. For example, burning grass has a particular sharp smell, while certain conifers create smoke that smells kind of sweet.

The height and shape of a smoke plume can reveal information about how hot the burn might be. Most Surface Fires run at about 600 to 800 degrees at ground level. Crown Fires can burn at twice that temperature or more. Ground Fires just sort of seep smoke, but not necessarily show where the actual burn might be.

Estimation of flame length was tricky without something, like nearby trees, to use for comparison. I got better at this as time passed. I experienced respectful awe learning how really dangerous a "simple" grass fire can be … with almost instant flames taller than a tall man and moving faster than a running deer even without wind.

Grass fires are not simple! They may sound mild, but are nothing to sneeze at.

I tried to soak up as much information as possible from the Hotshot Foreman without asking too many questions. I discovered that he wasn't the only guy around that knew about building hand trail. I watched him carefully, but took my questions elsewhere. Besides, he was kind of a pain to be around. When at Headquarters, I stuck to my older, veteran friends. On the other hand, the Hotshot Foreman knew a lot about building hand-trail.

The summer may have been a mellow one in regard to bigger fires, but it was a busy time for me. I learned a lot about leadership, hand trailing and fires in general.

In September, ODF again asked me to come back the next June.

CHAPTER 12

Most of the more experienced older guys that I worked with when I was a teenaged wildland **firefighter were about 25 to 40 years of age.** They pretty much treated the youngsters, the teenagers, with a toughness that had an underlining kindness and level of respect.

The jobs held by the kids required muscle, endurance, and a healthy share of bravery at key moments. As such, the first encounter with the flaming "monster" was a Rite- of- Passage for most. Just as my dad had modeled how to function and not panic when a dangerous situation caused bewilderment and fear, the fire vets filled this role for the other young guys. It was a very important moment for all involved.

The older men on the staff usually had at least one fire season of experience – others had decades. Their experience and the steadiness displayed were and still are traits that are a vital part of the excellent capability of ODF and other effective fire agencies. The veterans I knew had faced the fear, felt the sweat and sore muscles, and knew the rush of challenging the fire as it battled to live. For all the required parts of the job, I felt they were good role models.

There were exceptions.

NEW SEASON – NEW LESSONS

I looked forward to the next fire season, going into my third year this time. A second winter of ho-hum college in Ashland hadn't cooled my enthusiasm for the job of firefighting.

I distinctly remember the crew boss who led the Hotshots in the 1964 fire season. After the first day or two of the new fire-season, I believed him to be sorely lacking in leadership skills. He also had an overall unpleasant and arrogant personality.

The Superintendent of the Hotshots that year had his original fire training at one of the two ODF-run crew camps in the Willamette Valley. The camps had grown out of the old pre-WWII Civilian Conservation Corps. The training was essentially that used by the USFS. From that this guy knew a lot about building fire-line. All good, but still he came up short in the personal character and leadership departments.

There was no dispute that in the first fifty years of the 20th century the USFS was the very Best of the Best throughout the entire world in forest fire control. Even in the 1960s their training program was still excellent. Today ODF, several other state agencies plus some private contractors, have wildfire fighting skills that meet and quite likely are far beyond USFS in current wildfire suppression. Now days, the main difference may appear to be in the depth of resources. USFS is, without doubt the agency with the most revenue and supplies. When comparing the performance differences, these revolve mostly around Direct Attack philosophies and general management of large fire suppression efforts. Basic sound training is the basis of these components.

When I joined ODF, the agency had earned and was extremely proud of their exceptional record in fire control. Since the infamous Tillamook Burn fires a few decades earlier, ODF had put extraordinary effort into wildland fire issues. Acres burned were notably low in relation to total number of fire incidents, with both costs and personnel injuries also kept to a minimum. They've continued to build on their excellent record since then.

When I returned to ODF for the 1964 summer season, I was still obsessed by wildland fire and still trying to learn everything I could. By careful observation of the Hotshot Supervisor and referring back to the other older vets on the GP staff whenever I had questions, I'd gleaned a lot of good information about hand trail construction and excellent useful wildland fire lore. Not all I witnessed was 100% accurate or continued from season to season, but I was very open to suggestions and correction. To get the job of Fire Killing done, the concepts of innovation and flexibility seemed very obvious to me.

For example, some things that have changed around were right in front of me. At one time fourteen-man crews were in use. In 1964 the local ODF Hotshot crews were 9-man teams, counting the two straw bosses and the crew supervisor (or Warden/Fire Officer). I've since witnessed crews with twenty or more members, some using a buddy-system and some with a more military hierarchy in command.

In the Crummy, the head guy drove. On the line he usually marked the route for the fire line or handled a power saw. During travel one straw boss rode shotgun, with duties to help locate the route to the incident, read maps, handle the radio and watch out for traffic or other road hazards. The second straw boss rode with crew to relay information and keep order, plus he had special duties, like calling the "Bump" (move the whole crew forward at once) on the line when the crew was working.

I felt a crew boss and one straw boss was adequate, but was most familiar with our single boss/two straw boss arrangement. Our crew could easily divide into twin units when fire conditions called for such a split. Usually the group remained intact with the supervisor or one straw boss at the front of the line and the second straw boss at the rear. Our dual hand-held radios gave us added safety by allowing continual communication within the group. This was very important when involved in direct attack where sometimes visibility might be an issue. Our call numbers on the two radios were 443 and 444.

Our process followed a set plan. Upon arrival at an incident, once the truck was safely parked, the crew would exit through the rear doors and arrange themselves in planned order facing the rear of the truck. The exception was the Tool Man (or Toolie) who had long before been designated. This person sat near the front and stayed inside when the rig was parked. As the rest of the crew left their seats, he'd raise the hinged tops and prepared to distribute the tools out the back doors. Sometimes a straw boss did this job, but more often it was a crewman.

The Supervisor would have decided what would be the best assortment of tools to use according to the fire and the terrain. Some of this information came from HQ Dispatch in-route, but also the Supervisor on hand made his own assessment of the fire and terrain on arrival. Whoever was acting Toolie would distribute the tools as directed in the appropriate order to the crew.

In general, tools for cutting – like axes and power saws - went before the body of the crew. These went next to the bumper of the rig, to be picked up by the Superintendent and whomever was named as his helper – often the first straw boss. When the crew lined out to hike to their starting spot, the superintendent and first guy were in front. The crew following would receive their assigned tools in order and each member would move away from the truck. The first man with a digging tool in line was called the Head Hoe without regard to what tool he held. The last man, called the Ass Hoe or Back Hoe was usually the second straw boss. His job was vital to the effectiveness of the crew. This position was generally held by a very effective and stronger trail builder in the crew.

The crew boss would lead the hike to wherever the fire line was to begin, mark the spot and move with his helper into the rough ground. Building trail, the supervisor would take the lead, marking the path for the crew to follow – usually hacking with a machete' or leaving flagging as a marker. If the fuels were heavier, the supervisor might take a straw boss (with a saw) and move ahead on the proposed trail route. Bigger fuels and thick brush were cut and wrestled out of the general path of the crew behind them. The boss might use a chainsaw or a Hazel hoe depending on conditions, or have his helper work the saw. They would begin to rough out the heavier fuels like smaller trees or thick brush so the body of the crew could maintain their rhythm and speed using a tried and true digging system to clear the line.

The Head Hoe would begin at the marked spot and pace off the first section of trail according to how many workers were actively digging at that time. Each man's segment was marked with a hacked spot in the dirt. The next couple of guys in the crew line often carried digging and chopping tools, suitable for removing roots and medium sized brush. Next came those with tools for grubbing and digging. It wasn't uncommon for each man to carry more than one type of tool. The more common fuels in SWO called for use of Hazel Hoes and sharpened shovels.

The last man in line might be equipped with a shovel, a Pulaski or Hazel hoe depending, again, what the fuels called for. His job was to ensure that a totally bare and finished trail was left when the crew moved onto the next section of the line. The signal to move was bellowed out by the last guy – he would call-out "Bump!" - and the whole line moved forward. As everyone paced the distance to a new spot on the marked line to dig, that last fellow also had the job to both scan and repair smaller problem areas on the trail. If there were larger parts left undone, he may call out a signal for a shorter move to a new workspace or even a backward move. This was to allow extra time for total clearing of anything in the previously worked part that would burn. After the first couple of "Bumps", the end straw boss would have a feel for the fuels and the needed time for each crewman to totally clear his allotted line segment.

While building line, the first radio was either the Supervisor or lead straw boss Whomever had the radio would keep contact with either HQ Dispatch or radio-to-radio if the person calling the strategy on the fire was an Incident Commander, not the crew supervisor. The end man on the Hotshots would carry the second crew radio so that the Supe (as he was sometimes called), and the other straw boss up front, were always aware of any issues with real or even potential problem spots on the line.

I was still learning the basics of hand trail building this new year of 1964, as the previous summer the Hotshot crew functioned shorthanded with only one straw boss. The new Hotshot Crew this year had different faces than those from '63. A few of the new guys had been on an engine the year before, but most were completely new to all parts of the wildland fire job.

Our Supervisor was maybe twenty-two or twenty-three, I would turn twenty in July, and the new guys ranged from sixteen to nineteen. A second straw boss was named as well. He was a year younger than I was.

Like the year before, the Hotshot Supervisor wasn't shy pointing out all the shortcomings of the crew, though this guy was willing and able to buddy-up to the HQ supervisors whenever they were around. Often these insincere encounters were in the presence of the crew. He was always highly critical and opinionated mostly at the expense of the crew he was supposed to lead. Listening to his unending negative views and often taking blame for his screw-ups was not something that endeared him to anybody.

Some of his training ideas again seemed questionable to me, especially so early in the season. I recall the abrupt retrieval of an old telephone line strung up to the abandoned Kerby Peak Lookout. Our boss guy directed the crew to hike straight up to the mountain top via an overgrown six-mile long foot trail, then turn around and take down the wire while hiking back down; coiling and carrying recovered wire as we went. The early summer humidity and heat had arrived just in time to make the assignment completely miserable.

Every crewman lugged the necessary tools plus lunches. All hands were completely filled with some kind of gear. The straw bosses were each burdened that same way, as well as both carrying the extra 10-15 pounds of two-way radios looped with a strap over one shoulder. The boss-man chose to tote only his own lunch. Humm.

No rest breaks were involved on the hike up or during the work going down except for a very short lunch. This was a grueling hike under the best of circumstances and the crew boss seemed to like pushing everyone harder and harder. Often yelling and berating us to keep up with him when anybody lagged back even a little.

It took nearly a week's work for the crew to complete this job – up to the top everyday and working our way back down. Back then it was believed that water in-take should be at intervals of two to three hours apart, to avoid getting "water-logged". Since neither rest, nor water breaks were included much in the phone-line removal assignment, we struggled on a long and very steep trail with only minimal hydration in hot, humid weather day after day.

As my peers on the crew and I labored back down that brushy trail with the added weight of the inconvenient wire and sweating buckets, a thought came to me.

"What if the crew is called out while on this hike?"

Except for the supervisor, I was pretty much the only guy with active fire line experience. I realized this crew would be useless on a line at this point. The conditions we were struggling under were so much more extreme than any likely fire incident that everyone was suffering from rubbery legs and muscle cramps. These conditions lasted for even a couple of days after the job was finished. Luckily no real injuries occurred and no demanding fire calls came.

Our crew boss seemed to enjoy putting the crew through the most difficult training scenarios. He gave us the feeling that he felt we were much beneath him in every way. The sudden demand for such an outlay of effort day after day without the benefit of gradual increments gave our group no time to build stamina and recover physically. This wasn't just unfair, it was dangerous.

His stated purpose was to get us into shape, but we decided that he mostly wanted to show everyone how he was in better physical condition than any of the lowly crew. Add in his habit of choosing the most inopportune times – when in the company of Unit supervisors - to note what he saw as errors, omissions or deviation from his instructions – well, an inevitable reaction by the crew occurred.

This was not the same group who had quietly endured the Foreman of 1963. After the wire retrieval assignment, this crew may have been pooped-out, but every one of us was also very angry. The lead guy probably didn't know he was well on the way to building a "team" attitude among members on the crew, but he wasn't included on the squad! Being kids, we chose our own way of correcting the situation.

After some discussion the crew decided to try to alter things for the better. No thought was even considered going to the Unit boss.

Our focus was to find a way to tone down the training hikes. We already knew that as a group we were actually in pretty good shape … several in our midst were notably skilled in various types of high school athletics. It was obvious that the crew boss was using the training hikes mostly to prove that he was able to hike longer and harder than the crew members. Maybe a poor showing by him while hiking would show that extreme daily hikes weren't all that productive?

Following the fire-line structure, my straw boss partner and I occupied the 2nd and last positions on the trail when hiking for training. This logistical fact was important. The task of humbling our Supervisor, without being too obvious, would require effort by everyone but a little more by the two of us.

It was decided to push our boss as hard as we could while hiking during training. We also had to be sure that the whole crew out-hiked the boss. A strategy was planned.

The first straw boss that generally stayed directly behind the Supervisor (me) would push the beginning pace quite hard until feeling tired out. This should create a bit of a gap behind me in the crew line, but they needed to stay within sight. I'd send a signal down the line when I needed a break and the rear end straw boss was to move up. I'd ease my pace as the backend straw boss moved into my place. I'd drop back beyond sight of the front of the line as the crew line maintained a fairly steady march. I might even have time to stop for a brief rest before moving into the last place. The other straw boss would now be using a fast pace in the number two spot, again pushing the crew boss. We'd repeat our shrewd switch-off maneuver until the hike was finished.

The basic idea was that whoever was on the boss's heels had the job to keep right on his six. The other tired-out guy could take it a little easier for a few minutes, catch his breath then pick up at the tail end of the line. The crew's job was to keep a fairly regular pace, stay between the two straw bosses and not leave huge gaps in the line that might be too noticeable.

On the next couple of training hikes, we successfully switched the second and tail positions again and again without the boss really noticing. We discovered we were in even better shape than we realized. It might be that in our zeal to be successful, we even pushed ourselves more than usual. That we all were in the scheme together was evidence of a complete variance in how this new crew functioned.

Before we reached the end of the second day of our plan, our tough-guy boss man was hanging onto a tree as we all gathered in a circle and watched him puking his guts up. We didn't laugh or in any way taunt him. We were, however, merciless. It took about six training hikes to accomplish our total plan, but the last four days of those six weren't nearly as bad as earlier. He slowed down a lot. After that the hills the Supervisor chose for hiking practice also weren't quite as steep and his hiking pace was much more modest.

Best of all, the crass and ill-chosen remarks by the boss ebbed enough in venom to be semi-tolerable to all on the crew. Still, as a leader of the group, the supervisor was disagreeable at best. It was a good thing that the fire season that year was another fairly quiet summer similar to the year before. As such, the fires were on the smaller size and generally followed the expected behaviors.

With that crew I remember that as the season died away, the end of the summer turned really cool that year. One of our last fires near the end was somewhere far out into the Illinois Valley near the California boarder at higher elevation. As was so often the norm, that fire call came late in the afternoon. It wasn't a really big fire, but large enough to keep the Hotshot crew busy for several hours – well past dark.

It was after midnight when we finished the containment trail. The fuels were kind of mixed, so that when we moved from the hand trail to mop-up chores inside the burned-over space, there were a few medium sized snags and larger stumps that needed care. The night was so cold that our crew nursed some of the snags back to active flames so two or three guys at a time could huddle around and get warmed up.

That hand trail crew wasn't really tested with extreme conditions where the need for strong leadership was apparent. My straw-boss counter-part and I were able to go with the flow, not forced to cope with what we realized was a glaring leadership problem for the Hotshots. I'm sure glad nothing happened, as that crew had something of a chip on its collective shoulder where the crew boss was concerned. The Unit bosses never asked our opinions about the guy.

Fifty years ago, hard working older schoolboys and young men manned fire lines. In spite of technology, today's wildland fire lines are also filled with younger people. It has to be that way and probably always will be, as the human body can only do so much. Older people with experience should call the shots, but the resilience of youth is an important component when physical strength and stamina are vital in getting the job done. Line jobs are a young-person's game.

The fire season isn't long enough to use a military type of training to build leadership. Finding young people with the physical requirements, the experience and savvy plus the needed skills to lead a fire fighting crew is a challenge. Keeping them on the job over more than a season or two is very difficult.

One thing that has changed is that those under age 18 years are not used like they were in the early 1960s. This is because laws now forbid use of power equipment and sharp tools in the hands of those not at least 18 years old.

What a waste. Wildland firefighting is great for building pride and confidence, plus creating a strong work ethic and an excellent team mentality. These are good things for young people to know. Today by age 18 years, so many young people shun hard physical work.

Fighting wildland fire is very physically demanding, but it is simple for those on the line. We were well paid in comparison to other jobs at that time, (a benefit that most kids that hold jobs today do not receive), and willingly did what was necessary. By starting at a younger age, important fire-lore was learned by those who were interested, building a knowing group who could move into Overhead roles while still young enough to handle the physical demands.

All together, the job provided good experience across the board.

Explosive crown fires move quickly, especially when ground and ladder fuels plus wind give support.
Courtesy of ODF Grants Pass Unit

CHAPTER 13

A couple of mild summer seasons in a row can develop problems for wildland fire agencies. Everything seems to get topsy-turvy. Bad fire seasons make good fire fighters. The opposite can also be true.

Serious personnel issues are possible when fire seasons aren't too demanding. The very nature of the firefighting job lends to the use of a temporary work force. When fires are few, many experienced young people move on to other types of work. The really good ones find permanent jobs where their work ethic and common sense are assets. Their unique fire suppression skills are lost when they leave and are not so easily replaced.

Agencies that have a lot of skill with wildland fire fighting can get cocky about their past success and let their guard down during less demanding times. Their personnel may resist vigorous training, feeling they have no need. This lowers effectiveness and creates unnecessary hazards for crews. The holes in the full set of required skills would not be apparent until another really bad fire occurs. The lack of general preparedness can bring on disaster.

The only possible way for a fire agency to fill the gaps in their systems in quiet years is the insistence by Overhead staff to increase training. This is expensive, but cheaper than having everyone just sit around waiting for fires that don't happen. The bosses will likely have to continually defend the training without apparent justification to those in executive control who see no apparent need.

It's unfortunate that training cannot completely replace experience. If not done with care, crews become jaded when training becomes too repetitive.

Then there is another issue. Public assistance in maintaining a watchful attitude is an important part of reducing fire hazards. Man-caused incidents account for most fires at all times. When fire danger is high there tends to be fewer man-caused fires. Numbers increase again when weather and temperatures are mild. It's hard to maintain top performance when demand is low.

A BAD WINTER – A GREAT SPRING

That next winter was pretty hard on the Pacific Northwest. The heavy snow in early December, then torrents of rain brought on the infamous 1964 Floods a day or two before Christmas. Bridges and road washouts were everywhere. With even more snow laid down in January and February, the upper elevations were taking a beating, while the valleys were awash with down trees and mud flows.

I'd had sort of a rough winter myself. I had transferred to Oregon State University School of Forestry in the fall. I'd been unconcerned about school when attending Southern Oregon College. Assignments were completed and I seldom ditched classes, but mostly I was indifferent about my performance.

OSU was much more demanding than SOC. The curriculum didn't lend itself to a nonchalant approach. Before the first quarter was over I was in deep trouble academically. After the holiday break I was determined to mend my ways, but the hole I'd dug was too deep. Near the end of January, I decided to withdraw from school until spring term rather than flunk out. I decided I would return in late March with the personal resolution to be studious to a fault.

In the mean time I needed to find some winter work to make up for the money wasted by my shiftless behavior. Once again, I ended up breaking my back and freezing my butt in the mud on a mountainside planting trees in the late winter cold rain and snow. This time I was on a contract tree planting crew that was working above Wonder in the Hayes Hill area south of Grants Pass.

As per my intention, I returned to Corvallis in late March and finished up the school year at OSU. I worked my rear off there as well, but in a different way. The time off put a hole in my knowledge. I was able to earn barely passing grades in particularly nasty classes like Technical Report Writing and Plant Physiology. I even survived a complete term with a half-day Saturday lab connected to another difficult class. A six-day school week was rough!

I was a very chastised individual when I contacted the GP ODF office about returning to summer work in June 1965. I assumed that I would be returned to my Hotshot straw boss assignment. I learned that last year's Hotshot headman had been switched to an engine assignment. His new patrol area was the Merlin/Hugo spot my dad had left open with his resignation.

There was no one yet named to the Hotshot leadership role. I was stunned when the Unit Supervision asked if I was interested in the job. The unexpected offer really lifted my battered self-esteem. Still I was really torn about what to do. Being fully aware how unprepared I was for that job, I almost turned down the opportunity. I was scared to the core that I couldn't handle the crew training, the required fire evaluation, the assessment of tool needs, and most important, the team leadership the job demanded. I knew I was pretty young for the responsibility too.

A couple of the older staff guys and the Unit boss talked me into accepting the offer. They assured me they'd keep an eye on how I was doing and be available to give whatever help I might need. They did too.

I was not yet age 21 with my mid-July birthday, so I could not hold a full Warden/Fire Officer certification. I was named as a "Crew Supervisor", but would receive the higher Warden's pay for the required six weeks interval. When my birthday came, the Warden's title would become official. The only real difference was I could not write citations for fire violations or issue burn permits for the interim. Big Deal!

Even after my birthday, I was still the youngest Warden in the state. I felt proud and humbled all at the same time. I desperately wanted to do well. The bigger paychecks were nice too.

My somewhat bruised ego really gained a much-needed boost of confidence the new assignment provided. The new job also healed some of the strained relationship with my Mom. She was still pretty upset about my withdrawal from school back in January, giving me the dickens pretty regularly.

I came into the summer fire season cheerful but cautious. The 1964 Hotshot crew had evolved into the new 1965 crew, losing only a few members. This was good. The early fire season progressed as expected with mid-June Fire School and early season training routines. I was pleased with the way "my" Hot Shots were working together.

The two guys who were named as straw bosses for the crew were both good workers, but tended to goof off a lot during downtime. This caused me much worry. Since I'd been on sort of a peer basis the year before, I found it really hard to walk that narrow line between friend and Supervisor. It was much harder than I had imagined.

Just when to get tough and demand they put all joking aside was tricky. I was lucky that both of them usually snapped to adult mode in the nick-of-time. I let my guys swagger a bit, but expected them to act the part of an elite crew when at HQ. Mostly they came through with flying colors.

I came to really enjoy the company of that crew. For six days every week we were based at the HQ Compound, of course. Like the two permanent in-town engine crews, the elite Hotshots stooped to the simple HQ Compound daily chores. On days when we were not too busy with training or had other assigned projects, we'd virtually fuel, check oil, wash and shine every non-fire ODF rig that came into the compound. I expected our own vehicle to look the best and brightest.

I made a big deal about tool care. Tools were checked every morning even when they hadn't been used overnight. Whenever the Hotshots made use of their tools, whether for training or for an actual fire incident, all edges were examined for nicks and gouges. Everything was cleaned and oiled. Those implements in need were honed either by hand or on the HQ Shop grinders, then wrapped again in thick canvas fire hose segments held in place by extra heavy bands of rubber inner tube segments stretched to hold tight. Great care had to be taken when handling the tools.

I really promoted an attitude of our crew as a special team. Little things began to indicate that the crew was willing to buy into my plan. I very much discouraged any guy on the Hotshots to participate in the water fights, letting the engine crews get themselves into trouble with the Unit bosses. We came to mostly avoid doing much grounds-keeping duty. It became a personal challenge to find productive work for my crew that didn't tarnish the image.

The Grants Pass ODF Headquarters was located on NW 12th Street about two blocks uphill from today's Grants Pass Shopping Center. For all who were assigned to the main compound as their base station (like the Hotshots), driving through town for fast fire response to the south side of the Unit was a big problem. Navigating traffic through town to go south of the Rogue River was especially hard because only the Sixth Street Bridge for crossing that direction was available then. Since the Hotshots were an initial response team, the traffic issue in Grants Pass was a constant irritation, almost always slowing us down.

We had no colored lights or siren attached to our Crummy. Blinking the headlights didn't do much to encourage drivers to make a path for our fire equipment in the downtown section. Peak traffic times could mean a back up for blocks. Sometimes slow trains moving through town completely stopped the flow of cars at several crossings, costing us precious response time.

That 1965 Hotshot crew was a cheerful bunch and very enterprising. A couple of the more gifted members took on the Grants Pass traffic challenge by hanging their heads out the vehicle windows and making siren sounds as loud as they could bellow. The younger straw boss that year was particularly good at this. He was without doubt the very best of the human vocal sirens we had available. Drivers would often head for the curb when they heard his call echo off the buildings more than a block away. It was unbelievable how well this worked. Good enough to make a way through clogged streets!

As a group we tackled our fires, but I made it clear that final strategy was my decision to make. Sometimes hand trail crews worked a good distance in front of the head of the fire (Indirect Attack) or on the flanks. Other times work was done within a few feet of the blaze (Direct Attack). If the fire was low lying and slow, Direct Attack worked well.

I've always preferred working near the fire. The added heat can be physically uncomfortable but I like to see the fire and know what it is doing. Those with experience assessing fuels don't get blindsided too often with surprise flare-ups when working close to the flames. My crew began to copy my style of Direct Attack. They became very accustomed to working close to the fire.

It wasn't long before we were known to be a gutsy crew, but not fool-hearty. Near the flames, if there was a small flare-up, a shovel full of loose dirt directed at the problem spot knocked down the fire, cooling things off. Soon the crew made this move as a matter of course, allowing the trail construction to continue without loosing their rhythm. As our reputation grew, the behavior of the guys on the line became totally businesslike when working. This made my job as leader easier.

Still the pranks that occurred during downtime never really stopped. The tried and true lizard or snake in someone's lunch box was standard stuff. Soon our more knowing crewmembers refused to react much when stray critters popped up unexpectedly. This may have worked in our favor once or twice.

Sometimes when we came off a fire to ride back to town exhausted, the guys would relax on the ride home. Some removed their hot and heavy boots leaving stocking feet to cool off in the delicious fresh air. Some would even fall asleep. If the mood was right, those who were still awake might take advantage of the snoozers. A quick flick with a match would light the tiny balls of fluff on the exposed woolen sox of an unsuspecting victim.

I knew what was happening as I drove the crew home, but usually let it go. The straw boss with the crew could handle anything that went awry – although sometimes he was the culprit. Whoever was at fault, the glow of burning sock-fuzz made a pleasant gentle gleam in the darkened crew truck at night. An occasional entertaining yelp of a now wide-awake crewman experiencing a hot foot would add to the entertainment.

It was probably my fault that the crew became cocky during downtime. We were a very young crew and maybe needed to blow steam sometimes.

Maybe because we were in the vicinity of fire so much, acting a little too casual in its presence could be expected. On the other hand, I shared a lot of what I'd learned with that bunch of guys. They came to know a lot more than most about how fire would likely react under different conditions.

I will admit, there was swagger about that Hotshot crew – myself included. We were good and we knew it

CHAPTER 14

I look back on that **1965 Fire Season and see myself as a kind of a mix of man and boy.** At work I was a grown-up, making decisions that could have life or death outcomes. Away from work, I wasn't finished with being a kid. Some decisions there weren't so good.

That summer was different from all the others. My personal life and home situation both entered new territories that year where I didn't have much experience. My job at ODF was the rock that anchored all the rest. The Hotshot crew that year was the best.

The summer is very clear in my memory. A number of unique events that occurred turned into milestones.

A VERY SPECIAL SUMMER

Somehow during that summer of 1965, I acquired a steady girlfriend. This didn't start up immediately. It just evolved naturally, with no conscious decisions up to that point that I recall. Even the beginning was sort of indifferent.

It had happened more than a year earlier.

I'd come home from Ashland over the Halloween weekend in 1963. I had replaced the not so reliable Plymouth several months before with a nice little 4-door '56 Ford. After dinner that evening, my two younger sibs were on their way to a teen dance and hayride held at the old Hugo Elementary School. I didn't have any other plans for the evening, so gave them a ride in my car, and stayed for the whole shebang.

I met the girl at that dance. She had hair the color of dark chocolate, big friendly brown eyes and a smile that lit up the room. At that point, though, she was just a girl I didn't know. We danced a lot and talked even more.

Over the next eighteen months I invited her to a couple of movies when at home in Grants Pass, but not often. Mostly my social life was centered at college in Ashland. The girl was only a junior in high school, okay for a date when around home but not really suitable girl-friend material. I thought college guys should stick with college co-eds.

Coming into June 1965, I hadn't thought very much about the Brown-eyed girl since a handful of my friends and I had invited several hometown girls to an impromptu picnic over Spring Break in March.

The weather on that day in late March was clear and sunny, but colder than a Christmas swim on the Oregon Coast. At the picnic our group had explored the damage from the '64 December floods at Indian Mary Park near Galice. We were all suitably awed by the highwater marks on the restroom walls and the driftwood suspended thirty feet up in the treetops in the picnic area. The cold and windy afternoon outing included a gut-wrenching menu purchased by the guys in route to the park – half-cooked hot dogs on dry buns, soda pop and potato chips. Yummy!

We'd paired off with the girls huddling around an open fire, talking and sharing blankets that usually covered the torn seats in our older cars. There are perks to wrapping up with a girl in a blanket on a cold day, but I probably got too fresh. Being a college man and all, I'll admit to being kind of brash.

My date wasn't really happy with me. She already had voiced her discomfort with the lack of inside door handles on my car. That had been a coincidence. I had just finished painting the Ford a pretty metallic maroon but wasn't quite finished getting everything put back together. Her comment about the missing appliances to open the car from the inside was a bit irritating.

Things between we two had continued to quickly cool off a whole lot, closely matching the air temperature. I'd dropped her at home without regrets. At the time I really didn't care all that much, as only a few days later after Spring Break ended, I was in Corvallis back at OSU. For the new term I really buckled down academically with a focus on good grades. I used whatever extra time I had left after classes and studying to finish the fix-up on my car. There wasn't much time left for dating, and I was mostly broke to boot.

Flash-forward to June. My dad had decided to quit the fire fighting business, giving up the Merlin/Hugo patrol. My younger brother really liked the work I'd done on the now gussied-up little Ford. The previous summer he'd nabbed my old engine crewman job with my dad, and earned enough money to buy the pretty Ford from me. As usual, I had needed money for tuition, but no last-minute job appeared. I was down to buying gas to get home with pennies from trading in pop cans.

The financial climate around our Hugo farm had improved a great deal since I'd gone off to my first two years of college in Ashland. Our mom had finally finished up her own college education during my last year of high school. She'd been teaching school for a couple of years since. Mom's regular paychecks had pulled our family out of poverty. Now my family was firmly part of the middle class.

The year before, Dad had purchased a really nice used '59 Ford Fairlane as the family car. That spring he was about to replace that car with a spanking new Pontiac straight off the dealer's lot. Since my brother now owned my Ford, I needed a car to get to work over the summer. When the new Pontiac came home, my parents let me work out a way to buy their Fairlane. A series of payments were worked out, with the first one due after my July paycheck.

I loved that Fairlane! At last I owned the car of my dreams. The Fairlane was a terrific car – the best I ever had. It was a two-door; had a 352-cu. in. engine that purred at an idle and roared when I gave it the gas. Even the black and gold upholstery was perfect. It was a beautiful car in terrific condition inside and out.

This perfect combination of things led my parents to plan something unbelievably rare in our family. They had cash in the bank, nearly three months ahead with no job entanglements, two almost grown sons to pick up the slack with the daily farm chores, and a new car. It was an invitation for them to take a vacation. Such a holiday was so unusual, they decided to do it up right. A lengthy tour of the lake states, the northeast and the southwest to visit distant relatives was planned. A return to Oregon would occur near the end of

August. They bemoaned the fact that all five of us could not go. Our sister, only fifteen until mid-September, wanted to stay home for summer, but they loaded her into the back seat well supplied with lap games to keep her entertained. Off they went just after school closed.

Just a day or two before Mom and Dad left on their trip, I met up with that Brown-eyed girl. It was our first meeting since the picnic debacle.

I believe ODF had just started Fire School, so it was just about the first week of summer work. I was driving home, going to Hugo via Monument Drive (old Hwy 99). I was wearing my spiffy new supervisor suntans complete with new ODF arm patch. My spirits were high with the ego boost of my job promotion erasing the disappointments of academic disgrace from the winter before.

My big shinny white Fairlane was rumbling along near the new junior high school. It was a beautiful early summer afternoon. Ahead, on a long open turn I saw a car just pulling over at a wide spot. It had an obvious flat tire. The two ladies inside were in the process of climbing out as I pulled over behind their car. The damsels in distress were the girl I'd offended at the park and her mom.

I didn't think of it so much as a chance to show off; more like a Good Samaritan – right? There wasn't much conversation at all. Her mom was really nice, but after I changed the flat, it was that girl's 500-Watt smile that made me feel really good. Short story, I felt that maybe my earlier not so polite behavior was forgiven; hopefully forgotten.

This meeting was just a quick crossing of paths with a duration of around ten minutes. Still I wondered, did she notice my new uniform and my flashy car?

Within the week that girl and I accidentally met up three more times.

CHAPTER 15

Summertime in southwestern Oregon is not consistent. The days of terrific weather happen often enough so that people remember them the most. The other days seem to just fade away. The days of wonder are when the sky will be such a deep blue it almost hurts your eyes. In early morning hours the birds begin to chirp around five AM, making such a racket that most people can't sleep too late.

The afternoons are warm and sleepy, filled with the sounds of buzzing insects. The hottest time of day is around 5 PM, when the summer warmth begins to be challenged by a nice little flutter of air. Gentle breezes start moving up the many canyons and valleys of the area, taking the sharp edge off the heat. Slowly, dusk comes soft and purple, changing into calm leisurely evenings. The outdoors is a wonderful place to be.

Usually there is also an ugly part to the summer too. Many people tend to kind of forget it when it's over. Around the end of July there is almost always a hot spell that may be a few days in length or could last for two or three weeks and even more. It gets hot – really hot.

After the first day or so of hellish heat, most people seek out some kind of relief. Outdoor shady areas are soon abandoned for indoor air conditioning. Daily afternoon temperatures move past the nineties into the three-digit range. An occasional late afternoon can get to over 110 degrees, and the daily breeze that cuts the heat most of the time, abandons southwestern Oregon.

If any kind of damp weather system comes off the ocean during this time, powerful thunderstorm systems build above the mountain tops. This is when literally thousands of lightning strikes attack the landscape, igniting remote fires everywhere. The stale valley air is fouled even more when the blue sky turns brassy, smelling of old smoke. This is an uncomfortable period, especially for those whose outdoor work is located within spitting distance of a wildland fire.

Sometimes a summer or two may skip the hot interval all together. Other years must suffer through the nasty heat well into September and October. Many people rave only about how great the weather is in southern Oregon. Sometimes it is excellent – but just as often, it is downright awful. Those who claim it's always wonderful are either newer residents, or just have short memories.

ADJUSTING TO CHANGE

The summers had been fairly gentle in 1963 and 1964, but the next year went right back to normal, at least where the hot weather was concerned.

The winter weather had been pretty severe. Everyone embraced the springtime weather. There were big changes ahead for me that summer of '65 that I had yet to adjust to. The pending responsibilities of my job lay heavy on my mind. I spent much time mulling over these problems and their possible solutions. Adjusting to being a boss was very strange. Acting the part wasn't so difficult, but I didn't feel really comfortable being an adult so abruptly.

Then there was the empty house that I came home to after work every day. The absence of sixty percent of our family left the house in echoing silence. The foremost change, was that my brother and I were to be home alone in that empty house for over two months time. This required adjustment too. We'd always had our parents there, ready to answer any question or offer correction to any mistakes.

Supposedly my brother and I would divide the basic farm chores that usually Dad handled. It was intended that we two would work around our ODF jobs and keep the farm going until the folks returned.

My brother, now seventeen, was driving my now pretty maroon '56 Ford into Grants Pass daily. He rode an ODF patrol engine for his second fire season. I had my white '59 Fairlane purchased a few weeks before from my folks to use for my transportation to work. It's a good thing gasoline was cheap then, because our ODF schedules were different and didn't really encourage ride sharing. Besides, we both reveled in unaccustomed freedom.

During our parents' long road-trip our accountability was limited to only the feeding of livestock and milking of cows. There was also a short irrigation line to tend, pumping water from the creek. On paper the list of daily chores looked very short – really quite do-able.

Within days, though, my brother and I discovered that getting even the short list of jobs done was hard for us. Neither our work nor social schedules were convenient for the responsibilities at home, forcing a continual trade-off back and forth. This led to some pretty spectacular arguments about who did or didn't do what. At least one of these spats turned into a wrestling match under the kitchen table.

Mom must have been aware of the unlikely success of leaving her two sons home alone for a couple of months. She had hired a lady to come in to cook for us, keep house and maintain some order. After a few days, though, our caretaker was no longer in the picture. I'm not sure exactly why. I do not recall any misdeeds by my brother or me that would prompt the lady to walk out on the job.

My mom was forced to switch to Plan B. She tried to keep in control over the telephone, but was only marginally on top of the situation. Wildland fires keep odd hours, so we two orphans at home had a ready-made excuse for being hard to track down. Also, when one or the other of us was around when Mom phoned, sometimes we knowingly chose to not share some things that might cause her to worry. Realistically, there wasn't much she could do to keep order anyway.

Mostly I saw my brother when sharing the bathroom getting ready for work in the morning or around bedtime at night. In truth, we did really pretty well on our own. The expected chores at home were completed more often than not, although not always on time. Once in a while the chickens had to settle for half-rations and the cows were milked long after dark, but at least no livestock died or disappeared. We two managed to eat regularly, got to bed almost on time, and arrived at work as we should all on our own. There were, of course, many other things that led us to miscellaneous transgressions.

What a huge temptation for two red-blooded American farm boys, to have the best part of a complete summer with our own wheels and income, a roof over our heads, a freezer full of food, and no parental supervision. Less than stellar behaviors began to creep in the longer Mom and Dad were on their road trip.

About a week before our parents left, I'd started back at work. There was no break at all for me following my return from OSU. At the ODF office before the official fire season began, the older supervisory personnel (which now included me), had been busy getting equipment and materials ready for Fire School. This was completely new territory for me, but my association, albeit at the pinochle table, with many of the older guys was an asset. They were really helpful in sharing things I needed to know and correcting my many mistakes. My direct supervisor was now the Protection Supervisor for the north half of the GP Unit. I didn't bumble around too much and was still soaking up information like a sponge.

The next Monday, the sixty or so fellows on the patrol engines and hand trail crew reported to work. Fire School flew by. Before I was really ready, I was alone with my Hotshots leading their physical training activities. It was then that one of the first small fires of the new season was called in from the Mt. Sexton tower. It was mid-afternoon almost immediately after Fire School was finished. Later we knew the cause of the fire was from an electric fence that had shorted out in tall dry grass.

The smoke was located about half way between I-5 and old Hwy 99 near the eight-mile marker north of town. Today this is directly west and across the freeway from the Sportsmen's Park.

There was no access to the fire from the freeway side to the east, and only roundabout ways from the west side. The best access known for the Hotshot crew was beyond an old cemetery to a farmhouse driveway. Still, this route would need a good mile long hike through very thick brush. An alternate route from the south at about the seven-mile marker was via a paved road that came to a dead end. This choice also required an even longer hike over a notable spur ridge. Neither way allowed a quick arrival, which was always important.

When the fire call was made, both the Merlin/Hugo patrol engine and the Sunny Valley rig were at the wrong side of their areas of responsibility. My Hotshots would arrive first, but would still be delayed in our initial response by travel-time.

We were coming all the way from town, but at least traveling north, avoiding the bottle-neck of downtown traffic. Every minute that passed meant the fire was getting bigger and stronger, harder to put down. With several houses in the vicinity of the fire, we needed to hit that baby before it got ahead of us. Maybe we could find another, faster access than those suggested by Dispatch?

As I drove the Hotshot Crummy north on Monument Drive we entered my territory – we were deep in the Merlin/Hugo patrol area and only three miles from my home for the past twenty years. I knew that several small acreages had driveways going toward the fire's location from old Hwy 99/Monument Drive on the west side. Nothing on the map showed complete access cross-country through to the fire for the Hotshot Crummy.

The family of the girl whose flat tire I'd changed a day or two before, owned one of these properties. I'd kind of been thinking about her since our short meeting regarding the flat tire. Her family's place was directly west of the fire site indicated by HQ Dispatch from the location given by the Sexton Lookout. The house was less than a mile from the fire.

I decided to take a chance and check if there could be a way to drive into the fire across the twelve acres where the young lady lived ... it would save a lot of precious time if successful.

It was my lucky day in more than one way. That Brown-eyed girl was the only person at their house, along with their family dog. He was a really big German Shepherd, with an approximate size of your average kitchen table. That dog had golden eyes and a grin that brought to mind the wolf in the Little Red Riding-hood story – like he was wondering which one of your legs he might decide to eat first.

When we drove up, the girl came from the house holding the collar of that big smiling dog. When asked about a possible way to drive through the property going to the east, the two of them led our Hotshot Crummy on a narrow cat-trail through the brush to the back of their place where the neighbor's very old rusty field fence lay on the ground. There she pointed out the way.

She was wearing Levi shorts, cut-off at mid-thigh and had nice long tanned legs. It was pleasant to watch as she walked ahead of our crew truck filled to the roof with appreciative teen-aged guys.

I took more than a little ribbing about even knowing this girl. There was also a comment or two about dealing with the dog.

I drove across the downed wire onto another overgrown cat-trail. With directions from our guide, we left her at the fence-line with the dog. I wrestled the crew truck over the rough but flat ground, to follow another rickety fence through more buck brush, manzanita and poison oak. In a few minutes we broke out of the brush. About 200 feet ahead across open ground was the fire.

There wasn't much wind, so the total area burning was still small. Good fortune had located the loudly popping hot-wire fence on the edge of a natural wetland patch. It stretched all the way to the freeway's edge.

A shallow rock table on both sides of the freeway there keeps the light fuels to mostly thick native grasses and a few wide spaced runty wild plums and cherry trees. The meadow grass was quite heavy and very green, as the rock kept water in the soil from soaking deeper. Spots like this show up all over SWO. The almost swampy ground was sour from the mineral content and too much moisture. The grass was well rooted, but the scrawny trees had not developed healthy systems.

The Hotshots got right down to business. We quickly organized into a hard-working hand trail crew. All the naturally occurring factors were temporarily keeping the fire small, but we had to figure the wind would soon be on us. Building line in the thick grass and wet soil wasn't too hard. The weak root systems of the heavier fuels let my crew grub out the little trees along the fire line pathway with no trouble at all. We had the low flames and burned-over area completely encircled in about thirty minutes.

Almost as if someone pushed a button, just as the containment trail was finished the regular summer late afternoon breeze kicked up. If we'd followed either of the other access roads with their necessary hikes to the location, that small burn could have moved into the dry brush and taken a run toward the houses.

I pointed out this important timing fact to those on my crew who had teased me about the girl. My most professional boss-man tone of voice was used for these comments, trying to deflect any more teasing remarks from my crew. Inside our trailed circle of burned-over earth, the fire was dying down. That's when two patrol engines arrived almost together. They had come via the same overland route our crew truck had used and that we had identified over the radio. The timing was perfect for them to take over the mop up duties.

In a few minutes my crew was released by Dispatch. We were able to return back to the Grants Pass HQ at just about the regular time to ready the crew truck for tomorrow and then go home.

All in all, it had been a nice afternoon's work. I had enjoyed the short encounter with the girl, and the little fire was just the right size to limber up the crew on different soils and fuels from the norm – adding to their training. It had used up enough time to practice proper line building without adding any extra time to our day. Overall it was a positive start to my first fire season as the Hotshot Supervisor.

At the end of the week I had a night and following day off. The entire Hotshot crew was turned free almost every Sunday night and all day each Monday every week for the whole summer. I think we were starting on the second week of work when I went to see the new James Bond movie called "Gold Finger" that was showing at the Rogue Theater in town.

I usually would have taken my brother and sister along. My brother had to work the next day and had planned an early evening at home playing pool. My sister was somewhere on the way to Michigan. Instead I'd made arrangements to meet up with two town buddies at the theater.

Sitting in our favorite balcony seats next to the projection booth at the back wall, we had a great view of the screen and also of anyone else who came upstairs looking for seating too. Just as the lights dimmed, that same girl and some of her friends plopped down in the row immediately in front of my friends and me. We guys teased and pestered the girls throughout the film. It seemed the natural thing to do.

It's remarkable she didn't just flatten me right there for being such a jerk. I expected her to give me the brush-off when I offered her a ride home, since her parents' place was on my way. Back then it wasn't too unusual for kids living out of town to share rides with those who lived nearby. Still, I was surprised when she agreed to the ride I offered. Walking up to the Fairlane she admired my beloved car. I told her I appreciated her compliments as I drove toward Hugo. Mostly it was a quiet ride. She gave up that big smile with a polite Thank You leaving the car when I dropped her off.

A day or so later in the early evening after work, I was priming our irrigation pump in Bannister Creek. The creek bed roughly parallels the old highway along that stretch. I heard female voices nearby. Lo and behold, there she was again, walking south on Monument Drive with a couple of younger girls who lived at the local ma 'n pa store down the road.

The big trees along the creek effectively hid me from the girls, and I could just barely tell who was on the roadway up the bank above me.

Without really thinking I yelled a hearty "Hello". There was a quiet pause, then a cheerful shout answered. A brief but loud conversation went back and forth. It seems the girls were walking home from the local swimming hole on Jump Off Joe Creek that we all called The Falls.

I think I was as surprised as that girl was upon hearing words of invitation coming out of my mouth.

"Would you go to the movies with me tomorrow," I called out for everyone within a half-mile to hear.

"Sure", she yelled back. I gave a time when I'd pick her up. We each called out our Good-byes and she walked on with her friends.

How about that!

Looking back, I think once again maybe Destiny or Fate was fiddling around in my life – and maybe hers too. Before that flat-tire situation, I hadn't seen or thought about that girl in months ... not since that unpleasant picnic back in March. Our parting then had definitely been on the unfriendly side. I hadn't really been thinking about dating or any girl at all. Now the crossing of our paths four times within a few days had put this young lady back in my mind in a very big way. Plus - surprise, surprise – I had a date with her with no planning or worrying involved!

The happy connection between this girl and me came from this batch of chance meetings. These led to going out, soon on a regular but not necessarily exclusive basis. Maybe I was a little lonely with our usually full house now nearly empty. Something new and very important – this relationship - grew that summer.

At least I wasn't getting any razza-ma-tazz from my family about how most of my very limited free time for the next two months was spent in the company of just one nice girl. Our time together wasn't exactly exclusive, but more like an inevitable drawing together. We went on a couple of picnics and saw a few movies. I gave her rides home after work from her in-town job fairly often. When together we sometimes just sat and talked. Literally hours passed as we talked about anything and everything. There was some smooching thrown in here and there as well. By the time my twenty-first birthday arrived just a few weeks later most everyone, including my whole crew, considered us a couple. Still, I'm very sure neither she nor I felt particularly committed to the other. Spending time together just seemed natural, the way things were supposed to be.

Our dating continued all summer but never with any obligations spoken. We became good friends, usually very comfortable when in each other's company.

CHAPTER 16

*T*he Interstate Five freeway was almost new. In 1965 it was mostly complete from the bottom of Mt. Sexton all the way into Ashland near the California border to the south.

Going north there was only a two-lane winding challenge going for thirty miles or more over the mountains. This section began at the Hugo turn-off.

The finished parts had a posted speed limit of 70 MPH. It was considerably straighter than the old Hwy 99 roadway to the west. There was about a mile between the two roads that were almost parallel between Hugo and Grants Pass.

People didn't travel as much back in the 1960s as they do nowadays. The semi-truck traffic was a fraction of what we see now. Also, Josephine County housed a population 2/3 smaller then. And so, Interstate 5 had only the lightest use even in the summer. The combination of a broad empty roadway and a sleek muscle car driven by this 20-year-old guy, led to a certain kind of driving behavior.

BEING A KID IN HUGO

My parents had always been pretty strict about my behavior and that of my siblings. Yet here I was about as free as any kid could be. At home I was accountable to no one. My brother and I soon worked out most of the unpleasant aspects of our responsibilities.

At work I enjoyed the structure of the organization of the department, the company of the older fire veterans, and was coming to appreciate and even enjoy the leadership role I now held.

The daily drive to and from work was the best time of some of my days. During empty roadway periods early in the morning or late at night I often had the entire road to myself all the way from Grants Pass to the Hugo turn off. I was able to drive that stretch from home into GP in about 15 to 20 minutes, and often much less if I didn't pay too much attention to the speed laws.

Driving the Fairlane was a wonderful experience. There were a few times when the road was completely empty and I'd give into the temptation. I'd floor the gas pedal.

Wow! It almost felt like flying.

I was really beginning to enjoy my Fairlane and what its big engine could do. It had a great sound and would really respond when asked. State Police that patrolled the section of road between Hugo and north Grants Pass stopped me at least once, but when they saw my uniform and learned I was going to a fire (really!), they motioned me on. Over time, they just waved at me as I sped by.

How I avoided a speeding ticket is a mystery. I'd gotten into the habit of switching over to driving the old Hwy 99 (Monument Drive) sometimes to not push my luck.

The only complaint I really paid much heed to was from the father of that Brown-eyed girl. She shared that her dad said he "could hear that Dickerson kid's big Ford" as I topped the first slope coming down the hill toward the Joe Creek Bridge on Monument Drive. I had no doubt that what he said was true, even though that bridge is about a mile to the north of where their house was located.

The engine in my car sounded exactly like distant thunder! I loved it. Later when her dad and I became better acquainted, I found he was a guy that really appreciated the sound of a powerful engine. He had souped-up just about every vehicle he'd ever owned, including their current family station wagon. Her two older brothers had followed his lead with their cars too.

I'm not real sure about my brother's driving habits throughout that summer; I wasn't his keeper. There were some vague comments I picked up on while our parents were absent. If he did receive a speeding ticket, he had enough from his paycheck to pay the fine without having to spill the beans to me. I didn't ask.

Our work schedules were very limiting. To find time available for late night shenanigans of any type was kind of dicey to put together. This was probably a very good thing. Wildland fire fighting does not fit well with nighttime carousing. Party animals need not apply. It is a job that tends to wear a guy down – sleep becomes quite valuable. Just taking my almost girl friend to a double feature at the Rogue Theater all the way in town meant my bedtime was pushed to around mid-night. It made for a rough morning the next day. Needing enough sleep to handle my job six days each week made my one night off even more precious.

I don't recall just what day-off my brother had, Tuesday I think. For me, Monday of each week was when my Hotshots were "off" but "on call or stand by" – meaning we still had to be available to a telephone or carry a radio at all times. If there was a need, we had to get to the compound ASAP. Otherwise we had 24 hours more or less to ourselves. From whatever time we were able to clock out Sunday evening, until 9 AM Tuesday morning the GP Hotshot crew was essentially free.

Since we were paid a monthly salary, if we were called in, we worked 24/7 without any extra pay except the already allotted Comp Time bonus. If a night-fire stretched a regular day's tour until midnight we were still expected to stagger in at our next regular morning starting time.

In all fairness, when we did pull a lot of extra-duty hours, especially late into the night, our reporting time was usually extended by an understanding Overhead boss until late morning or even mid-afternoon the next day. If we worked through the night, we might not have to report until regular time the next day following. Still, the telephone/radio contact rule was in effect 24/7.

The schedule was intended to maintain an available well-trained workforce at all times. Since the Headquarters Crew House was closed up two years before, everyone on our crew could scatter to their own homes when on stand-by. No one was supposed to be unavailable. My guys were very good about staying near a telephone. I pretty well kept one of the crew's hand-held peanut radios with me all the time so HQ Dispatch could always call me.

As the Hotshot Supervisor, I'd receive a call-out notice first via HQ Dispatch, and then notify my guys myself. This was bothersome work and sometimes not completely successful. A side effect was that I sort of insisted the Hotshots spend a lot of our rare free time together whenever on stand-by. With my parents out of town, our empty home became a substitute over-night Crew House more than once.

The crew didn't exactly enjoy the chores at the GP HQ when waiting for a fire during the day, but at least there were things to do. Stand-by at night was better. Our evening hangouts included the Rogue Theater in downtown GP or the Redwood Drive-In Theater south of the river. Except for Larry's Drive-In restaurant and the roller-rink, that is pretty well the entire list of stuff to do in Grants Pass back then. I recall the crew disposing of one full day-off on boring stand-by playing a marathon game of 8-Ball at our place. More than a couple of guys on the crew used stand-by as a time to catch up on much needed sleep. Even when we were together, someone was usually sacked-out nearby.

We spent several hot weather days off at The Falls swimming hole. The Falls were easily the most favorite swimming hole for the older kids who lived at the north end of the valley. Most of my crew lived in town, so I introduced them to our local teen hangout. The Falls are on Jump Off Joe Creek about a mile up the canyon to the east of I-5. They are very easily found, snuggled up tightly at the bottom of barren looking Red Mountain, just southeast of Mt. Sexton.

At that time a deeply rutted roadway twisted through the buck brush giving us access to an open area on the top of the sheer bank of the creek. This was where we could park our cars, and sometimes an occasional horse could be found tied, awaiting its rider in the dense shade of large oak trees. The ruts in the access road were world-class and took out more than one car's oil pan.

The stream was about sixty feet below the parking area, down a rock face. Today an RV and camping resort are located there. There is a gate to control entry to the site with access available for a fee.

The swimming area included a large deep pool, fed by a long rocky chute kind of like a slide. The stream flow gave the chute a nice slick surface if one wanted to use it to get into the water. A smaller pool was immediately downstream from the big pool, more secluded but also much more shallow. Those not swimming could and did climb the surrounding rocks and jump or dive into the water of the bigger pool from several proven spots on the cliff face. Sometimes people would misjudge the depth, or stumble when climbing around, resulting in skinned knees and sometime foreheads.

The whole thing resembled pictures of places like Hawaii or other tropical pools, except surrounded with alders and conifers instead of palms and orchids.

Rag Tag was a favorite and probably dangerous game usually played only by the guys when a larger group was swimming at The Falls. A rolled up, wet, t-shirt was thrown at the other players to designate who was "IT". Scrambling like squirrels over the rocks to get close enough for a successful hit or to elude the stingy THOOWACK of the wet shirt required agility and tough feet.

We mostly left any girls present out of this activity except for peripheral splashing that brought howls of complaint. Once in a while a wild throw of the wet shirt nailed a girl by mistake.

I had gathered the GP Hotshots on stand-by status at the Falls on one of our mid-summer collective days off. We were busy with a rousing game of Rag Tag when we discovered a foot-long rattlesnake sunning itself on the very small sandy patch behind a rock formation we called The Turret. This was a taller, pointy rock that only the gutsiest guys would jump from.

Several of the guys on the crew couldn't resist teasing the reptile. The little viper was so young it didn't seem to know how to use its tiny single section rattle. With a stick of sufficient length for safety, a couple of the guys pestered, poked and prodded the young snake, trying to get it to buzz, without immediate success.

After a bit the group around the snake were rewarded with an angry high-pitched Z Z Z Z Z Z Z produced when, using the stick, someone lifted the snake from his resting place. Dumb, dumb, dumb! The sudden warning from the snake startled the crewman with the stick in hand. By mistake he flipped the baby rattler into a long, high, and gentle arc that thankfully landed it in the water of the pool below, close to the far shore. The snake swam to safety – but no one really wanted to jump into the water for a very, very long time after that.

On really warm days there could be up to ten, even twenty kids at The Falls at a time. Adults seldom made use of that swimming hole during the daytime, so it was ours alone. We kids all loved the place.

As that summer wore on, my twenty-first birthday was rapidly approaching. My brother and my crew made it clear to me that this landmark date was an excellent motive to kick up our heels. There were serious logistic issues, what with only the single 24-hour day-off per week. Great minds were handling the problematic issues.

The event was in the planning stages for some time. We all put our best efforts toward finding ways around the most obvious barriers. Sufficient supplies were being stockpiled next to my mom's washer and dryer on our back porch.

Three or four days before B-day, a first attempt to do something special was foiled by the weatherman and the ODF Unit Supervisor. As my Hotshot crew left the GP office to go their supposed separate ways for a potential next day-off, some ominous looking clouds were building into thunderstorms to the southeast along the Siskiyou Mountains crestline.

I rounded up my guys before time to leave the compound, telling them the event we'd all been planning for that night was cancelled. The crew was on stand-by, so all were advised to stay near their telephones. I made sure my peanut radio had fresh batteries in preparation for keeping it at hand that night and all the next day.

Up until then the "stand-by" designation hadn't had much affect on our one day-off. With the lightning storm literally on the horizon, things changed. I'd been directed by Overhead to keep the crew pretty much together and reachable. This was at a time when all use of the telephone was via landlines. Imagine - no cell phones.

We remained on call that night and the next day, but the storms blew over. Again, the next afternoon clouds began to build, and we were on stand-by once more. Before I'd been notified about the second evening on stand-by, I had called my almost girl friend and made plans to go to the drive-in theater that evening. This was still on the agenda, but we had to modify the initial design.

She seemed somewhat surprised that I showed up at her house with three Hotshot crew guys in the back seat of my car and the peanut radio on the dashboard. A promise of two more vehicles filled with the rest of the crew meeting up with us at the drive-in brought a somewhat strained smile to her face.

Nine guys escorting one girl was pretty irregular.

Nevertheless, with little choice at hand she accepted the situation for what it was. Off we all went to reunite with the rest of the crew. No smooching tonight.

The second cloud build-up blew over without any fireworks, but we all had a great evening that I'm sure most remember even now – fifty years later.

The crew located themselves in the three cars, with an occasional and on-going switch of seating for one or another reason. We were all parked next to the others, toward the back of the Drive-In grounds. Monday night wasn't a busy evening at the theater so there were perhaps two or three totally empty rows behind us. An overgrown wide space filled with dried grass and trash lay between the last row of speakers and the back fence. All cars entered the theater viewing area through that space.

Not long after, still in the purple twilight, just as the first movie began, a familiar smell of grass smoke wafted past our open car windows. Everyone was quickly on alert, tracking down the origin of the fresh smoke. It was located in record time by this savvy bunch.

A low-lying blaze was creeping its way through the weeds and trash in that open area behind all the parked cars, probably caused by a carelessly dropped cigarette from an arriving car.

The well-qualified and fully able GP ODF Hotshots were on the scene! Without much discussion and being rather bored anyway with the forgettable storyline unfolding on the screen, all the crew sprang to action.

Armed with nothing more than feet shod in sandals and tennis shoes, and carrying a couple of backseat blankets, my crew burst out of our respective cars and attacked that pitiful little fire. Even through we had no tools whatsoever, we had it knocked down and fully out in record time.

Only minutes following our initial attack, we were back in our cars, our casual clothes now smelling like we often did after a hard day's work of fire fighting. Everyone was laughing, comparing the burned spots on the soles of our shoes and trying to catch up on the few minutes of the movie we'd missed. No one thought to notify the theater staff about the fire – it was out and no longer a problem.

Our evening's entertainment was not yet over! About ten minutes passed when the wail of a siren was heard approaching. It was one of the well-used Grants Pass Rural Fire Department tankers. Everyone with ODF was merciless in their assessment of these well-meaning but sorely under-trained laymen and their rickety equipment. The GP RFD was supposed to focus exclusively on structure fires, with any effectiveness while fighting wildland fire always in question.

Keeping the siren echoing and all of its pretty lights flashing, that dented and nearly worn-out truck searched the drive-in and the adjoining roadway for the blaze we'd just stomped out. Once, twice, three times that tanker cruised the road and the theater area, irritating most of the movie patrons with every pass. The quest was, of course, fruitless, as the flames were out and the burned area invisible in the dark.

The Hotshots, to a man, could not avoid the giggles and guffaws each time the RFD vehicle passed. It was more entertaining to watch the unsuccessful search for the fire than to flag them down and share that the action was over. We probably should have let them dowse the black space to avoid a possible flare-up – but we didn't.

Probably in response to multiple complaints, the manager of the drive-in finally asked the driver to leave the grounds. I do not believe they ever found out what happened or who did what.

My not-girl friend presented me with a really nice fully iced birthday cake that she had carried along that evening. I figured the guys with us would devour the cake on the spot – but restraint was found. They decided I should take it home and keep it in the frig until at least my Real Birthday arrived later in the week. It spent the evening at the movies safely stored in the car's gigantic trunk space.

The following week the crew was NOT on active stand-by when our day-off arrived. The actual date of celebration had passed, but my brother, my crew and several of our friends from ODF ranks as well as others from our Hugo neighborhood, put together a wiz-bang birthday party for me on the non-committed Sunday night. The locale was our family home in Hugo – sans parents of course, who were still on their east coast trip.

We filled the whole inside of the house and pretty much the entire fenced yard outside. It's a good thing there were no houses very close to ours, as we were a noisy group. The guest list was entirely male, primarily between seventeen and twenty-one years of age. In case the Hotshots were called out, the whole crew was present and expected to spend the night.

The stockpile of refreshments was quite generous. Eventually we all got totally smashed. We didn't get caught for underage drinking, thank goodness, as that would have probably landed me in the company of the previously infamous Hotshot straw bosses fired back in 1963.

Unaware of the party and not present, my almost girl friend had earlier provided that lovely birthday cake. It was appropriately decorated and kept safely in the refrigerator for several days. It was perfect for the party because she had decorated it with a stubby bottle of Olympia beer imbedded in the iced top. (I don't know how an 18-year-old, fairly straight-laced girl got a hold of that!). My Hotshots gave me a really nice 16-inch genuine German beer stein complete with molded metal flip top lid. It is currently sitting on a bookshelf in my living room.

It was a challenge, but my brother and I kept all the guys contained that night, mostly within the fenced space around the house. Eventually everyone fell safely asleep – many in some pretty strange places, such as on the pool table, the middle of the front yard and on the roof.

When dawn rose on the scene, we realized one of our crew was missing. It took about an hour of searching to find one fellow partier. He was a couple hundred feet from the house and snoring deeply next to the chicken yard near my dad's equipment shop.

It's a very good thing there were no urgent and unexpected fire calls that night. I had been prepared to take any such calls with the peanut on my hip all the while, but there was no way that bunch of sots could have handled a fire.

Considering our ages and the circumstances of our situation that summer, I think my brother and I kept pretty good control of a potentially bad experience. That was an unforgettable 21st Birthday party.

I absolutely do not condone a teen-aged beer bust as a team-building exercise for fire crews. I will say though, as a group, that crew could build fire line better than most any other I've seen. They also put together a great party as well.

CHAPTER 17

One of the more interesting things about the SWO District, is the phenomenal diversity of landscape. A big part of that is because of the Siskiyou - Klamath Mountains that roughly parallel the East-West orientation of the Oregon/California borderline. This mountainous area is very old geologically. There are unique metamorphic soil and rock types that restrict or promote growth of particular plant species.

The Oregon Coast Range and the Cascade Mountains both run mostly north and south. Although mostly running east and west, the Siskiyou - Klamath Mountains have ridges going off in all four directions. That impacts the angle of sunlight and rain-shadow effect altering humidity, total precipitation, and air-flow dependent on the direction of the mountain face. All this confusion with the terrain really promotes the unusual diversity of the district.

LEADING THE HOTSHOTS

That 1965 Hotshot crew seemed to develop a bond that was unlike any I'd experienced. I don't condone the use of an underage beer bust as a team-building ploy, but after my birthday the crew grew even closer.

That was a really great crew of guys without regard to how it happened. All of us were kids, but when working everybody was very serious and mature. The focus when on a fire was all on the job.

That was one tight-knit group. Several adventures were yet to be experienced by the crew that summer – a couple of these events particularly tested me, helping my leadership skills grow.

It was my fourth summer to fight wildfire in SWO. I had just been promoted as the Hotshot crew boss a little over a month before. Sometimes I worried if I was ready for the job, but with most of two previous fire seasons as a straw boss on this crew, I was getting more confident in the leadership position every day.

So far that summer, I'd had a good feel for planning sufficient physical training and fire attack strategies. The guys on the crew were out-spoken offering lots of valued input, yet they followed my leadership without too many negative comments. As a crew we'd built a lot of trust. Socially we'd also bonded very well, enjoying each other's company.

Both of my straw bosses persisted with childish pranks. Their timing was well chosen, avoiding interference with the serious nature of our job. Nothing they did was really over the line, just little things like a lizard in someone's hardhat or an occasional hotfoot. I couldn't slam them too hard, as one of the Unit mid-tier supervisors had a thing about practical jokes too. Once or twice I had to caution my young offenders. At least the lighter moments kept the outlook of the crew pretty much on the positive side.

Nobody was particularly targeted. With everyone as a potential victim, we all became wary and occasionally turned the tables on the culprit. And when a successful caper came to fruit, we all shared in the laughter. We also managed to get pretty far into the season without entanglement in any really sticky situation when on a fire.

One of our experiences gave the crew a good opportunity to razz me – but they never did. We had been called out of the Grants Pass HQ to help the Williams Warden and crewman with a lightning fire on a ridge several miles south of the Murphy/Williams area. In the mid-afternoon, smoke had begun to show enough to draw the attention of a distant mountain top Lookout tower.

When the Williams engine arrived at the scene they found a fire at about an acre or two in size and quickly growing. Most district engines and equipment were involved with other lightning strike investigations or fires.

There was no close road access that would allow the Williams guys to use their water supply, leaving hand-trail as their only attack strategy. The size of the incident led to the Hotshots being sent to help them with the necessary trail building.

To get to the fire we took a logging road that mostly followed a ridgeline that ran generally south to north. We'd circled around and were coming in from a southern approach. When the road ended, we'd parked our crew truck, gathered our tools and hiked another couple of miles north along the ridge top before finding the fire. The Williams crew was hard at work, but the fire's size put them at a big disadvantage.

All of that late afternoon was used to encircle the blaze with a secure hand line. We spent the early evening starting mop up on the burned-over space, starting from the trail we'd built and working into the black to the ignition location.

Earlier, one of my crewmen seemed to be in the early stages of heat exhaustion, as the mid-summer day was very hot and humid. His condition wasn't too serious, but to be on the safe side I relieved him from the line. I felt we were fairly close to finishing up, so I'd sent the injured guy with another crewman as an escort, back to the crew truck. I'd sent our extra radio with them in case our man got to feeling worse and needed more help.

Instructions were for the over-heated guy to get hydrated, rest up and wait for the remainder of the crew to return. The extra crewman who was assisting was told to return to us and bring additional water bottles back with him, plus a couple of flashlights as darkness was beginning to fall. He returned in about an hour, leaving the second radio behind with the sick guy as told.

The after-fire mop up took longer than I'd expected, and full dark had arrived. The Williams Warden released us from the burn around midnight. He and his crewman would stay on the fire until morning.

I wasn't concerned about getting back to the crew truck in spite of the dark. The hike back was over fairly even ground and we now had the two flashlights to help keep our footing. Even though there was no real trail, as long as we took some care and kept to the ridge top we'd hiked in on, there should be no problem finding our way.

We all knew it would have to be a slow trek in the darkness. No one wanted to trip and fall on their face. I told the guys to keep in a fairly tight line to keep someone from wandering from the group by mistake.

Gathering our tools, we set out expecting a slow walk of about thirty minutes or so. I took one flashlight at the front and gave the second to the straw boss at the rear of the crew line. I was sure all we had to do was follow the contour of the crest of the ridge going south straight to the truck.

The hike on the ridge wasn't strenuous but seemed to be taking longer than I thought it should. When this thought came to me I gathered the crew around me calling a halt.

Direct radio contact was made with the ailing crewman I'd sent back to the rig. It took a while to get an answer to my call because, being exhausted, he had fallen deeply asleep. When he was finally awake and alert, I asked him to honk the horn and flash the headlights. We were all sure the rig would be within earshot of our location.

The crew quieted down, everyone on the lookout and listening.

I was honestly surprised when not one of us heard any sound or saw a light in any direction. What could have happened?

We could not have passed the truck in the dark, as we would have hit the access road our Crummy drove in on. We should have at least heard the horn even if a half mile away.

With a sinking feeling in my stomach, it came to me that I had managed to get the crew lost in remote mountains on a dark night.

Well, that wasn't really accurate. We weren't actually lost – I just didn't know exactly where we were.

To keep walking in the dark was plain stupid; it would just compound our current problem. I was immediately sure we had no choice but to wait for daylight.

The kids on the crew expected me to provide reassurance and a solution to our shared dilemma. A very brief wave of despair hit me, where I felt the full weight of the responsibility of leadership lay heavily on me. For a moment I wished someone else were in charge. Thinking out the problem was hard. I was so doggone tired from working the fire, plus the heat and humidity. Also, I was suddenly aware of being famished!

I forced my weary mind to make a review of all that we had done and what we might yet do to get ourselves out of this mess, or at least make the best of it. No matter how I studied it, just waiting was still the most favorable choice. Once I came to this realization, I told the crew and called HQ Dispatch, telling our situation.

We would camp out for the night – everyone was safe and accounted for, but we would obviously be hours late with our arrival at HQ. I was a little surprised that there were no comments or even grumbling from any of the crew. Every pocket was turned out checking for snacks that might be shared. We did have a few aluminum canteens half-filled with tepid and stale water.

I radioed to the crewman at the truck and also shared my final decision with him. If I was going to get any heat from the Unit Forester about keeping the crew out all night, at least it wouldn't be because there was anybody who was left to worry needlessly about our safety. I told our sick guy to stay put and get some sleep; we'd be there in the morning.

One by one the seven guys with me leaned heads against tree trunks or curled up on the mixture of pine needles, brushy debris and lumpy dirt trying to find any comfortable position. Even though the hour was very late and every fellow there was physically worn out, I didn't figure any of us would manage more than a few fitful naps on the hard ground before dawn. All present were very dirty and very, very hungry. Dawn was several hours ahead of us.

At least at this elevation there weren't too many mosquitoes to make the situation worse. There was no need to build a warming fire either, as it was a pleasant enough August night. As the bright stars slowly passed overhead I could feel the air temperature cooling a bit – it must be very late.

As I lay there in the dirt and longed for much needed sleep, my mind would not rest. I've always been one to worry over problems, seeking some solution. Over and over I thought through what I needed to do in the morning. Finally blessed sleep came.

The night didn't turn out to be as long as I feared it would, and we all slept more than we expected. Dawn arrived as always; it was quite early on top of that crest line. Since the ridge we followed ran south on our way out of the fire, I had expected the sun to rise on my left as I faced back along the hilltop. Surprisingly, the sun was on my back. We had been hiking toward the WEST!

Everybody uncurled and stretched stiff arms and legs. After a couple of radio messages to our ailing crewman at the truck, the rest of us set out to find our vehicle. We would need to backtrack, find where we'd strayed and then hike to the truck using visual clues unusable the night before.

After plodding back along the ridge about ½ mile or so, I found where we had deviated last night to get around some especially heavy brush. A wide circle down hill and around was necessary. We worked our way back to the higher ground once out of the brush and came to a place that appeared to be the same ridge we had lost in the dark. After a very short false start while well able to see our way, we found that this was actually a spur ridge veering off to the west. It was easy to see how we'd lost our way especially in the dark.

I questioned the crewman who'd successfully hiked to and from the rig the evening before, but he said it looked different in the morning light. Even if we'd had a map, we probably would have missed the intersection of ridge-tops.

At that point I radioed our crewman at the truck telling him to honk the horn again. This time we could easily hear it in the clear morning air. With a tired cheer, everyone turned down the correct route along the main ridge. Weary legs carried us about another mile and we found the crew truck just as we'd left it the afternoon before.

We trooped up to our parked vehicle happy to see its dusty sides and windows reflecting the early morning sun. As tools were secured, I radioed HQ that we would be on our way back to Grants Pass in just a few minutes.

It was so early that after we left the dusty logging roads and headed past the mill and over Murphy Hill nearing downtown GP, hardly any traffic was to be seen on Williams Highway.

By now growling stomachs were loudly making their protests. The scent of bacon frying led us to a restaurant that opened early and gave them more breakfast business than they could handle.

It isn't every day that nine starved and filthy teenage kids, each one smelling like the Devil's own wiener-roast walk, into a café. We were covered in soot, ashes and dirt. Some of the guys still had leaves and pine needles in their hair. It was still a bit before 6 AM and my crew ordered just about everything on the menu.

Stacks of pancakes, biscuits and gravy, chicken fried steak, bacon, hash-browns, ham, sausage and dozens of eggs disappeared. We even destroyed a couple of freshly baked pies. The amount of food devoured was astonishing. It was a delicious breakfast long to be remembered by all!

Best of all, my whole crew was safe, sound and present.

One large lightning storm that rolled through Southwest Oregon in 1965 created a large number of smokes that needed attention. In order to get the most coverage with the resources available, the unit supervisor decided it would be best to temporarily cut down the size of the Hotshots. My crew was left with just three crewmen, leaving a total of four guys. The other five were dispersed to five patrol engines, increasing their crews to three on each rig.

This was good thinking. Lightning caused fires are often up on some ridge top and not very accessible for engines. When that happens, engine crews must resort to using only hand tools to control the fire. Having another set of hands available can really decrease the amount of time to control each blaze, then move on to the next down-strike as quickly as possible. In this way, more fires were controlled with the same number of personnel.

Those of us remaining of the Hotshots were dispatched to a fire about fifteen miles south to south west of Grants Pass. When we located our smoke, it was up on a ridge top but not overly far from the access road. It was on state-protected land, but not very far from a USFS property line. We loaded up an assortment of tools - one Pulaski, a couple of Hazel hoes, a shovel, and our chainsaw (in case we had to fell a burning snag, as is often the case with lightning fires), and hiked up the slope to the fire location.

The fire had burned about a tenth of an acre, and was not moving fast. It appeared to have started from a ground strike in dry pine needles and grass, so no felling was required. We jumped into the job of building a hand line around the perimeter, which took about 45 minutes to an hour. We just started with some mop-up of a few hot spots to make it safe to leave temporarily, and move on to another assignment. All fires controlled and left in this manner were checked again at the first opportunity to be sure they stayed safe.

Just as we got started with working the hot spots, we heard a fast moving, low flying aircraft come overhead. It flew right over our fire, banked around and made another pass. We could see it was a mid-sized, twin-engine plane flying low enough that we identified someone peering out the open side door. It was a Smoke Jumper plane, with a crew about to make a jump onto our fire. Since the incident was contained, that action wasn't needed.

Although the ODF didn't directly employ Smoke Jumpers, we had some familiarity with them. Sometimes USFS visited our office to recruit experienced folks from our crews to become jumpers. I think they succeeded in getting a couple of recruits this way over the years. Not me, though. It was my belief that it wasn't a good idea to jump out of a perfectly good airplane.

Anyway, my short-handed crew ran into a nearby open area where we could be seen and tried to wave off the jumpers. This was to no avail. On the next pass at a higher altitude, here they came, one by one out the side door.

It was quite a sight to behold, with their colorful chutes bellowing out as each fellow left the plane. They free-fell a short distance before the chutes opened. I recall that there were four of them, then a couple extra equipment packs, also with chutes attached.

We watched as they made their descent to the ground into another open area also near to our fire. As they gathered their chutes and equipment, we hurried over to greet them and exchange information. They were from the Cave Junction base about twenty-five miles southeast of Grants Pass.

We told them we tried to wave them off, but they just grinned, saying they had interpreted our actions as an invitation. It is my belief that they just hated to go back to their base on the plane. At any rate, they joined us in making sure the fire was safe to leave.

One of the jumpers was a younger guy, closer in age to our crew. He was rather small in stature, but a good or better line-builder that any of his bigger cohorts. We learned his name was "Peewee", or something like that. Apparently, he was something of a legend amongst his trade. Very well respected by his peers.

Once the fire was safe enough to leave, we all trooped down to where our Hotshot Crummy was parked, and hauled the jumpers back to where they could be picked up by their support vehicle. They were glad to avoid the usual long hike they often faced trying to get back to their base after a jump.

A few years later, I heard the unwelcome news that Peewee had died in a parachuting accident. The forests of Oregon had claimed another young life.

CHAPTER 18

Selecting strategies when on initial response to a fire is not something that is easily learned from a book or class. There is a lot of instinct involved that combines with understanding how fires usually behave, an accurate assessment of the fire and fuels, the potential of the location, plus a healthy dose of luck.

Review of decisions made by command personnel after a fire seldom gives a totally accurate picture of the reasoning why certain strategies are used. Still the examinations are good exercises.

A small fire with one Incident Commander and one or two crews may include many choices made as the situation evolves. A modest sized fire would have demanded dozens of coordinated and individual decisions by a handful of Overhead people. A very large fire would multiply the complexities and the number of decisions needed. At that point, those in charge may be faced with an on-going multi-crisis reality throughout the whole suppression process.

Review is good, mostly as a training tool. Since much detail will be lost forever as the urgency of the situation fades and memories become clouded, review for disciplinary action would be invalid. What appears wrong, may have been right at just that moment; what appears right, could have seemed completely wrong.

FIRE BEHAVIORS

Later in the 1965 fire season our crew went on another fire that has especially lodged in my memory. This one was in the Medford Unit, just above and to the west from the old Gold Ray Dam, just outside of Gold Hill. When my crew arrived, the blaze had already moved well up the side-slope and approaching the nearby ridge top. The low but steep ridge was maybe ½ mile above the Sam's Valley Highway.

After a quick assessment I started our access hike, moving quickly up the hill on the south flank of the fire. I had an idea for a strategy, but it was dependent upon the crew moving as fast as possible to a specific place I envisioned on the hillside above us. I urged them into a near run up the flank. They followed my bidding without question.

Every so often we moved past marks on the ground where short stretches of abandoned fresh hand trail had been put in. It was very here and there and seemed to be completely unorganized. These trails wouldn't be from engine crews, because if any were at the incident the steep ground would confine them to working the lower edge near the road. Cat trails also weren't possible, as there were no unique track marks of any kind to give evidence of a dozer on the fire as of yet.

The mystery was solved as we kept moving at double time and met up with several pairs of crewmembers from the Medford Hotshots. They had been hidden from our view below by patches of brush.

It appeared our Medford cohorts were working in two's and three's, each group independent of the other. A very brief conversation revealed that they had been called in on their stand-by day and were short of several crewmen including their crew boss. I quickly suggested that they join up with our crew so as to be more effective. They declined. Time was urgent to my attack plan and I didn't want to waste any with arguing. At my direction our crew continued our fast-paced hike up the slope without any last-minute additions to our regular group.

My scheme was to reach the ridge top before the fire that was moving off to our right. We would dig a quick hand-line beyond and about eye height just over on the other side of the ridge's rim. Our line would start well beyond the existing south flank of the fire and would continue well beyond the north flank. We would turn there, come back over the edge and start down toward the highway, digging at an angle along that north side of the fire. This was a lot of line and we would need to be at the top of our game. Hopefully, if we got our line in place fast enough, the Medford crews and any others arriving would cut off the fire on the south side and then tie into our line near the hilltop.

My strategy was based on the knowledge that fires in some fuels such as these, when reaching a ridge-top, will suddenly die down and then begin creeping down the other side of the hill at a much-reduced rate – but only for the first several feet. This is because as the fire is going up slope, both the slope and the air movement that the fire is creating by its own draft give it added punch as it travels. But when the fire reaches the ridgeline, it begins to draw air from the other side of the hill to feed the flames. At that point it is burning against the new airflow, and is also suddenly without the aid of the incline when moving. The combined result is a lull in the intensity – a short interval in vigor that can be used by firefighters IF they are in the right place at the right time.

My crew was hiking very fast, and all of us kept an eye on the progress of the flames off to our right. The fuels were scattered, but volatile with low to medium height brush and sometimes knee-high dry grass. The traveling fire was starting to look downright scary, now exhibiting up to ten-foot flame lengths. It was beginning to make some noise that seemed kind of ominous. I know the hair on the back of my neck was at attention and sending signals about forgetting the whole idea.

Still I ignored my own qualms as best as possible and urged more speed by the crew. No one questioned the pace; all energy went into scrambling and clawing up the steep incline as fast as possible – no small fete as we were much encumbered by our tools.

The result of our supreme effort was that good crew reached the ridge-top well ahead of the fire. We quickly worked our way along the ridge-top, still panting as I selected a good starting point. The spot I chose had very little fuel except low sparse grass. This would give us a jump-start on the trail building and a little bit of a breather at the same time.

We began digging just below the ridgeline and quickly worked up to and over the lip as planned. The curve in the line was toward the fire and built where I directed. We began to contour along the slope on the opposite side of the ridge top from the fire, just a few feet below the crest.

We were now working directly in the path of the fire. The view of the fire as we worked was mostly blocked by the ridge-top, but the whole crew knew it was coming up fast on the other side of the slope.

Everyone had a clear and vivid memory of the ten-foot flames on the other side of the ridge and everyone was getting more and more nervous, me included. A comment here and there showed some of the crewmen were now growing hesitant to move forward putting themselves directly in the cross hairs of the flaming fury they had last seen while climbing. Soon we could hear it snapping and popping.

I encouraged them with as much assurance I could muster, explaining calmly that the fire would soon die down when it topped the ridgeline. In my mind I was hoping like crazy that I was 100% right.

As we all worked with great energy, I shared why I predicted the fire behavior. The info was quickly passed down the line. Some guys nodded in understanding and a couple grumbled a little, but all kept resolutely at the job. There was no sign of bolting.

Within moments, sure enough, the fire did exactly as I had described. It hit the ridge top with a loud last gasp, and then suddenly lay down like a sleeping baby, slowly creeping forward with tiny flames only an inch or two high.

Quickly we continued the trail out the ridge until we had a clear shot to head downhill toward the highway. The crew was now sharing grins and an occasional quip as we all efficiently and rapidly built trail, as per the original plan.

We weren't done though. About that time the ODF Medford dozer had arrived and reached the top of the same ridge, beyond the fire a distance away but moving toward us. The dozer was building line as it approached.

When the operator came up to us he commented that he was a little surprised that the fire was nearly dead along the top-line. This was, of course, due to our fire trail in the right spot at exactly the right time. If we'd abandoned our efforts, without the hand line to reinforce the expected die-down, the fire would have passed over the ridge top and rebuilt momentum. By now it would be some distance down the other side. That would have interrupted the fire line construction by the dozer and forced everyone to fall back to a new strategy, costing valuable time and adding many more burned acres and hours of work.

After a short confab with the Medford dozer operator, he confirmed with my plan that we should continue our trail down the slope. He would reinforce our line at the top and then work down-slope behind our crew, widening our hand trail. Fire trail construction continued pretty normally, at a much less frantic pace from there on down to the highway.

Still a little more excitement was lurking ahead.

The line building had become pretty routine now that the urgency was past. We switched to a different style of crew configuration more suitable to the mixed fuels now at hand.

I was ahead marking the trail and cutting smaller fuels with my machete. There was a gap of ten feet or so. Then one of the straw bosses and the head hoe were together between me and the main body of the crew, where several of the guys were working close together

Behind me, the straw boss/saw-man was using our small brush chainsaw cutting larger fuels. The head hoe was helping him on the farther side, moving the cut-up debris to the outside of our line to lower fire intensity as much as possible. The was another much smaller space, then the rest of the crew was aligned using Hazel hoes to reveal bare earth a few more feet behind the Head Hoe.

I was about halfway downhill toward the highway when I heard a loud excited yell uphill behind me. It's always smart to check out a whoop coming from a line crew. When I looked up, it was just in time to see the whole bunch scattering on the slope above where just moments before I had stepped over a down log about twelve inches in diameter and the saw man also had twice just cut that same log creating the chunk to be rolled aside.

The next guy, the head hoe to the right of the saw man, had rolled that cutout bit of log aside. This move uncovered a nicely sized rattlesnake that had hidden itself underneath the now missing piece.

The head hoe's reaction was an excellent loud howl of startled surprise – better than any reaction to afore mentioned mice, lizards or other livestock hidden in hard hats or boots. The leap into the air was easily four feet straight back and included a nicely done twist that allowed him, upon landing, to take off on a quick short run. The second hoe a few feet away had reacted quickly to defend his crew-mate. He took a big step forward and gave an effective whack or two with his Hazel hoe. Result? A quick end to the snake problem.

With that little serge of adrenaline, a few moments were needed for the crew to move back into line building formation. Busy chatter and a couple of back-pats were exchanged up and down the line. Perhaps a bit more care than usual went into the turning of rocks and tossing of brush until the remainder of that trail was completed.

We monitored our trail until the shift was complete and we were released to go back to our HQ in GP. There was a lot for the crew to talk about on the trip home that day. The excitement while racing the tall flames to the hilltop had faded somewhat, but the alternative subject took center- stage. The main topic was exactly how two of our group, those of us in the front of the line, avoided the up-close and too personal rattlesnake encounter. Altogether it had been another satisfying day for our group to tuck away into our collective memories.

CHAPTER 19

*L*ike all specialized occupations, wildland fire fighting has its own language. This jargon is mostly consistent across agencies and geographical regions; there are a few exceptions. There are many public agencies that must work together across the multiple ownerships just in Southwest Oregon. Use of the same terminology helps avoid a lot of confusion when clarity is pretty important.

The USFS had tried to generalize firefighting language by creating a somewhat standardized glossary of terms before I began working for ODF. This reference guide was revised again around 2000. In the new publication, I like the change in some lingo – such as calling fully trailed fires "contained" instead of "controlled". In my mind, the only really controlled fire is one that is out. . .

Since I retired the year before that most recent glossary was released, some of my own fire-line terminology may be out-of-date. I apologize to the reader for any confusion.

NOT SO BORING MOP-UP

Still later in the same 1965 season another thunder-bust went through the SWO district. A down-strike started a small sized incident on a ridge top somewhere near the City of Rogue River. This section of real estate really takes a beating from thunderstorms – or at least did then.

I don't think the blaze ever grew to even a half-acre in size. Our Hotshots were sent out and we had the thing trailed and supposedly out in short order.

As with every fire incident, this wasn't the end of the situation. As a matter of course, part of our assignment was after-fire daily monitoring of the burned area (and several others from the same storm). Necessary dry mop-up included that daily check for smokes and dealing with them. Tedious, mostly just dirty and boring, but a required part of the job.

The burned ground had been a bit of a challenge to gain access for our initial response. We originally had to hike in for considerable distance after driving existing roads in a round-about search to find the blaze. After the fire was trailed and out, my crew stumbled on a very rough but serviceable cat trail running from near the blackened ridge-top to a service road nearly at the valley floor.

To eliminate a long hike after an even longer drive every morning for what might very well be just be a very quick walk-through of the site, I decided to try using the steep and unimproved cat trail to get daily access up the hill and then back down. It was a smart decision, but only if our vehicle could handle the steep incline and unimproved surface.

Our crew Crummy, fully loaded with nine strapping young men plus tools and other equipment, was a pretty heavy vehicle. It was not four-wheel drive. To successfully ascend the hill, I put the Chevy into its lowest granny gear and kepting a steady feed on the gas pedal. This tactic effectively moved the whole outfit up what had never been intended to be a road. We traveled at a slow pace, what with a whole lot of bouncing around and occasional tire-slippage included. Use of the cat trail eliminated the need to drive several out-of-the-way miles, and it was better, for sure, than hiking that incline through scratchy brush and nasty batches of poison oak.

For about a week after the fire, each day's workday began with the fully loaded Hotshot Crummy making the slow-motion, but bumpy drive to that hilltop using the cat trail. As taught, we dutifully checked the burned area for potentially smoldering stump-holes, snags and active smokes. Scraping and smothering with dirt dealt with the hot spots found. Our assignment continued until no combustion evidence could be found for a 48-hour length of time.

Some folks accuse wildland firefighters of being hooked on the adrenaline rush that comes with regularly going nose-to-nose with a vicious crackling blaze, having only hand tools for defense. I'm not saying this is true or not, but I will note that there are many other parts of the job that offer ways to get a good surge of excitement besides on the fire line. My crew had stumbled onto one of these.

That daily trip UP that mountainside was nothing special – kind of fun and bouncy enough to encourage everyone in the rig to wear their hard hats and hang on tight to avoid a few lumps on the skull from smacking into the headliner. It was mostly a nice little shake-up first thing every morning for several days.

On the other hand, the drive DOWN that hill was worthy of a first-class roller coaster ride ...1

... and we actually got paid to do it.

I had to keep the transmission in the lowest and screaming gear all the way down. A touch to the clutch and we'd be free-wheeling in a second. Not good. To keep steady pressure on the foot pedals was really hard. The steering wheel whipped around with a vengeance with every bounce. That extra heavy rig on that steep ground was a real test of both brakes and diving skill! The Crummy spent about half the trip air-borne.

As we neared the lower part, our rig wasn't traveling all that slow. From about half-way down until we hit the service road the entire crew began to call out rebel yells and yee-haws like bronco riders. The multitude of tools we carried boomed and clanked with every jolt, and combined with the happy bellowing of the crew just behind my head, it was hard to concentrate.

Each safe return to the flat at the base of the hill was met with grins, cheers and congratulatory pats on my back. We and our rig managed to survive every trip. It never got old.

Such a goofy bunch – we all thought it was great fun!

When schools opened just after Labor Day, we lost a few of the younger guys on the crew. We continued as a smaller workforce until late September. The rest of the crew, me included, nearly finished out the entire 1965 Fire Season. The average closure date then was October 1, dependent on the weather.

It had been a very satisfactory season for me and apparently for other guys too. At the end of our last day together, the various members still working on that excellent Hotshot crew, each went their different ways with sincere good-luck wishes and hardy thumps on each other's backs.

I still occasionally cross paths with some of those guys at times – good memories are shared.

The day following our final workday I packed up my school clothes and personal things. Off I went to Corvallis once more. Fall registration began at 8 AM the next day, a Monday, in the big OSU coliseum. Tuesday was the first day of classes.

CHAPTER 20

Oregon State University is one of many Land Grant Colleges. This system of high prestige learning and research institutions is nationwide. Every state has at least one, with a select few having more. The focus of study is an amalgam of science, math, engineering and technology, including extensive agricultural and natural resource studies and research. The knowledge base is unlimited.

Academically, the School of Forestry at OSU is second only to one other university in the United States. The front-runner has been Syracuse in New York State for as long as I can remember.

DISTRACTIONS AND DECISIONS

The 1965 fall term at Oregon State University was another chance for me to become a very conscientious and hopefully successful student. I was determined to get it right this time.

I was now a full year behind my high school graduation classmates. I had selected a course of study, without realizing, that required about 20 extra credits for graduation when compared to most other fields. My choice of classes at Southern Oregon had also left gaps in my undergraduate preparation. In total, if I worked very hard and kept focused, I should be able to graduate in June of 1967. I still had a long slog to go. My status as a "college junior" seemed to last forever.

I'd been in touch with two roomies from my previous disastrous school year. We three had found a place to rent only a block from campus. It was the second floor of a two-story house, complete with a nosy grandma-type downstairs. We discovered the problem with our elderly landlady within days of moving in. The location was great but the lady was such a bother that we immediately began looking for another place to rent.

Maybe it was a coincidence or Fate was again involved, as my not-girl friend, now also at OSU, ended up in a dorm on the edge of campus closest to our apartment. A walk of about two city blocks. The potential distraction of a regular girlfriend so close-by was a very real problem for me. She and I had several long discussions that revealed that she also had strong feelings about doing well academically.

Soon after classes began, about mid-October, we agreed we were getting too serious when we each wanted to concentrate on our studies. Our regular dating, though enjoyable, seemed to require too much time that should be used for studious activities. By mutual agreement, we both decided to go our separate ways. With sadness we officially agreed on a break up.

I guess Destiny wouldn't be denied. The reluctant split lasted less than twelve hours. The next morning, a Sunday, we literally bumped into one another going opposite directions through a door at the student union. With happy smiles and a warm lingering embrace, we were immediately back together. We just couldn't stay separated for any length of time.

More discussion resulted in acceptance that our connection had real depth. This led to an exchange of rings and a sincere mutual proposal. Once we decided on marriage, a long engagement seemed no different than simply dating. The outcome was that when the new term began after Christmas break, we were newlyweds.

We found a tiny row apartment on Witham Hill – about two miles from campus. My grades improved a lot, and quickly too. My new bride was good in some of the subjects where I had problems. It was a real bonus to have in-house corrections before my written work was even turned in.

We were together when not in class or at work, and owned neither a TV nor much else to take time away from studying. If we wanted to simply listen to the radio we had to go sit in the car. Also, since my main distraction was now usually right there in the same room, it was easy to give her a kiss and turn back to the books.

We were perpetually broke and a few extra dollars meant a lot. My bride found a few baby-sitting jobs. I ventured into Work-Study offered by the University. This work program was great for struggling students like us. Hours worked per week were limited, but the pay was reasonable. Another advantage was that the hours were flexible to fit around class schedules. I worked in the College of Forestry's Self-Learning Center, located in the basement of the old Peavy Forestry Building across the street from the big Memorial Union. New buildings to the west have since replaced that old boxy brownstone where I worked and attended most classes.

When Spring Break arrived in March 1966, I left my bride with her parents in Hugo. Six of the nine days of the vacation were spent planting trees in the Coast Range Mountains above Waldport. This was again on a contract crew working on private land belonging to a timber company. Two of the crew were my friends from the previous summer, one from the Medford Hotshots and the other one of my prankster straw bosses. We three went to the job together and shared expenses.

The work was very hard, much more so than any tree planting I'd done previously. About six months had passed since summer – six months of sitting in classrooms and getting out of shape. Our foreman required that we each plant 800 – 1,000 tree seedlings a day. If we did not reach our quota by the end of the shift, we kept staggering along until finished. Near the week's end all three of us had improved enough to meet the daily goal, but the days still seemed incredibly long.

That was a cold and miserable six days of really hard work! Muscle sore and pooped I picked up my smiling lady on the last Sunday evening in Hugo. I slept long and hard for several nights when school resumed.

My beloved Fairlane suffered a horrible and unfixable disfigurement on May 31 – Memorial Day that spring. We'd come home for the "Boatnick" holiday, and ended up bashed on both sides when a car ran the light at 7th and A Street. A younger teen driver speeding up 7th Street hit us on the right side, just at the rear wheel as we passed through the intersection on A Street. The impact spun our rear around to the left and into the path of a car traveling the other way on A Street, hitting us again in almost the same spot on the driver's rear side. This bounced us around to the right where we slid up hard against the curb near the corner nearly tipping our car over.

The Fairlane, like most cars then, had no seatbelts. A friend was riding with us in the front passenger seat, and I was driving. My buddy and I rode the actual wreck through by holding tight to the armrests on the side doors. My wife was in the backseat alone. As the result of the series of collisions, she was sent flying against the right inside wall of the backseat with the first impact, and then tossed to the left side. Impact with the second car slammed us into the street curb. That jolt brought her back to the right a second time, where she came to a rest with her head on the seat.

The unexpected bouncing around inside the car wasn't particularly pleasant, but the sudden quiet when it stopped was ominous. As soon as I gathered my wits, I was half over the front seat checking on my now pregnant wife. We still had the whole summer to go, but this kind of shake-up couldn't be all that good for her. There were some scary moments as she lay very still on the seat for a few moments. Soon it was determined that she had only suffered from getting the wind knocked out.

Our drive to Corvallis was postponed until after sorting out this mess the next afternoon. We had to cope using our wounded car for the trip, as Finals Week was about to begin. Our beautiful sleek Fairlane was finally replaced sometime in the middle of the summer more than two months later. A similar model of the same year became ours, but was not anywhere as nice. The replacement car had been badly kept. It was high on miles and rust spots, and low on performance and appeal. It always had a vague smell of stale cigarettes with a touch of mold.

Truth be told, the importance of a dream car was fading away in my thinking. Now we needed reliable transportation. Somehow the sad shadow that replaced the best car I ever owned limped along, fulfilling our transportation needs for the time being.

The author and wife mid-July 1966.
Photo courtesy of CC Dickerson

CHAPTER 21

Finals Week closes every term in the Oregon college calendar. The schedule of tests is set before school even begins each September.

During my time at OSU, some final exams took over three hours to complete. Some required detailed written essay type answers. Evaluation by the instructors must have been a real chore. Grades for the term were usually calculated as a combination of class work, quizzes, tests, and lengthy research papers. The ending grades were mailed to students, with delivery taking up to three weeks.

SOME FINAL TOUCHES TO GROWING UP

We moved back to Hugo in June as soon as we both finished our last scheduled finals. I stepped back into the Hotshot Superintendent position with the GP ODF a day or two later. I was a little disappointed reading the list of names assigned to my crew. Only a couple of the same crewman from the year before had returned.

My 1966 crew had mostly new replacements; almost all were younger kids, either just out of high school or still needing a year or two until graduation. I will say, they really did try their best. They were rightfully proud to be on the crew and did possess a whole lot of heart. Their knowledge of fire lore was on the lean side though, and physically they just couldn't meet the performance level of the '65 group. The instinctual feel for fire behavior or any tendency toward catching the fire fighter's Bug weren't obvious.

I spent a lot of extra time with this novice crew, sharing information and working with stamina training. Luckily most of the fire season was pretty tame. Temperatures were a bit cooler that summer and it rained hard a couple of times, keeping the SWO fire danger at lower levels than usual. There were still the average number of several smaller fires (over 200 in-district), but almost all of these were within the abilities of the fledgling skills of my very, very young Hotshots.

During the closing days of the summer I especially remember a couple of larger fires – only a couple of weeks before the youngest kids went back to high school. Weather conditions had changed for the worse as they so often do at that time in the fire season.

The first of the bigger fires was a really nasty piece of work, demanding the best from everyone present. The incident was way out to the north and above Graves Creek beyond Mt. Bolivar. It was in the DFPA protection area across the Douglas County line. In a felled and bucked logging unit about sixty to eighty acres in size, a fire had burned through most of the upper part.

The cable carriage on the logger's yarder had caught fire, and a couple of the big and very expensive machines, a yarder and loader, had already burned up. This was before our crew even arrived. Our north-end Unit Supervisor was there already, as well as several DFPA engines, and the logging crew of course. For some reason the dozers were delayed.

Our access directions from Dispatch brought the Hotshots to a ridge-top yarder landing where the fire had started. My Supervisor stood with me on the rim of the landing as the young Hotshot crew unloaded tools and other equipment from the crew truck parked behind us. The boss gave me specific directions as we scanned the view spread beneath us down a steep mountainside.

The felled unit was laid out below us with an excellent panorama of the whole site. It was an untidy jumble of fairly large logs, many already bucked (limbs removed) by the fallers. A mix of green and dried tops and limbs with other fuels was lying underneath and around the newly dropped logs. Everything on the hillside was on a pronounced tilt and unstable.

The boss pointed out how and what he wanted us to attack. The blaze had already burned all the upper ground, so most of the fire movement was now well down the steep mountainside moving toward un-cut timber. The rapid movement of the flames going downhill was a result of a lot of burning debris rolling beyond the head of the fire down the slant, starting spot fires.

We could see another cut road off to the side and a long way down the mountain well off to the right. It did not provide immediate entry into the felled area but was something to note. The boss told me to move down the left flank from where we stood, building trail as we went, then work under the active front of the fire trying to tie into the road we could see far below.

The crew had quickly unloaded what we would need to do the job, as the boss and I discussed plans at the landing. We took mostly Hazel hoes, as I felt they would work best in those conditions. Another very important and much needed tool was our largest chainsaw, with a good supply of gas and oil. I could see we would have to literally cut our way through the unit's big logs to get a trail established. This would be a challenge, as those had been big trees. Our saw was much smaller than those used by the fallers. I would have to make two to four wedge cuts, as compared to a single cut by the loggers.

This was going to be a long haul and probably would keep us out all night. I felt very uneasy about the whole set-up. I was running the conditions over and over in my mind, trying to focus on the fire. The big downed timber worried me a lot. There was also all the loose debris, and those big logs were obviously unstable.

Eventually we would have to work on the hillside below the felled trees. On the steep slope those fresh cut limbs were all that held the logs in place. The idea of all those big logs rolling around uphill while we worked below them wasn't a pleasant thought.

Since the situation made me so uncomfortable, I put some real brainwork into consideration of escape routes. If things got bad I knew it would be fastest to take the crew across and down the hill rather than back up to the yarder landing where we were to begin our hike.

I took the crew back down the road by which we had arrived, hiking a short distance and came to where the Overhead guy had indicated that the crew was to begin working. We turned to building the fire trail following the planned route and began digging on the downhill incline.

As we moved farther down, I pulled a man from the crew and stationed him where he had a good view of the area above our hand trailing operation. I gave him specific instructions, being especially clear that his very important role was to act as a lookout for any danger from moving debris of any size coming our way. I was worried.

Just as I'd imagined, as we moved further across the hillside into more dangerous territory, the loose limbs and smaller burning debris were beginning to lose hold on the underside of the logs above. Some of the movement was of smaller stuff, but the big timbers began to shift around here and there too. Mostly one at a time, a log within the actively burning area would stir, then roll a few feet. The organic trash on the ground would then grab at the log, and it would get hung up again and stop. At that time none was near enough nor traveled far enough to endanger my crew. Still, I made a point to gather the guys around me and gave serious caution for all to remain wary.

To speed things up and get the crew across the more dangerous ground as quickly as possible, I took our saw and a crewman, moving about 50 feet ahead of the crew farther into the dangerous zone. I used my machete' to mark the trail route, then my helper and I began cutting short sections from logs lying in the pathway of the crew's progress. Working as fast as possible, the two of us tossed smaller limbs and large pieces of peeled-back bark out of the trail line. When we came to a log too big to move, I'd cut out a couple of donuts and we'd roll the segments from the planned route the crew was digging out. These pieces would roll sluggishly over the unstable slash, never more than a grudging few feet.

After the crew had built a couple hundred feet of trail into this dangerous section, it became apparent to me that there was a huge amount of big wood blocking the trail route. The Hazel hoes couldn't handle the job. I was having to saw so much out front of the crew to rough it out of the way, the crew behind was being badly held up.

I called our supervisor on my hand-held radio and asked if we could move the trail farther down the hill and out of the thicker felled and bucked timber. This would speed up our operation, but would sacrifice almost all of the felled logs. I indicated that at our current rate of progress the fire would beat us to the bottom of the slope anyhow, so we would likely not be able to save any of the down logs even if we continued with the line as he had instructed.

Approval to abandon this trail and start lower downhill was given by the boss immediately. We quickly shifted location and modified the direction of our trail to meet the new plan. This change lifted everyone's spirits a lot. Still, even with the new route there were several downed logs in our path and a few smaller trees left standing by the fallers that I would have to cut through.

Since we were still working below the burning cutover part of the unit, the precaution of posting a lookout for burning debris on the move remained. As we worked, every so often our watchman on the hill above gave a cry of alarm. Whenever he called out, we'd all pause from our work for a moment to check whatever was descending on us from above.

Pretty good progress was being made in spite of the frequent interruptions. The kids were doing a good job, coping with some very rough terrain and downright awful trail building conditions. Nearing sundown I was running low on saw gas and oil, and the crew's drinking water was almost gone. I pulled one of the straw bosses loose from the line with directions for him to return to the crew truck far up the hill. He was told to bring more saw gas and oil, plus drinking water back to the rest of us.

It took well over an hour or so before our re-supply guy returned. He was coming up to us from below, wearing a necklace of filled canteens over his shoulder that made a musical sound banging together as he climbed toward us. He explained as he handed over a can of saw gas, that one of the Overhead fellows at the landing had told him it would be much quicker to take our crew truck around via the road and landing visible from the ridge top before we started work on the trail. He'd driven the Crummy around, parking it below us. Since the road was where we planned to end up once this new trail segment was completed, his actions made sense and were good with the new trail location.

We went back to work. The sun had set, but there was still enough light that we could see well. Then my worst fears became reality.

I was atop a rather large downed log, sawing a way through for our trail when another whooped warning was sounded by our lookout.

Checking out the threat, I saw a good-sized burning log that had broken loose and was now sliding butt-end first down that hill – and this time it didn't stop or ever slow down. It was picking up speed! I could see that it was heading toward dead center of the line where my young crew worked on the hillside.

The guy with me and I were probably sixty feet in front of the head hoe and unable to do anything but yell additional warnings to the crew. The log didn't hang up on the slash like the others we'd watched before. It just kept sliding and picking up more and more speed as it traveled.

The kids on the hillside straightened up and stared as the log quickly approached them. It seemed they expected it to stop as all those before had. In my best boss man bellow I screamed, "MOVE!"

In the dusk of the early evening that log soon looked like a big rocket sled with fire shooting off the sides and out the back. It was actively burning with sizable flames in the wind like something from a cartoon drawing. At last the crew split in the middle leaving a wide pathway for the log, with guys running and going both directions.

All but one. A single crewman from right in the center of the line stood motionless, eyes glued onto the oncoming log.

It was one of those nightmare moments where people seem frozen to the spot and can't make their feet move. That one kid stood there like a deer caught in headlights. The rest of the crew was either scrambling to safety or yelling or both. By this time there was a lot of empty space on either side of the lone guy; all he had to do was leap one way or the other to be clear – but he couldn't seem to decide which way to go.

At the last moment, he turned throwing his tool to the ground and began to run. I was horrified to see he was running straight downhill.

That log quickly caught up to him, even though he was taking leaps that probably would have won gold medals at any track meet. That burning log smacked him in the behind and lifted him off his feet. For a few seconds he was totally air-borne, making a complete body flip as though it was planned. Hard hat flying, he landed astride that big log, riding it like a horse.

I watched in a wash of great fear as my young crewman rode that burning, bucking log down the hill for easily another fifty feet or more. Only gravity and the contours of the hillside dictated what that log was going to do. The entire crew now watched in groaning awe as the front end of the log swerved slightly to one side and began to roll. It tossed our colleague off to the downhill side, promptly rolled over him and continued on down the hill, ending its wild downhill trip about seventy-five feet below us.

I was in total shock with my gut in a gigantic knot. I was sure that the kid could not have survived. That log likely weighed a ton, more than enough to have squashed him flat. I've never been a squeamish person, but as I jumped over a few downed trees and piles of debris hurrying to the location where I'd last seen the kid in one piece, I was sure I was going to puke. I fully expected to see nothing but bloody pulp lying where he had landed.

When I was about ten feet away, imagine my surprise and instant delight when up popped the crewman's head looking squarely at me, eyes about as big as light bulbs and just as bright. In a few moments the rest of the crew joined me gathering around him. He'd landed in a natural depression just large and deep enough to save his life as the log rolled over him.

We carefully helped him from the life-saving ditch. He wasn't unscathed, but he wasn't butchered either. Short of stripping him down to his skivvies, we assessed his most apparent injuries there in the blue-gray dusk on the mountain side. A few cuts and scratches, a bloody spot here and there, some minor burns on his hands and legs.

This was one incredibly lucky young man!

His left shoulder seemed very sore. As he began to move painfully around, it was obvious that one knee was badly sprained and he would not be able to walk any distance without help.

Our crew still had a big job to complete - we weren't done for the day, but this kid sure was. I got onto the radio and happily reported to the Command Center about our still living casualty. We had an urgent need for an evacuation with medical assistance PDQ.

One of the Overhead supervisors who'd just arrived at the fire hiked all the way to us from the roadway below. By this time, we weren't all that far from that lower access road. Another couple of people I didn't know also showed up and helped our wounded crewman off down the hill and away into the growing darkness.

CHAPTER 22

The very nasty fire my Hotshot crew was battling on Douglas Forest Protective Association lands had its origin from a logging operation. Overall, wildland fire starts from logging were pretty unusual back then.

Statistically, in the last half of the 20th Century, loggers had a stellar record of woodland fire safety, estimated well below a 5% rate of origin. Compared to lighting starts at about one-third or 33%, that isn't too bad at all.

From the view of a fire fighter, the presence of loggers in the forest gave many benefits. There were a whole lot of knowing eyes out there everyday, watching for smokes. Plus, even the most primitive roads built to reach remote operations gave us access too. (Today, in SWO many of these roads are no longer usable.)

The larger number of woodland jobs put more people who were at least familiar with the demands of the landscape often in the vicinity of burns we had to fight. As such, these guys were semi- trained in fire suppression and nearby with their big machines when most needed. They were a potentially vital work force that might be called quickly to task when things were critical.

The loggers were busy on the fire that day, for sure.

MISFORTUNE MULTIPLIED

Of course, that fire didn't just quit because of the problems that were plaguing my Hotshots. Before very long those of us who were still able, were back at work wondering what possible new disaster might befall us in the dark on this hellish fire.

Time is always a factor on fires and we didn't have any to waste. One of our first chores was to take care of the burning log that had intruded into our space with our guy aboard. It had to be quickly trailed and put out or else it would cause a spot fire that could burn back up the hill behind us. We were dealing with enough danger already and sure didn't need to invite more. We attacked that log with a vengeance.

When that important business was completed, we next had to get back to work on the fire line up the hill. Back we went. On the positive side, we'd built enough trail to put us in a safer position on the slope. On the negative, full darkness had arrived and visibility was now very limited, slowing us down.

As I'd feared when assessing the terrain and fuels when we first arrived, we spent the whole night on that hand trail, nervous and on edge the whole time.

Several engine crews and dozers came on the fire as the day and then night progressed. We could hear vehicles of all kinds and sizes come and go on the lower road as our work brought us closer to our goal during the night. At about dawn's first gray light, we were still at work on trail building, weary beyond description. I marveled at how well this crew of pups was doing. They were doggedly getting a man-sized job done and done well.

We were quite near to our ultimate goal, the lower cut road, when a very loud cracking noise came clearly to our ears. The CRAAACCKKK – THUMP sound was accompanied by a strange discordant metallic screeching ka-pow noise that none of us could identify. It resembled the sound when someone stomps on a pop can lying on hard pavement – only this was much deeper in tone. The origin of the sound seemed to be somewhere along that lower road. Perhaps a dozer had broken free and slipped from its trailer?

We had a fire trail finished almost to the high bank above the cut road that awaited us. Our line was completed nearly at the same time we were relieved about 5 AM; not quite light enough to see well. The fire was still burning above but was nearly in the corral of hand and dozer trails.

We each slid on our rears, down the loose dirt bank to the road below. Thoroughly done-in, everyone trudged with staggering weariness behind the straw boss who'd moved and parked the crew truck the evening before. We were really looking forward to packing up the Crummy and heading home. But our rig wasn't there.

It was common policy on fires to leave the keys in parked vehicles so they could be moved if necessary. At first, we weren't too concerned about the missing Crummy, figuring we'd find the crew truck parked nearby. Everyone lined out slowly walking down the road looking all directions in the dim morning light for our ride. Several other vehicles and lowboy trailers were parked willie-nellie on the landing and in wider spots along the road. Many dozers and other vehicles had used the lower road as access into the fire above.

We hadn't gone far when our Crummy came into view through the early rather smoky gray morning.

It stood out from all the other rigs – in that it now had a very large Port Orford cedar snag lying across it just about dead center.

With a unified group groan we gathered around our squashed crew truck. The snag had burned off on the uphill side of the cut road and fallen almost as if the location of the fall was intentional. All the side windows were blown or busted out and were now on the ground in a neat circle of broken glass. The roof was mashed down within about two or three feet above the interior floor, and the back doors were sprung.

Our straw boss that had parked the crew truck emphatically swore to me and anyone on the crew that chose to listen that he'd chosen a safe place for the vehicle – and this spot was NOT the place he'd selected. Many of the crew offered comments or suggestions to me for transportation back to HQ.

My tired brain was sorting through the small barrage of words just as a DFPA supervisor showed up from a huddle of parked vehicles farther down the road. He apologized about our rig and explained that he had moved our crew truck to make room for a lowboy to turn around. He had parked our Crummy right behind his own pickup, which he gestured at. It sat a few feet away totally untouched.

Although appreciated, the apology didn't help me solve our newest problem – transporting our tools and exhausted bodies back to Grants Pass. At that point I don't think the explanations or ideas mattered much to me. I knew I'd be filling out a pile of accident report forms as it was, but first there was this one big problem to work through.

The crew had really done an excellent night's work, but was beat and moving in slow motion. The only way back to HQ required at least another hour's work on the truck for us just to even fit inside. I know I sighed. No one would be doing this for us – it was our problem to fix.

It was almost painful to think through what actions were necessary to make the Crummy usable. The work wasn't particularly easy either. Removing the errant log on top of our rig was done by cutting off short segments with the chain saw. These chunks were each lifted free by one or two guys. We then used the stacked-up sections together with the hydraulic wheel jack from the Crummy to pry the roof up far enough to open the seats tops in the back. This allowed us to load up most of our tools. What didn't fit, the guys very carefully wrapped and put on the floor under their feet.

More prying bent the roof up enough for the crew to sit on the seats more or less upright. At last we all loaded up and pulled the back doors mostly shut, holding them with corded straps. I worried about the vehicle's suspension on the road, but in its wounded condition the crew truck drove fairly well considering. It wandered around some, but that was understandable.

As was normal after a long fire, some of the guys tried to nap on the way back to town. Without windows, though, we all got to feeling mighty cold what with all that ventilation. It was late summer and still pretty early in the morning. At least the cold air blowing in helped me to stay awake as I drove. It was a grim ride back to Grants Pass.

We were a pretty dejected bunch coming into GP that morning. Even after a big breakfast on the state ticket, everyone was still very down. That was one of the most difficult fires to attack that I've been on - ever. I usually felt satisfaction after a fire – not so this time. Just unbelievably tired.

The next day, the Unit Supervisor called me in – I was in dread of what he was going to say. I was still exhausted. My worrywart nature meant I'd hashed over all that had happened on that fire – not sleeping well at all - to figure if there was something that could have been done to avoid any of our accidents. First of all, I was extremely proud of my crew's performance. I wasn't so generous with my own actions, but upon review was sure I had taken all reasonable precautions to avoid the sliding and rolling debris by posting a lookout and by moving our fire line downhill to avoid the excessive amount of heavy material to cut through. This had also given us more escape room. We'd parked our rig in a safe place, but it was moved by another person to make more turn-around room, which was the reasonable thing to do. Was there anything else that I'd missed or forgotten?

After repeated reviews within my mind, I think the situation would have to be chalked up to old-fashioned Bad Luck. As it was, I did not receive any reprimands for our actions. The boss man cautioned me to keep safety to the foremost, but we all agreed that it had been a uniquely difficult fire incident, with several unusual and unforeseen issues.

Our injured crewman showed up a day or two later to relate his experience after he left us at the fire. Apparently, one of the scrapes on his chest turned out to be a puncture wound about 3 inches deep into the muscle near his left arm-pit, which required the doctor to probe around, quite to the crewman's discomfort. After a few more days, his knee sprain had improved enough that he was released to return to work.

I've thought about that really ugly fire over the years. From the get-go it was a problem. Maybe with a more experienced crew it would have made a difference in how the crew might have reacted, or maybe I should have anticipated someone might panic and freeze. I've never felt I've found any real answer but Bad Luck in regard to that fire. But then I shouldn't complain. The whole set-up was potentially very dangerous. We really had been very lucky no one was killed or even seriously injured. Of course, that possibility is always there with every call-out.

About ten days passed with no more mishaps. Then our tool man, while taking tools out of the storage boxes for sharpening at HQ, lost his grip on an unsheathed Pulaski. As it fell, it hit him across the wrist with the cutting edge. A trip to the emergency room with several required stitches was the result. A loose cover on the sharp edge had caused this accident. Seems like it's so often something small. I'd been a real bear with constant emphasis on safety in all work and training with the Hotshots.

There were other incidents at the station and with the patrol engines overall that were outside my area, that altogether led to a decision by the headman to shake things up. A general change for the final few weeks of the season found many of the crewmen and Wardens reassigned. This shifting around coincided with the annual thinning of manpower as the summer wound down and local schools reopened.

The rash of problems wasn't restricted to our crew, so the restructure was maybe also in preparation for the end-of-season drop in manpower. Some of the guys on the Hotshots were moved to engines. I was re-assigned as the Forest Officer for the Merlin area, the post my Dad had held up until two years ago. I probably wouldn't have even minded my change of assignment for the few weeks left of that fire season except for one thing - I didn't much like who was named headman of the now really mixed up Hotshots. The poor kids that remained or were newly placed on the crew (including my brother), were now under the arrogant thumb of my previous Hotshot crew boss. His attitude and leadership skills hadn't improved one bit either.

CHAPTER 23

Occasional visitors like tourists and the campers with less experience tend to have an idealistic perspective about wildland spaces. The peace and beauty can detract from the potential dangers lurking everywhere, even in areas built just for recreation and tourism. No matter how woodland workers try, many of these occasional visitors resist understanding when presented with the realities of the forest. Offense is taken.

Those whose daily work is in the forest environment know it is a very dangerous place to be, even on a good day. When fire increases the hazardous conditions, general safety standards must be multiplied. Constant attention to detail and the serious consideration of possible hazards from any action is vital. Even those with experience and training are brought up short upon occasion.

I've read about concerns that more urban residents are seeking out wild places to experience the freedom offered. They come unprepared in their dress and physical conditioning, depending on their cell phones as both a guide and emergency communication. Sometimes I think they leave their Common Sense at home.

Wild places are not forgiving. Rescues require more than the dispatch of an ambulance.

A PERSISTENCE OF BAD LUCK

I was reassigned back to the Merlin/Hugo patrol engine as the Forest Officer/Warden for the end of the 1966 Fire Season. My new crewman came from the Hotshot crew with me. He had graduated from GPHS in June, so would not be leaving the position as early as some of the other youngsters. We got along great, as he was an excellent crewman with a terrific attitude and a lot of skill. On the Merlin/Hugo patrol, we still worked the same old six-day schedule, with one day of stand-by.

It was in these last days of the fire season when my wife and I were surprised by the birth of our first child. Our baby girl arrived a couple of weeks before the expected due date the doctor named, coming into the world just before Labor Day. We weren't the only ones surprised.

My wife didn't feel well that morning when I left for work. She insisted she was only experiencing an upset stomach, so I went into HQ about 8 AM as usual. An hour later, when her doctor was contacted by my Mother-in-law for advice, he explained that no real rush to the hospital was needed. First babies not only often gave false symptoms of pending birth, he explained, but also even when on the way, are most always very slow in coming.

That was not the case this time. In spite of it being her first experience, my wife's instincts were better than those of the doctor. After another difficult half-hour, she declared that anyone else present was welcome to stay, but she was going to the hospital even if traveling alone. Her parents knew her to be a realistic type and loaded her up. The actual delivery occurred about fifteen minutes later in the back seat of my in-law's car in-route to Grants Pass from Hugo. Our baby arrived on the southbound side of I-5 of Merlin Hill.

It was around 10 AM on a cool and foggy Saturday morning. I received the remarkable and downright scary news at work just minutes later – ODF gave me the rest of that day off, but nothing more.

Early September of 1966, the author, wife and their week-old daughter pose
with his assigned Ford patrol engine at the end of fire season.

Photo courtesy of CC Dickerson

A couple of weeks of the fire season remained. Mostly the college aged and older, permanent staff at ODF only remained working. The younger crewmen were at home, released from their long, hard-working summer. Now they were getting ready for high school to begin within just a few hours.

That summer was particularly bad for yellow jackets. Our new baby was about a week old and awakened two or three times every night to be fed. One night the baby, whose crib was next to our bed, cried and awakened both my wife and me for a two AM meal. Just as mommy and child came back to our bed where I was lying awake, a yellow jacket landed on the baby's head just above the temple. Both my wife and I reacted, instinctively trying to protect our child. We almost counter-acted each other's attempt to brush the wasp away, but only ended up irritating the evil-tempered little critter. The tiny beastie bit, but thankfully didn't sting the baby on the forehead.

My second swipe at the bug was more accurate, flipping the yellow jacket to the floor on my side of the bed. I grabbed a book on the bedside table and gave that bug an extra half dozen whacks!

It took a very long time to quiet our wounded and unhappy baby! When I woke again around six, my wife was once more involved in feeding the baby. I began dressing for work – Warden's uniform and of course, heavy boots. I noticed that $%#!* yellow jacket lying dead on the floor from the incident the night before. It had robbed all three of us of more than a little precious sleep, and caused a red welt the size of a quarter just at the edge of the baby's silky dark hair, which was still tender. The sight made me angry all over again!

I was probably cranky from lack of sleep, but I felt a little better after giving that dang insect a couple of good stomps with my work boots, even though it had been dead for hours. It was unnecessary and pure revenge; but I was a very good stomper. My sleepy wife and I shared a laugh over my early morning "dead-bee dance" as I left for another day at work.

By now it was late into the fire season. The weather turned again from cool to hot and dry. Bigger and more frequent fires came at us with many call-outs daily, sometimes twice or three times during an 8-hour tour.

The Merlin/Hugo engine was called out to another fire in the Rogue River area. This time it was on Wards Creek, and it was big. The potential was very bad and most of the available resources were activated

– but so late in the summer there were several holes in the ranks where the youngsters were missing. In another week when the college classes began, it would be worse.

The driving time from the Merlin/Hugo area to the farther side of the City of Rogue River to Wards Creek insured that when my crewman and I arrived, the fire was already well beyond initial attack. It was likely that more than five acres had already been blackened up a steep hill to the east. Fuels were dry grass, sparse brush and occasional small groves of mixed oaks and conifers. The area tended to just grow back enough fuel to burn hard and hot.

Our engine arrived at about the same time as the GP unit's TD 14 dozer. It was logical that my crewman and I were assigned to swamper support for the dozer on foot. We stashed our rig safely on a distant access road.

As my crewman and I hoofed it over to where the dozer was unloading, we passed near the GP Hotshots who were building a trail on the side-hill. Various other engine crews had been drafted onto hand-trail duty to bolster the short-handed Hotshot crew. My younger brother was one of those working the hand line.

My crewman and I spent some time assisting the dozer operator unload the big machine. Soon the dozer was lumbering farther up the hill from where the Hotshots had been working, building trail as fast as the driver dare travel. Almost sprinting behind the dozer, we continued at double-time up the hill, trying to keep up.

There was a fellow above us on the hillside who also fell in behind the dozer. He must have been with one of the rural fire departments or maybe pick-up labor or a volunteer. We surmised this as we climbed, because he didn't appear to be well trained at all. Like us, he'd started following the dozer, but he was too close behind. He was in danger of getting run over if the dozer suddenly went into reverse for some unseen hazard. Dozers often do this, and ODF people are trained to give the dozers extra space, keeping back.

Being so close and in the dust swirl, the guy was unable to see when the dozer had just scraped over a yellow jacket nest, cutting it in half. My crewman and I saw the insect danger at the same time, each yelling a warning to the other, but not likely to be heard over the dozer noise by the other man who was much closer to the machine.

Staying clear and from below, we could see the black cloud of wasps come boiling out of their nest in the ground and start after the stranger on the hillside above. He was yelling and ran up directly to the dozer, bringing the wasps with him. When the dozer operator hollered at him to get away, the guy turned and ran blindly back down the hill, right through the seething wasp nest again. This hazard turned him to the side running across the hill toward a couple of Overhead guys near the flank of the fire.

Eventually the man was far enough away, and clear of the wasps. He was able to swat and bat most of the stubborn ones off, but we could see, even at a distance, that his face was all bloody from the many stings and bites he received. The Overhead guys got to him quickly, escorting him to a nearby vehicle for a much-needed fast trip to the hospital.

During all this, the newly assigned Hotshot crew boss pulled his crew to him on the newly built cat trail. He was the same guy who'd held the Hotshot Foreman position when I'd been a straw boss. Now he repositioned the whole bunch on the fresh dozer line, apparently to watch for flare-ups and slop over.

From where I was working uphill from him, I could see that he was pulling Fusees from his pockets to start a fire for burning out along the hand line. It appeared that he had decided to make the best use of the earlier poorly placed hand trail by burning-out between it and the more effective cat trail on the steep slope above. This was a good decision on his part. I figured he knew what he was doing.

As I worked along behind the cat I casually followed the Hotshot Foreman's actions. I had some experience with burnout action, but watched for something new to add to my store of fire knowledge. The Superintendent lit up several spots, moving quickly at a near trot along the trail line. In only a short time the Fusee stick in his hand grew too short for more use. He casually threw it down and moved to get a fresh one from his pocket as he continued trotting along in the fresh turned dirt of the cat line.

His actions caught my attention immediately. With astonishment from my distant locale, I stopped in my tracks and looked intently, unsure what I'd seen. In just a moment I realized I'd witnessed the Foreman toss the still lit Fusee butt down in mixed fuels on the WRONG side of the fire line!

He seemed totally unaware of his error, as he kept moving away from the spot without so much as a backward glance. I would have yelled, but the distance was too far to get his attention. Besides, now this was MY problem.

A lot of what was afire that day was dry grass with waxy manzanita and explosive buck brush. The Fusee lit spot immediately blew up and began to spread quickly. Within seconds there now was a fast moving and very dangerous mostly grass fire coming up the hill below my crewman, me and the rear-end of the dozer.

It was mostly by chance and our good fortune that I'd seen this happen. As it was, that flare-up was really moving and time to get everyone clear was very short. I gave a quick "Whoop!" to my crewman. When he turned to face me, I gestured at the flames and shouted at him to move down into the already burned-over, safe area to our left. I would come and meet him there in a bit. Then I pointed at the dozer working up the trail from me, indicating I was going to warn the operator first. He nodded and didn't hesitate to follow my instructions at a run. I paused just long enough to make sure he was moving toward safety, and then took off too.

I turned up hill, and with a scrambling run up the fresh trail went to warn the dozer operator of the fire coming up on his six. Dozers are noisy machines, so getting the driver's attention with the radio could take extra time we didn't have to spare. I figured direct action was quicker. So instead, as soon as I was within throwing range, I hucked more than a couple of dirt clods against the backside of the driver's cage while still at a run. He looked around after about the second or third dirt clod landed behind his head.

I gestured wildly at the blaze below. When he saw the raging and fast-moving grass fire on his blind side coming uphill, he gave me a nod and thumbs-up, quickly shifted into reverse and tore back down hill out of the path of the flames. I made a quick side-hill sprint for the burned area off to the left.

The quick action of the dozer operator let him reposition and restart another trail from below the unintentional Fusee blaze. The dozer snuffed the new blaze pretty quickly. At that time, I was gasping for breath after reaching safety in the burned over section.

Later, when the operator and I compared notes, both of us were pretty ticked off about the unnecessary danger to us from the thoughtless action by someone who most certainly should have known better. Not to mention the extra work and time lost to get the resulting problem flames under control.

The new-again Hotshot boss received a not so great rating from both the dozer driver and me on this potentially very serious mistake. Errors in judgment were one thing, but such a careless action was pretty serious. It's very important to alert other workers about such actions – a serious over-sight. I already disliked the guy, and this little snafu sure didn't improve my feelings about him.

The bad luck of the previous few weeks seemed to be continuing. That fire ended up being pretty rough on the Unit dozer. It was like an on-going cloud of bad luck hanging over the GP Unit in general.

My crewman and I remained with the dozer assignment all that night.

At one point, the fire moved onto ground so steep the dozer work was getting really dangerous. As the operator was maneuvering his machine on the side hill, he backed onto a log he couldn't see in the dark. This caused the dozer to become high-centered. The tracks were barely touching the ground on both sides.

While the operator worked to get his machine free, the log he straddled started to slide down hill taking the dozer with it. It slid backwards about 100 feet, but it finally came to a fairly safe rest between two large fir trees and up against a third growing in a clump.

Obviously, the dozer couldn't just park there. Somehow it had to be freed to continue work. My crewman and I, along with some of the Hotshots who were now maintaining the dozer line along with us, went over to see if we could help the dozer escape.

A first ploy was tried. The driver would use the hydraulic blade to push down, causing the front nose of the dozer to rise up on its tracks. We would then stack as many big limbs and small logs as we could find in the dark under the tracks. Down would come the dozer's front end, and the operator would try to drive the machine back up the hill. Mostly the chunks of wood were just pushed out the back by the tracks without the dozer moving more than a foot or two.

About then another slightly larger dozer, an HD 21 if I recall correctly, showed up working the fire nearby. To free our dozer, we went to a different plan. Our skinner sent me to flag down the bigger machine and ask its driver to build a short side hill flat space as near as possible to be under the blade of the TD 14.

Once the excavation was accomplished, we hooked the winch from the HD 21 onto the front of the TD 14 and pulled the smaller machine up onto the partially flattened out space.

Then bad luck hit again. Unfortunately, as the TD 14 came past the big firs in the group of trees where it was trapped, one of its hydraulic lines for the blade control caught on a limb. This broke the hose, spewing fluid everywhere. Within minutes the TD 14 was now on safe ground with tracks clear, but there was a new problem. Without hydraulic fluid the driver couldn't lift the massive blade so the dozer could move all the way back to the lowboy parked down the hill for repair.

With a quick confab between the two operators and those of us on the ground, we decided to make use of the 14's own winch line to hold up its blade. The HD 21 operator carefully maneuvered so his blade caught under and lifted the TD 14 blade. Three or four of the guys on the ground scrambled over the cage and manhandled the rear mounted winch line of the GP dozer up and over the top of the canopy.

That line was very heavy and hard to handle. By attaching the winch-hook onto the lower edge of the blade, when the winch was cranked it held the blade far enough off the ground so the dozer could move downhill.

All these maneuvers and a hose replacement took until daylight the following morning before the TD 14 was back on the fire building line. About the same time, around 6 AM, a fresh dozer operator arrived. At the shift change he was put onto the machine so that the regular GP skinner could get some rest. The ground crews were also given a twelve-hour respite. Everyone was called back late in the day to begin mop-up on the burned over areas.

When we reported back onto the fire that evening, we learned that during the day shift, the new dozer operator managed to get the unfortunate TD 14 into a severe nose-down position on the steep slope. Everywhere that hillside was very much on the tilt. To avoid a rollover, extensive and tricky moves were needed to get the machine turned around.

With that particular dozer, any lengthy time with the front end well below the rear was not a good move. Since the oil pump was located at the rear of the engine, gravity would not let the pump pick up enough oil to get to the crankshaft. The substitute skinner managed to burn out the bearings while trying to turn around safely on the hillside.

When we saw our original skinner coming back for nightshift, he was really upset about his dozer. The dozer operators were very careful with their machines, keeping the engines in tip-top condition. This was because it always took a long while to get engine repairs done on the dozers. With this snafu, the GP Unit dozer was now on the blink indefinitely. I think it was around then that the Unit decided to replace the TD 14 with a newer, more powerful and more modern D 6. That fire on Wards Creek ended up to be almost 700 acres. The district personnel handled it pretty much on their own, short-handed and all.

CHAPTER 24

In Southwestern Oregon there are summers when thunderstorms just don't build at all. Other summers have storms from beginning to end. Most years are some-where between the two extremes. The worst, as far as fires are concerned, are those years when only lightning and rumbling thunder come about. With no rain getting to the ground to cool things down, the fire agencies are run to a frazzle trying to track all the lightning strikes. This is called Chasing Smokes. When the storms occurred after the younger personnel had returned to school it could get really wicked for those still on the job.

The tail end of the 1966 Fire Season forced the district to deal with the annual drop in manpower at precisely the same time as a series of storms zapped the area with over a thousand down-strikes with almost no rain at all Today's weather equipment can print-out maps of the district that pinpoint every lightning strike. What a wonderful invention. We could have really used that kind of tracking in 1966.

Although every strike does not result in a fire, I would estimate something lights up in about one of every ten hits. (This is just a personal guess.) If rain falls, it may put out fires that do catch. Other times, a strike that results in fire may first smolder for many days before it breaks out unexpectedly. Either way, it's a problem that can't be ignored.

CHASING SMOKES

The Fire Season was bad 'til the end that year. Very late that summer there was a strong lightning bust in the mid-afternoon. I do not recall how many starts occurred, but it must have been a bunch, as we were sent way out of our Merlin/Hugo area to several smokes and reported fires. That only happens when things are really popping.

A blaze had been reported in the south part of the Unit, I think by a resident in the Williams area. When we couldn't locate the smoke, we stopped at the old Williams Store. Dispatch had provided the contact phone number for the guy who'd reported the smoke on his property. A local farmer answered our call and told us there was no close road access to the burn. He was on his way to check on it and was eager for us to meet him farther out in the country at a road junction. From there he led us to the fire location cross-country.

The fire was about ½ an acre in size, mostly on the surface near a stand of pole-sized trees with a few bunches of brush. It was spreading at a modest pace and showed a couple of flare-ups where ladder fuels led to some topping out in the young trees. The trees weren't really big enough to call it a Crown Fire at that point, but it was vigorous and scary looking, with flame length of eight feet or more overhead.

We took action with our hand tools, knocking down the hot spots first with the help of the farmer. He was an older guy, but game and really helped. When we had things back on the ground, we began to quickly trail the perimeter and cooled any flare-ups with dirt as we went. At some point the farmer had to leave. We finished the containment line with just the two of us.

Once the line was completed, we reported our status to Dispatch and the condition of the fire. It was contained, but there was one hot area that had a large, tall snag actively on fire. It was located near the line, so the fire would need to be closely tended until that spot died down. When the intensity cooled off, it would be safe to take down the snag, and kill the flames and embers with direct attack on the ground.

Considering how busy the lightning bust had kept us, we weren't surprised when Dispatch immediately sent us to another down-strike. Our fire wasn't quite yet safe to leave untended, so Dispatch instructed us to wait until a Bureau of Land Management (BLM) crew arrived. We were told they were a patched together crew, pulled from the BLM office ranks to help cover the manpower shortage. They were doing extra fire duty because of the many incidents the storm had caused. This was important information to know.

My crewman and I began to dry mop the burned-over ground, keeping a close watch on the burning snag. It took about 30 minutes before the BLM folks arrived, and the snag was still burning with vigor.

We had to talk the new crew into the tricky access through Dispatch, as their agency used a different radio frequency so we couldn't talk rig to rig. I took special care sharing the situation and what was to be done. The briskly burning snag was the main point, plus a close patrol of the hand trail.

When I felt the inexperienced BLM crew understood what was required with the fire, I called Dispatch. Careful details about the fire and instructions to the BLM crew were shared before we left heading out on our next assignment.

We had a long drive to the next smoke. It was mid to late afternoon when we arrived at what became the last call of the day. Once more it was a smoke on the north side and above I-5 about half way between Grants Pass and Rogue River.

The location of the fire was on the nose of a high spur ridge, running toward the freeway about ½ mile from off the main crest. Fortunately, there was a well-maintained road on the top of the main ridge that we could use for access. We still had to hike down most of the spur to the fire with our tools in hand.

Once more the incident was well outside our patrol area, but Overhead was obviously desperate with personnel spread so thin to cover so many smokes. This time the fire was less than an acre and not spreading very fast.

The landscape was favorable and we quickly put in a good hand trail to contain the low flames. A little mop up was needed, but mostly the black area was clear. The snag that had drawn the down-strike that started the whole burn needed our attention. We took down what was left of the still flaming tree. This job was done with our hand tools, as we didn't carry a chainsaw. More mop up was needed after the snag was on the ground.

If we'd left the snag standing it would likely burn through and eventually fall most any direction. The impact would scatter the embers when no one would be on hand to smother them. Any stray breeze could bring the coals back to life and defeat all earlier suppression efforts. We took care to kill all visible smokes and flare-ups inside our perimeter line. We were doing exactly the same as what I'd told the BLM crew was necessary at the other locale.

We had been working so hard that we had not noticed some weather changes that were occurring. We were almost finished, when looking up to take a breather we could see a thunderhead coming over the high ridge on the other side of I-5 to the southwest. It was a huge, very black and ominous formation looming and moving fast in our direction. About then that cloud started to crackle with frequent bolts flashing and one very loud CRRACKK! There was hardly a pause when several more with loud bangs and booms followed, flashing lightning and the sounds echoing away into the distance.

With the snag down, our fire was in good shape and safe. At this point we were not! Being on that high ridge like that, we were exposed targets for the now very active lightning in that cloud cell. It was time to grab our tools and vacate the premises to the relative safety of our rig a half-mile away.

A quick gathering of our gear was followed by an urgent jog back to the truck. We arrived at the engine just moments before the storm got to us. It was very humid and we both arrived soaked with sweat, and panting like dogs chasing crows on a hot day. Distantly spaced raindrops the size of my fist spat out of the sky once or twice onto our backs making loud SPLAT sounds.

Tools were tossed into the back and we clamored into the cab. The following twenty minutes or so, we rode out the booming and flashing storm. It was a spectacular show and we had the best seats in the house. Before long the lightning began to come with longer gaps between strikes. In spite of the first promising splattering of moisture from the sky, no significant rain fell.

After awhile I felt it was safe to use the radio. We reported to Dispatch about our fire and our current status. They directed us back to GP HQ keeping an alert watch for any new smokes on the ridge-tops as we drove.

I don't recall that we saw anything on our way back into Grants Pass, nor were we reassigned to another fire from the bust. Maybe any blow-ups were finally all successfully manned. Maybe locations across the river below us were accompanied by heavy rain. Maybe the down strikes were smoldering away, ready to test the district's crews tomorrow.

This busy day had been my last for the season. I am pretty sure that was my last fire that year.

I came into HQ late the next morning to turn in my keys and pick up my paycheck. Signing out, I noticed the active status of the Williams patrol rig on the assignment board. That crew and another engine were working the fire my crewman and I had turned over to the green BLM crew the afternoon before.

When I asked, the Dispatch people described what had happened, and I was completely disgusted. Either the crew that relieved us had been poorly trained or was just lazy. It appeared that those guys had underestimated the potential for the snag to re-ignite the fire. When their regular time to go home arrived, they'd left the incident obviously without a complete mop-up.

I hoped some supervisor somewhere was burning their ears off. My crewman and I had put a good portion of sweat and muscle into putting that fire down. It really twisted my tail that they'd botched it up by leaving early. That old farmer who owned the land and who'd helped us as best he could, had deserved better. I went away grumbling. Why do something so important only halfway, then leaving it for others to complete? These were my dad's words echoing in my head.

Other things quickly caught my attention, though. It was time for my brand-new family to take up residence in Corvallis until next June. I needed to finish my Forest Management studies at OSU.

I didn't know it then, but that had been my last day as a seasonal wildland fire fighter. In the years ahead, I would spend a lot of time on many more fires, but it would never again be my day-to-day job.

Plodding through the final year of college that year was just plain hard work. I was under the gun to finish everything by June to graduate. I needed that diploma to find a full-time job to support my family. Voluntarily I skipped things I really enjoyed like football games and even half-hour TV shows, hitting the books. Time was limited. It had to be allotted with care.

Several weeks before graduation, a group of potential employers sent representatives to the university to interview the soon-to-be graduates. About that same time my wife shared that our family would soon be growing. We were expecting our second child to be born near Christmas at the end of 1967.

To me, a job with a level of security was now the most important factor. I was not very interested in working in the private forestry sector. I thought that being a public employee, while offering lower pay, had more staying power and maybe better benefits in the long run. It seemed that private forest industry jobs were more likely to be affected by the ups and downs of market conditions. With another baby coming, those benefits were particularly important just then.

With these things in mind, I interviewed with three government agencies including the US Forest Service (USFS), the Washington Department of Natural Resources (WDNR), and the Oregon Department of Forestry (ODF).

From my fire experiences, there had been many times ODF crews worked under the directive of other agency Overhead. The attitude of so many of the ranking federal people I'd come in contact with had kind of turned me off. It didn't help that their interviewer exhibited a similar mind-set. He was mostly interested in super students with the highest classroom grades, hardly looking at work records, experience and recommendations.

The federal agencies probably had some great people working for them. Somehow, though, I didn't feel really comfortable with their people – never had. There seemed to be too much emphasis on things I considered less important. My interview with the feds went okay, but from my earlier contacts, I felt I wouldn't be a good fit in their employ.

Many of the people I worked alongside in the woods and fighting fire were really savvy. Their know-how came from experience, not college. I really did value my college education and certainly worked hard enough to acquire it. The basic truth for me at least, is I had learned that the information in the books added to the practical daily, down and dirty work with my hands.

All together this served me very well. School and books were mostly faster ways to learn, but easier to take lightly. When I goofed up, what was learned in school was much more forgiving. Real life experiences were more thorough and lasting, and usually demanded positive results or else.

Or maybe I was just being my father's son. He only finished eighth grade, but could do almost anything. He most certainly wasn't stupid nor ignorant. I was a blue-collar guy from a blue-collar background.

In college I 'd known several really smart guys who earned very good grades all the time. When we would work side-by-side, these fellows had no idea how to even begin an innovative issue in the real world, where muscle, sweat and soiled hands were necessary. My grades weren't all that bad, but I certainly was not an overly impressive academic. That was okay. I knew how to handle complex, real-life problems.

Besides, I'd been an ODF guy for several years. The department had been pretty good to me for those five fire seasons. Mostly I hoped to secure a permanent job with them. I just felt I was better suited for either ODF or maybe the Washington DNR.

My wife and I sweated with worry for two weeks after the interviews. Days before graduation, I received a job offer from Washington DNR as a Reforestation Forester. The location was in Alder, Washington on the southwest slopes of Mt. Rainier.

Alder was a very small, high-elevation community and I heard that residents there were often snowed in for a time in the winter. The closest town of any size where a person could shop for most of their needs was about sixty miles away, (if you could get there). With a baby due in mid-December, this didn't seem too safe. The DNR people wanted a reply from me within fourteen days. I'd heard nothing yet from the Oregon people. What to do?

Another day or two went by. I still had not received any response of any kind from ODF, my employer of choice. With no response, I decided to take matters into my own hand by contacting the Personnel Director for the department in Salem.

The state director was not available when I called, but did return my call the following morning. I explained that I was really interested in employment with ODF, but did have a job offer from WDNR and needed to reply to them in a day or so.

He told me that staffing was changing within the ODF main office, so he hadn't had time to look at any of the new candidates for open jobs. He said he would check and get back to me promptly. True to his word, the next day the Personnel Director called back and with a job offer for me. It was as the Reforestation Forester for the Astoria District. The location was the extreme northwestern corner of Oregon at the mouth of the Columbia River on the Pacific Coast. After an evening confab with my wife, I telephoned in my acceptance the following morning.

Within the week my parents and two siblings proudly traveled to Corvallis. It was a warm early-June day in 1967. I lined up with more than a thousand other grads along the beautiful flowered sidewalks that grace the OSU campus each spring. All in line were wearing long black robes and tassels of various colors hanging from our flat mortarboard hats. Each color represented a different field of study. Mine was golden brown for Forestry.

My mom's dream of me earning a college education came true that day. I had achieved a Bachelor of Science degree in Forest Management from Oregon State University. The grand ceremony was held in Gill Coliseum in front of a packed house.

I will never pretend college was easy. Almost every dollar of the expense was earned through hard physical labor. The schoolwork was not so much about being smart enough – more about being just too stubborn to quit.

I didn't successfully over-come the academic challenge until I matured enough to force myself to stop goofing off. Getting downright serious about the whole thing changed the way I approached school. The academic demand was just like any physical daily work - a certain level of performance was needed to do any job right.

I always had a level of pride about doing physical jobs well. To me, that same pride eventually came to be equally important about the academic effort at college as well. In the long run, the same qualities that I eventually adopted about college, evolved to become exactly the same as my perceptions about work. Just as both my college studies and the earning money to pay for them had taken real effort, but of totally different kinds, so did my need to both thoroughly know my daily work, and the delivery of the highest quality of application every day. I guess my dad's work-ethic was part of me too.

At the end, I wasn't a kid anymore.

PART TWO

*The Coast Range Mountains
and Other Places*

CHAPTER 25

In the far northwestern part of Oregon, consistently bad weather really makes an impact on the lives of the residents. In Astoria, close to one hundred inches of rain falls each year, winter and summer. The rain is seldom gentle and often accompanied by very notable winds. A few gentle days sneak in here and there, usually in the fall, and then the coastal area of northern Oregon becomes spectacular in its lush and deeply green beauty.

In the late 1960s harvesting the rich natural resources of the region called for hearty people willing to brave the grouchy weather. Loggers and fishermen living near the mouth of the mighty Columbia River were mostly of Scandinavian decent, with a scattering of various Asian and Germans mixed in. It wasn't uncommon to hear native Swedish, Norwegian, and Finnish languages, with occasional Japanese and Chinese spoken on the streets and in the stores in town. A lot of the older generations, grand and great-grand parents, spoke little or no English. Many of the younger set were bi-lingual.

Heavy rain gear and caulked (spiked) soles on loggers' boots were working-attire for a goodly share of the population. In spite of the rain, umbrellas were rare, as the stiff winds granted only a very limited lifespan to such accessories.

A NEW JOB – A FRANTIC TIME

I felt constantly pushed for our first year or more in Northwestern Oregon. It really began just before leaving Corvallis. It seemed that every other week since June 1967 new pressures and changes popped up, mostly at my new job, but some in my personal life as well. Before we moved to the NWO job I had been buried in studying for the last round of final exams before college graduation. When the exams were done, next came the huge graduation ceremony with more than a thousand university students on parade in long robes, waving to family members, feeling proud. Thankfully I landed a much-needed job in my field of study. The job assignment meant my wife and I had to find a place to live in a town nearly two hundred miles away from the place we called home. Also, we only a handful of days to get settled in. By July 1 I needed to be at my new desk and ready to go.

Our car was a piece of junk and we had no money for gas or rent money. More pressure. Soon I felt guilty too. Neither my parents nor in-laws had much extra cash, so the small loan from my dad and help getting moved from my father-in-law put a strain on everyone.

The few extra dollars got a roof over our heads in far away Astoria. My in-laws stepped up with a small trailer used to transfer our meager belongings. They also filled our third-hand, new to us, refrigerator with groceries. Glory Be, our wreck of a car survived the trip getting us moved.

Unknown to us, the summer weather that year of 1967 was unusually dry and hot for the region. Since we were used to the hot, triple digit summer temperatures of SWO, only the added humidity was of note to us. The local residents made on-going complaints about the discomfort of beautiful sunny days with temperatures in the low 80's all summer long. We thought it was terrific weather and didn't understand their discontent. We pretty much had to take the first rental we found. It was a snug farmhouse on forty acres, ten miles east of Astoria, but closer to fifteen miles from the ODF office on the farther west side of the city. The farmhouse was nice, but from the start the cost was beyond our means.

The mild nature of our initial experience with good weather only lasted a couple of months – it was a very unusual situation in that part of the state. Soon enough fall arrived. We quickly learned about the weather, finding it safe to assume pretty much there would be rotten weather daily from then on. We broke out our winter clothes for use pretty much the entire time we lived there. Over the next four years we witnessed the weather extremes common to the area, but all new to us. For the first time in my life I saw snow on a sandy Pacific Coast beach.

That first beautiful summer we watched as the swallows swooped and dove through the air around the farmhouse. They built mud nests and raised their young under the eaves of the old barn standing on a low rise near the house. It was almost idyllic.

In the early Fall the local boss bull elk immerged from the woodsy area beyond the barn. He gathered his harem of cows in the back pasture and prepared to fight off all other rival males. I could walk out to the old barn and through gaps in the walls, sit there watching the ritual up close. Elk are a bit shy. Their presence so close gave inkling into how remote our new home actually was. I worried some about my pregnant wife and baby girl left on their own as I drove off to work in our beat-up car every morning.

I had felt some pride to be hired as the head of Reforestation for the Astoria District, but choked down more than I little fear of potential failure. I was within two weeks of my twenty-third birthday on my first day of work.

From the onset, much of the basic nuts and bolts of my new work were almost overwhelming. To function at all in those first weeks, I was dependent on whatever I could remember from college and my limited personal experience working on tree-planting crews during the winter months. I was facing a very steep learning curve needing to cram information into my brain as I went, as quickly and accurately as possible.

I wasn't a complete novice, but I sure was painfully aware that I was no veteran either. I greatly appreciated the experienced local technicians and timber-sale people in the unit office who were willing to share what they could. Often though, I didn't know enough to even ask the right questions. Most of my lack of information was in the area of procedures and schedules devised by the Department. These included numerous plans and reports created for Area and Salem staff review. My worrying nature was both an asset and a bother. From the first day, much of the basic nuts and bolts of my new work were almost overwhelming. The job seemed huge.

There was so much. Coming into the reforestation job was kind of like watching a whole wall of TV sets, each tuned to a different program, and trying to follow all the different storylines at the same time. There were many, many forested acres in the Astoria area that were each in a somewhat different place within the cycle of renewal, from newly created bare ground to places with younger trees of various species, ages and density. Every square foot of the 140,000 acres was partly my responsibility to manage. Ouch!

Astoria District Office where the author worked 1967-1971.
Courtesy of ODF Fire History Museum

Within my first week on the job, I was notified that I would be absent from the office for a weeklong New Forester's Tour starting in August. A group of newly hired foresters with varied assignments from around the state would visit several outlying District offices, plus the Salem Headquarters. I hated to lose more time from my desk, but later I realized the tour was a jump-start on the huge educational task ahead of me. Besides, it turned out to be a lot of fun on the State's dime.

The trip was an annual affair, planned and presented by the Personnel Director and the Training Officer. Every year the format changed to include different areas of the state. The 1967 tour both began and ended at the ODF Salem Office Headquarters. As I recall, there were ten new foresters on that tour with the director and his assistant as guides and chauffeurs.

We traveled in two station wagons, driving from office to office, visiting two, sometimes three each day. The atmosphere as we traveled rapidly changed from stiff to relaxed to kind of fun within the first few hours.

The two leaders from Salem were jolly and personable. We looped from Salem to Philomath to Tillamook on day one, and managed Astoria, Forest Grove and Cascade Locks on the second. On day three we were over the Cascade Mountains in the high elevation Oregon desert, stopping at The Dalles, Prineville and Redmond. The last day was a leisurely trip back over the high Santiam Pass to Salem.

Someone at each stop talked about their district, it's major functions, current issues and biggest problem areas. At times there was a quick trip into the nearby woods to help illustrate some of the more vital issues. It was good stuff to know, and the opportunity to connect with fellow workers was great.

The Department of Forestry is still one of the smaller state agencies, and it has almost a family feel to it even today, fifty years later. Parents and grown children, even grandchildren, siblings, cousins, other extended family members, plus old school-mates cross paths in the field of Forestry, work that is very common in Oregon.

After a lifetime in Oregon, this tour gave me an opportunity to really know my home state. I discovered that Oregon is a state filled with small towns. Excepting for Salem, every office where we stopped was located in a town with a population of 10,000 or less. Evenings after dinner were our own. Mostly our bunch behaved ourselves, only getting a little rowdy once or twice. Nobody told us to leave town

Beyond the casual times as miles were put on the cars, there were two little incidents that brought us closer to our tour guides. After lunch on the opening day, the Personnel Director took it on himself to fill the fuel tank on our car at the HQ compound pump in Tillamook. By accident he used diesel instead of gasoline at the unfamiliar fuel shed. We got only about three blocks from the office before the car began to cough and sputter, forcing a quick return. We took a lengthy pause in our travel as the Tillamook HQ mechanic had to drain and refill the car's fuel tank. The boss-man accepted gentle ribbing for this faux pas with grace and humor. Ever after to the guys on that trip he was known as "Jimmy Diesel".

The second situation involved the Training Officer. We stopped at a back-woodsy eatery called the Elderberry Inn for lunch on our second day. The food was less than good, the prices were higher than anywhere else on the trip, and the service was awful. For example, when one of the guys asked for a fork, he was rudely informed he didn't need one. Each of us had our own complaint about the food - my own chiliburger included several small rocks in with the beans. We all would probably have let it lie, but the Training Officer had raved about the place before we arrived and strongly defended after we left. We dubbed him "The Elderberry Hound". The nickname stuck.

In general, on that tour all members had a good time. We newly hired gained a better feel for our agency and the districts where we were now employed. We also came to know people much like ourselves dealing with similar situations. We each gleaned names and contacts with potential resource people at the Salem and other offices. Help was there to aid in our success, and we were obviously expected to use it when in need.

Also, the job description for everyone at ODF has a fire suppression role, even today. The department has an imposing record of success with fire suppression. In part this is due to the aggressive attitude of the agency. During summer fire season, virtually every department employee may be called upon to drop what he or she may be doing and switch to an active role in fire control as needed. All this is an out-growth of the catastrophic conditions the state endured with the Tillamook Burns during the 1930s. Not too long after the tour I learned first-hand that such unexpected call-outs also give opportunities for meeting and working with old – and new - acquaintances.

A master-list of permanent personnel and their fire qualifications is available to Overhead for reference when emergencies occur. Even those on staff who may be untrained and physically unable to work directly on a fire line may find themselves in fire support roles when things get bad.

Back home in Astoria after the tour of districts, I dug into the work piled on my desk, uninterrupted for another couple of weeks. It was now late summer, the very height of fire season across the state. My five years of fire experience was on record.

Once more I was plucked from my work-laden desk, still worrying about leaving when there was so much to do. This time the call-out was for a big fire not too far south of the Columbia River, but far away to the east of the Cascade Mountains. The incident was near a town called The Dalles, one of the stopping spots on the tour a few weeks before.

There were two of us from the NWO Unit dispatched from Astoria just at dark (about 9:30 PM) to help with this fire. My traveling companion was from one of our unit's timber teams, also a newer forester that had been on board only a year.

That night on our eastward drive, I think for the only time in my many years in the woods I saw a live cougar in the wild. Cougars are extremely wary and avoid humans as much as possible. This big cat was standing on a low cut-bank on the left side of the road as we drove past about midnight. We only noticed because of the reflection of bright green eyes in the headlights.

Our total travel time to the fire was well over four hours. We arrived at the scene in the early hours of pre-dawn, so were still able to get a little sleep before joining the 5 AM early morning briefing. Talk about dragging your rear out of bed! At that time, I was still a devoted coffee buff, thank goodness. I needed that caffeine kick.

This fire had quickly blasted from first ignition into Project Fire status. This term is used when a fire has overwhelmed the local resources in both personnel and equipment. During fire season, Initial Attack by local crews is vital and must be maintained. When situations exceed what the local unit can handle, a kind of All-Hands-On-Deck call goes into effect across the state. Incoming help takes on the problem fire, while locals drop back to Initial Response duties.

What my companion and I were doing, driving through the night, wasn't unusual. When a unit makes a Project Fire call-out, it isn't uncommon for personnel with certain skills to drive through the wee hours of the night to bring assistance. Additionally, Salem maintained a "Fire Cache" system and could load out one or more large trucks or "Semis" with needed materials and equipment. Delivery time from storage to a needy district is about eight to twelve hours.

It may seem that flying extra staff long distances would have been a faster means to deliver workers, but the additional equipment is usually as vital as the human resources inside. The downside with driving was that while the need for help on a big fire was important, new crews arriving weren't always able to get much quality sleep before their first shift. The necessary drive often forced the "fresh" arriving crews to be as sleep deprived as those they relieved, even before they began work on the fire.

Upon arrival, often the equipment went on the line immediately without regard to home unit – just new drivers. Equipment was hard used on fires, often with the only breaks coming during shift changes or for refueling.

This fire had started on mesa-like ground and quickly burned several hundred acres of wheat fields plus some brushy ground on the flat top. This kind of fire is hot and fast moving – very scary to observe and even worse to fight. It was beginning to burn down the steep surrounding rough slopes leading to lower ground on all perimeters. On the west side it was moving deeply into water-shed. The main watercourse was named Mill Creek, serving the City of The Dalles, an important area to protect.

Assignment to this fire was likely connected to my old Southwest Oregon (SWO) experiences. The Incident Commander (IC) that was brought in with the Project Fire status had been my top supervisor from the Grants Pass Unit while I worked there. Quite probably his words of advice had the most influence on my collegiate decisions - more than any other person. He even might have been called my mentor.

Upon arrival at Fire Camp, I was assigned to work as a Line Boss under the Division Boss on the west perimeter. The small world of ODF was also obvious, as that Division Boss was the very same Reforestation guru from the main Salem HQ that I'd met the month before on the new foresters' tour. He was an interesting fellow and was a WWII vet having been a Marine fighter pilot flying a Corsair.

I took over command of my part of the line at 6 AM that first morning. Just twelve hours before I'd been quietly eating dinner with my wife and little girl a few hundred miles to the west.

I had a dozer and a couple of hand crews at my disposal. We were to try our best to cut off the fire's advance downhill into a canyon with Mill Creek at the base. The going was tough, as much of the ground was rocky and way too steep for the dozer. Still we used it wherever it was able to safely get access to the proposed trail. The rest of the line was accomplished by hand. At end of shift (6 PM) we had made good progress and the fire was near containment on our side.

Just before the shift change the division boss called me directly on the radio. I was to meet him back on top of the steep slope, and we'd go to the Fire Camp together. The camp had been laid-out on the bank of the same stream, but downhill from our attack area where I had worked all day with my crews. I could debrief him as we traveled.

The end-of-shift hike up the side of that mesa was none too easy, especially after a long night's drive, only a little sleep and a very long, hard workday. I met up with the DB after I'd handed our equipment over to the night shift. We two sat in the dirt as I described what had been accomplished on my part of the line, marking his map. He seemed very pleased with the work the guys under my leadership had accomplished.

This fellow was an energetic type, with a very pleasant, upbeat way about him. I'd already found him very likable and eager to help with my reforestation questions. I was pretty wiped out after my shift, but his energy was contagious. When I finished my report, he said he'd secured a ride for the two of us to the Fire Camp in a recon helicopter that was temporarily not in use.

That was my very first of many rides in a helicopter. Even in my incredibly tired condition this was an exciting moment. It had once been my childhood dream to join the air force and become a pilot. The boss seemed to sense my feelings, reacting with a big grin at my enthusiastic response.

It was a very small copter. The pilot sat in the middle of the cabin and we two each squeezed in on the sides. I recall having only about one-half my rear on the seat and the rest of me hanging outside. I managed to stay partly in the machine by keeping my right foot firmly on the landing strut as we took off.

At first it felt like that moment when an elevator starts up to the next floor and your stomach seems to rise up into your chest. Then it smoothed out. With the fresh clean air in my face and the ground moving quickly below the machine, I was totally hooked!

I really enjoyed that ride. It ended way too quickly, as only a few minutes passed and we were at the LZ on the ground at the Fire Camp.

Over the next thirty-plus years working in management and protection, I would spend a lot of time in helicopters and fixed-wing craft, doing recon on many big fires, directing aerial spraying, seeding regeneration units and many other related forest projects. Although I'd always had a deep inner fear of heights, apparently it was somehow connected to having my feet on the ground. Strangely, while in flight, I didn't ever get even a queasy stomach. I loved every air-borne minute!

When we arrived at the Fire Camp that evening, our simple intention was to get cleaned up, eat some always-great Fire Camp chow and head for our bedrolls. The shower set-up was in a tarped-off area for privacy. As was common then, each shower was fed only with cold water pumped from an engine parked outside the tarp-sided stalls.

Our arrival though, was a bit of bad timing for us. Before we could gather our gear together for a wash, a spot fire was reported about a mile just upstream from the camp. The nearest available engine was the one feeding water to the showers. It was immediately commandeered. We watched with disappointment as our opportunity to clean up dashed away to put out the flare-up. Its return was indefinite.

There we were, left dry and dirty, each holding a bundle of clean clothes and toiletry kits. My now buddy-boss grabbed my arm and pointed to his personal state rig, a pickup parked in the motor pool area not too far away. Following his lead, I hopped in the truck and we headed out a road following the main waterway going upstream. My companion said we would find our own private spot where we could wash off the day's dirt and soot.

About a mile away from the camp we found a large pipe - maybe ten or twelve inches in diameter - coming out of the hillside alongside the creek. The pipe was gushing a full stream of water. This seemed like a good spot to both of us. Imagine our surprise when further inspection revealed the water coming out of that pipe was bathwater warm! This happy coincidence was because that area is known for its geo-thermal activity. The hot rocks far below the Earth's surface heated that water. We were delighted!

Our bathing did require some physical effort. We had to be sure to have a firm hold onto something solid so the considerable force of the water coming straight from the pipe didn't knock us down. To keep from being washed downstream, it took a lot of care to strip down to our under-shorts, get under that giant-sized water gush, climb out, soap up and get back under to rinse. All while holding on with one hand.

It sure felt good, especially compared to the usual coldwater bathing fire camps offered. I'm pretty sure my boss didn't know that the stream was part of the city water supply for The Dalles; I know I didn't. This bit of news was provided to us at a group meeting the following morning before the shift change. Everyone was told to be cautious about befouling the water of the nearby stream. We two kept mum about our earlier personal use.

Anyway, clean and refreshed, dried and dressed in fresh clothes, we headed back to Fire Camp. They served up a delicious dinner and after that we separated to our assigned beds looking forward to a good night's sleep.

It was not to be.

Every fire camp I've ever stayed in is kept very quiet at all hours both day and night. The reason is because you can bet a whole lot of people are sound asleep somewhere close by. But in the middle of that first night, there was a commotion lasting nearly two hours.

It seems that a few of the inmate (convict) fire crewmembers appeared to be missing. Bed and latrine checks had revealed that 2 or 3 empty bedrolls had no matching occupants. Then more thorough searching of the camp and further bed checks found that the original vacant beds were filled, but in the meantime some others were now empty. No one was forthcoming with an explanation. This rotational absence was repeated a couple of times, with the resulting searches waking people up every time.

Eventually, the guards that accompanied the inmate crews posted a stakeout on the sleeping area in question. Sure enough, another small stealthy group soon crept out of their bedrolls and were seen at the edge of camp. The guards tailed them quietly. The small wayward assemblage was found a couple of miles down the main road at a trailer parked and nearly hidden in the tall brush. Inside, two local women had set up a "shady business". The county sheriff was called, the impromptu enterprise was quickly closed down and the ladies escorted from the area. This let everybody finally get some much-needed sleep.

The rest of the fire and trip back to Astoria a couple of days later were pretty uneventful after that first exciting twenty-four hours. Beyond the first helicopter ride, The Dalles fire was my first Project Fire where I was an Overhead supervisor rather than a crewman on the line. It was also my first high dessert fire on the eastside of the Cascade Mountains. It was one to remember too. I learned some things about fighting fire in the much different terrain there.

CHAPTER 26

*E*asily two-thirds of all wildland fires have their origin from human actions. In my career field of Forest Management, fires are one of the more common tools. In fact, for hundreds of years, history records how fire intentionally set, has been used by humans to clean up or effect how forests grow.

These old-time fires were not exactly "controlled", but were primitive attempts at elementary forest management. Escapes were very common and often led to many catastrophic situations. Nowadays there is a lot of political discussion about controlled burns; the correct term is "prescribed" rather than controlled. I find these simplified opinions perplexing. To burn or to thin or to harvest are not actions that are inter-changeable.

As for prescribed burns, they have their uses, but are not new and not the miracle solution to forest management people seem to think. They are only one of many applications to achieve a healthy forest. Wildland fires that originate from escaped prescribed burns are very common even during wetter winter conditions. Intentional fires that act as planned can be helpful and economical, but are more uncertain than other good management actions. A long list of strict conditions must prevail, or the fire becomes a problem rather than a solution. Even a small escape brings issues.

Only the most experienced of forest managers can experience more success than failure with prescribed burns as a tool. Those in charge on site when the first flame is ignited must know the particulars of local fire behavior, plus have in-depth knowledge of the landscape, the fuels and the weather conditions. Such people are rare.

Forest conditions can change very quickly. An escaped fire easily becomes the same Mortal Enemy as any other wildland fire, even during winter months.

BACK ON THE LINE

It was the middle of summer 1968. About a year had passed since I took on the Reforestation job in the ODF Northwest Oregon (NWO) Astoria District. Wildland fires were very few in that area, but one afternoon I was told to respond to a call-out with several of my co-workers.

There was an escaped logging-show slash burn on the side of a very steep mountain in the south part of the unit. The Astoria supervisor had included my name on the list of our personnel to help in the Tillamook District, maybe sixty miles to the south. Our travel took us near to the rocky cliffs of the northern Pacific coastline.

In the NWO District any forest fire was rare. Mostly it was just too wet in that area for flames to grab hold, even in the summer months. Some people persist on calling this very damp corner of Oregon and Washington a Rain Forest. In fact, it is a Northern Temperate Forest type; not to be confused with the tropical forests thousands of miles closer to the equator. The big difference is the length of the growing season. Winter temperatures and shortened length of day-light forestall plant growth in a Northern Temperate Forest for several months. Still, the 90 plus inches of rain that falls every year thereabouts keeps it pretty green and lush – most of the time a lot more than was to my liking.

As a native of southern Oregon, I liked my summers dry and hot, and was accustomed to fighting wildland fires in triple digit temperatures. With my young family, we'd lived through one soggy and uncomfortable NWO winter. Weekend trips to the preferred dryer locale were few – too expensive. By this time, we were getting pretty homesick.

When sent by my supervisor to work on this fire near Tillamook, the change from my daily work was appealing. I was just beginning to feel mostly caught-up in my research work and with the needed personal educational quest. On the downside, there was still a huge pile of work for my daily job left untended. My nose was barely above the level of fatal drowning in the reforestation needs of the district.

Missing even one day might be a problem. I'd only had a couple of times to exercise my fire skills since I'd come to the NWO Unit, and missed the satisfaction I knew that would accompany the assignment. Following the instructions of the boss was a good idea, and so here I was, back on the line, busting my hump, digging hand trail – just like I'd been doing every summer since high school. It felt good – the reforestation work would wait.

In this case the fire was located high up on the steep slopes above the coast town of Garibaldi. This is very rough country. Time of day when we arrived was twilight near dark, but light enough to get a quick look at the lay of the land. It was bad, very bad. From my fire experience from the southern part of the state, fires on bad terrain were normal, but even so, this incline was one for the books. Parts of that mountainside were close to shear.

Access to the burn came in on a fairly steep ridge-top road that put our crew above the fire. The spread was modest in speed, moving downhill below us. There were several tender rigs coming and going on a modest sized landing, hauling water to keep an engine with a tank on its back full of water. The stationary truck was pumping down the hill through hose lays being used to work the fire far, far below.

Our crew had used the long drive to prepare, so without much delay, over the side and down we went, joining our cohorts in Direct Attack. Direct Attack means the crew is working within a few feet of the flames.

Actually "pumping" is not the correct way to describe the water delivery to the fire. Once the engine pump fed water into the hoses, gravity controlled the flow. The pump was used to simply keep the line filled. Any high school kid in a basic Physics class would know that the hose pressure on that set-up was directly affected by the diameter of the line, the length of the total drop, and the size of the nozzle at the discharge.

On flat ground the pump would supply the water pressure, but in this situation the pressure that was built up by gravity was maybe 100 to 200 psi (pounds per square inch). We dared not turn off the water anywhere below the landing for fear that any weak spot in the system would blow apart. Every connection at the lower end was in danger of going out at any time, plus any un-noticed worn spot in the hose could burst as well.

As it was, the hoses were very hard to handle, and the terrain added to the problem. Wrestling with a wild hose while tripping over rocks and brush on a steep hillside in the dark would not be considered favorable and safe fire fighting conditions. But then, wildland fire isn't ever a safe job, and "favorable conditions" is a relative term.

Sometimes the water needed to be off. There could be a need to add another hose length, or the hose-lay needed to be repositioned. To turn off the water, we had to radio the engine at the top and have them shut off the feed up there. Then there was considerable wait, letting the hose drain before we could change connections, add hose or move the lay more than a few feet. To resume the fight, even more delay was needed to reverse the process.

Fires always have an urgency factor, and this process wasn't really efficient in that regard at all. Anybody on a fire line tends to get a bit testy with these kinds of delays. I worked with the rest of the guys there coping with the less than perfect hose issue for a couple of hours. The increasing use of foul language indicated a growing level of irritation by all present.

We successfully put in a stretch of hand trail, but had several burning snags that were in need of being felled along the perimeter. The snags were near enough to the line that, if left alone, they could burn through and fall across the bare ground we had cleared. If that happened, there would be spot fires outside the fire line. Not good!

Since I had a fair amount of experience falling burning snags from my time in SWO, the job was mine to get done. At least it got me away from that frustrating hose-lay issue for a while.

What a strange job I had – using a chain-saw to cut down burning trees in the middle of the night on a steep coastal hillside. Well, it wasn't the first time I figured I was more than a little bit crazy.

I'd learned years before that judging a snag's lean at night was difficult. For some reason, in the darkness snags always seem to lean uphill. I'd not put down a burning snag for about a year, forgetting how easy it was to misjudge. That night the first one or two drops I worked caused me some grief, but I got them down without getting mashed to jelly or raining flaming debris on my head. It was kind of dicey; I guess I was out of practice. I doubt that I dazzled anyone with my skills.

After I finished with the snags, I rejoined the rest of the crew working with the goofy water setup on the tilt. I'd only been back a short time, when in the darkness we heard a lot of shouting coming from above. It's always smart to check out and take seriously whoops and hollers while on a fire line. As one we all looked up the 500 feet or so of slope to the landing to check out the yelling. There were several sets of headlights to be seen overhead and folks rushing in and out of the light beams.

One pair of headlights was slowly moving down what looked to be the access road and picking up speed quickly on the incline. The moving lights, obviously attached to some large vehicle invisible to us in the dark, turned to shine out over the steep bank way over our heads as it came to the flatter space above. For a moment it seemed the rig above us was stopping, as there seemed to be a very short pause. It was an illusion.

Suddenly the bright headlights slanted down the nearly sheer hillside coming straight toward us. The hose crews around me grumbled oaths that immediately turned into excited warnings to one another. We were all looking for a quick way to evacuate the immediate premises PDQ!

A loud chorus of crashing and crunching sounds now accompanied the scary headlights bearing down on us. An occasional boom and many bangs matched up with violent up and down movements of the light beams. There was one last pirouette, almost like a plea to the heavens. Then the sounds and movement stopped. Like movie premiere beacons, the light beams settled into a blind upward stare at the night sky. All of us on the lower hoses had cleared out of the expected pathway of the bright-eyed monster up slope. We carefully watched for several minutes to make sure that whatever vehicle had gone over the side above had truly come to a halt. In a moment there was a call over the radio telling us to stay put, as all the landing personnel were safe.

Since fires wait for no man, when we confirmed we were not about to be victims of some bizarre hit and run accident, everyone turned back to work. Despite rumors about stoic fire fighters, much speculation traveled along the line of workers around me in regard to whatever had happened. Later it was learned that the driver of a water-tender, in haste to unload his cargo to supply the pumping engine on the landing, had not secured his parking brake or blocked his wheels. When he got out to hook up the hose, his driver-less tanker took off with him running behind, yelling. Such scenes are for cartoons – but not so funny when it happens for real.

As is often the case, human error initiated the accident. Only thick brush and large boulders stopped the chain of events – and that big tender - before a larger tragedy that could have included those of us below. We were all happy enough to have been left out of the drama.

As the gray light of early morning began to define details around us, our shift ended. Only yesterday's travel to the fire had provided any time for our crew to sleep, so butts were dragging. We slowly slogged our tired way back up the burned-over hillside, a weary time for any fire crew. Generally, a guy's brain is numb with fatigue at that time, but I did notice the evidence of the runaway truck from hours before. Upside down, the tender lay on its back with four wheels in the air and looking pretty sorry. It strongly resembled a stranded turtle, all dinged up and dirty, no longer able to fulfill its role.

I didn't arrive home until late afternoon, bone-weary and filthy. After a clean-up and big dinner, a full night's sleep in my own bed was welcome.

The following morning, I was back at my loaded desk in the Astoria office. My huge pile of daily work was just as I'd left it.

CHAPTER 27

a great deal of the ground work in forest management makes use of gathering information. Reforestation is only one part of forest management, just as is fire suppression (Protection). Each, in itself, it is a complex science.

On-site observation and surveys provide numbers counting trees per acre, their girth size, height and so on. Dominant species in a specific location are identified. Ratios of species types are recorded and mapped. Certain mathematical formulas are applied to the survey numbers so the needs of each site can be analyzed. All this information is important to insure a management program is within the proper percentages representing a holistic ideal. Choices are made to select prescriptive actions to create a unique favorable environment for a healthy forest to grow. Most of this work is perfect for computers.

When I graduated from Oregon State University, a computer was available to forestry students to learn to use this new tool. An appointment was made for user- time. Handwritten data was carried to another building where the single computer took up most of the wall space. Input required a keypunch operator to enter our data onto cards, which were fed into the big machine. The results took a few minutes to print- out, accompanied by bright flashing lights and funky noises.

Back then computers, especially PCs were something for the future, not to be seen on foresters' desks for at least another twenty years. For handheld machines, add another decade. When I began in the Reforestation business, in-office work was done mostly using a ball-point pen, mathematics took a slide-rule or were done with the help of a lower function calculator. All reports and file data were written in longhand or on typewriters. It was slow and tedious indoor work, especially hard for so many people who came to the profession with an ingrained need to be out of doors. If copies of any documents were needed, a thermal fax process was used or flimsy carbon- paper. The former could turn out about 6 copies, and the latter about four, each of decreasing quality.

MY JOB

The prime ODF goal in reforestation was and still is, to quickly get healthy trees growing on any site where there are none. Combined with this was another big part of the job; to somehow identify why some sites resist healthy re-growth, and then apply specific treatment to favor more production. This was to be done without sacrificing what was of value and already there.

My education with wildland fire had taken place on the ground through experience in the diverse forests of Southwestern Oregon. I had the good fortune to learn that job in one of the best single environments in the state for the widest scope of instruction I could get. Now, as quickly as possible I needed to learn as much as I could about forest rehab and reforestation. College classes had given me the general basics, but practical experience was needed. Once more, I'd landed in one of the best places in Oregon to get an excellent level of instruction in the fastest possible time. Destiny was again giving me a little help, for which I was very grateful.

I came into the new job knowing I was in charge of Reforestation for the Astoria District. This was a very scary burden for a guy who worried a lot, like me. Aside from some collegiate mock-up stocking surveys, my few tree planting jobs while in college were the only hands-on job experience. Planting seedling trees is only a tiny part of the whole process.

I knew the general concepts, but was painfully aware that there was a heap of important stuff I needed to find out right now.

I had to rely on the experienced local timber teams of the Astoria Unit to share what they could. The Assistant District Forester was a big help to me and had been in the District for several years. He and his wife had four children, the youngest just slightly older than our daughter. We became good friends.

Over the first few months I had telephoned or made trips to the Area office in Forest Grove – also sometimes to the Salem HQ, as at each location were people that I could rely on for guidance in doing my job right. Three guys in Salem, in particular, were well-known reforestation veterans. They had been major players in the planning and process of the phenomenally successful reforestation for the massive Tillamook Burns more than twenty years before. They had a lot of pertinent knowledge, and thankfully liked to share.

The number one task was to learn what was already out in the forest. There were only two ways to do this – both vital. I needed to go and look, and I also needed to read all the background material available.

My predecessor in the job had left mountains of data for every unit that was under my responsibility. Each unit had its own file, some thin and others thick with information. This necessary flow of information over time was the foundation of the work. Reading at my desk while referring to maps and aerial photographs became tiresome for an outdoor type of person like myself.

Also, I had to make sure the process of gathering even more data continued, as someone would follow me as well. As summer drifted away I did add a third urgent task. When information in the files was not sufficient, I set up site surveys. Initially, I was the only one to get this work done. Out to the woods I went, conducting several surveys according to empirical standards, bringing back more charts filled with numbers. I got my first on-the-ground view of some of the lands that would eventually receive treatments I had yet to determine. As time passed I was able to find some fall and spring help in gathering information. By bringing to my team one or two of the better seasonal tree-planting staff a bit early, or holding them longer than normal to help with set-up plots and surveys, needed data was collected.

The foreman that ran my tree planting crews was a grizzled and grumpy old US Navy retired Chief Petty Officer and WWII vet. He was also a Fire Warden in the summer. He owned a small airplane and a bit of land he'd converted to a private airstrip. I liked the guy very much and he seemed to take a shine to me as well.

In the middle of that first long, dry summer my new friend and his plane were occasionally hired to conduct aerial fire detection patrols for the district. As I recall, there were only two or three active lookouts in Northwest Oregon. The aerial patrols were used to supplement the lookout towers for the detection phase of fire protection as the seasonal danger increased. I asked to tag along when he flew, helping as a spotter and to orient myself to the District, and to the many units that were my responsibility.

I discovered that in the future, completing just the survey work would take most of my time for two or three months each year. I began to set up a calendar, dedicating much of the summer for the survey work, as winters had to be used to do other field activities. Some things, such as tree planting, were already locked into the schedule. Tree planting had to be done within a small window of time when young trees are dormant in the cold months.

I needed at least one, sometimes two other people to get the survey work done within the seasonal limitations. This work included on-the-ground examination of every site that would be worked, recording conditions, drawing maps that included specifics, and then writing reports for submission to the area and Salem staff. The summary explained all the plans with all the details.

Additionally, it was necessary to also monitor all previous planting units until they were well established and in a "free to grow" condition. Meaning that it was unlikely that they would be again be threatened by competing vegetation or severe animal damage. On most planting units, semi-permanent plots were set out using three-foot tall stakes to mark about 50 tree seedlings across the unit. These were checked each fall for the survival of the seedlings, growth measurement, surrounding competition, any animal damage incurred, and overall general health. The most common animal damage was from browsing by deer and elk. Deer usually just clipped a few small twigs from the seedlings and elk did the same but would also sometimes pull the seedling out of the ground if it had not yet grown a well-anchored root system. Younger, smaller trees didn't have enough size to handle much of this kind of damage.

Once the survey issues were in process, I moved onto the analysis part of the job. Again, the crews' input was sought. After reviewing the survey information, I developed conclusions and decided on the necessary prescription options for each site. My projected calendar was filling up.

About then I began receiving information from the two timber-sales teams regarding planned timber sales. A percentage of the ODF land was managed for harvest to fund various state responsibilities, including our agency budget. The teams were setting up new units for sale as per the directives in the District Operations Plan. Each notice arrival was an alert to me of additional new sites that would likely be logged within a few years, and in need of my review. Since the prep time for successful tree planting or aerial seeding is also about two years, these notifications fell into the "urgent" category. I was already playing catch up, so knowing about more district ground in need of reforestation review before the trees now present were removed. These sites could not be ignored or the assessment postponed even a little while.

In spite of my fears, I soon discovered that the analysis and organization of tree planting or seeding operations coming from potential timber sales were probably the simplest parts of the reforestation job. Or at least they were for me, as it was pretty much just straight math calculation from the info available. How to figure the correct number, the species and age of seedlings for tree planting a logged area, or the rehab of an under-stocked piece of ground requires several steps and begins a couple of years before a site is cut. That was one reason why the timber sales teams were sending reports to me, so that my team could eventually do our job within the appropriate time constraints after logging.

The in-office work wasn't so bad - it was the supportive fieldwork that really took time and sweat. Beginning about two years out ahead, actual tree seed had to be collected from the strongest parent trees from near the unit chosen for sale. The genetic matching was vital. Also, those seeds of various species needed to match the calculated ideal percentage of species diversity.

This was no Mickey-Mouse job. Someone had to climb trees – sometimes up to eighty feet up - and secure cones at the proper stage of ripeness. The cones were not easily in reach to be pulled off like apples, and once picked had to hold viable seeds. This was hard to determine if the cone was fifteen feet out of reach at the ending-tip of a tiny branch!

When safely gathered in, cones were sent to our private state-owned nursery, along with instructions and specific dates for delivery. Thankfully we didn't have to grow, process and store our own baby trees.

Most folks think reforestation is planting trees, and it is. It's also making sure the right trees with the right genetics are planted in the right spot in the right numbers, plus a whole lot more. All the work would hopefully result in young trees that were attuned to the site in every possible way. Such Plus Factors are a boost to assist survival.

My workdays were dominated by fieldwork that produced paperwork that seemed endless, trapping me at my desk. The plot surveys and aerial recon took me deep into the forest or flying high above as I tried to ferret out information for analysis of just about everything. It was rough. I always felt like I was spending too much time at what I was doing, whether I was indoors or out.

Reviewing survey information sometimes revealed unforeseen problems at a certain site. When that happened, immediate prescriptive action was designed to protect the growth site, and shoe-horned into the schedule. Possible problems came from a long list of things like competitive grass or brush encroachment, insect infestations, animal damage, over-crowding and a lot more.

All the different types of work had to be somehow included into an always-crowded schedule stretching out into the future at least two years or more. Constant revision was required. My crew and I also took time to draw maps for work-crews to use along with the unit planting plan. Too often I had to make a trip to a site, because vital information was missing. The maps had to be accurate, or work might be done in the wrong place.

Just hiring the work-crews for projects was a challenge in itself. Sometimes I had to interview every potential worker that turned in an application. I didn't like to settle for just a warm able-body when hiring, but people that took a real interest in the work weren't always available. Once a crew was at work, I had to keep tabs on things to make sure expectations were met. Using proper tree planting techniques and correct spacing of seedlings were a couple of these vital points that needed checking.

The in-door work led to out-door work that sent me back in-doors. On any one day it was never a good bet to predict exactly where I would be.

During those early harrowing months in the NWO district, on a crystal-clear, and icy December day around noontime, a telephone call luckily found me working at my desk. My wife called to tell me I was needed at home as quickly as I could drive the necessary fifteen miles. She said we were going to be looking into the face of our second child within a few hours.

I left immediately. By three PM we were back in town. Our daughter, not much over a year old at the time, was safely in the care of the wife of one of the Forest Technicians from my office. I drove my wife to the hospital. Within the hour our second daughter followed in her older sister's footsteps, also rejecting the use of the maternity delivery room for her Premiere Appearance. While the older girl made a rather dramatic entrance into the world by showing up in the backseat of her grandparents' car, Daughter Number Two opted for the more modest hospital corridor. This was in spite of my wife very clearly describing the abruptness of her first delivery to the maternity nurses. She explained, with some frustration, that the baby was coming. All she got was a nice pat on the hand for her trouble. The doctor was barely able to keep our newborn daughter from hitting the floor as he arrived.

Without intending, once more we caught them all by surprise – kind of like before. A benefit was that without anesthesia and leaving the delivery room unused and pristine, our hospital bill was reduced considerably. Maybe all my girls were making an effort to reduce my stress level by not wasting precious time or money. My wife would likely laugh at such an idea. Those few minutes in the hospital corridor were kind of tense.

A month or so later I suffered through my own small medical crisis. After all those fires in SWO with no personal injuries to speak of, my good luck at work finally ran out. When I was hurt, it wasn't a fire or even an emergency situation. Thankfully it wasn't even a very big deal, and not a drop of blood was spilled.

After only a few months at work in Astoria I was using a pull-rope to start a pump motor on a small sprayer. We had a brush issue along a roadside needing a quick dose of herbicide. The motor backfired, jerked the rope handle through my fingers and broke the second knuckle of my middle finger on my left hand.

Because of the pain, I saw a doctor about the broken knuckle that same afternoon. I ended up with a splint to keep the finger immobile. It made for a semi-embarrassing look to that bandaged hand. The healing took about six weeks to complete.

When the splint came off, the pain was gone, but I was unable to make a fist or hardly bend the injured finger to simply touch my palm. The doctor said I'd never have full use of the finger or hand again. The diagnosis seemed a little extreme, so I asked to see a specialist. He indicated that he could do surgery on the finger to remove a bone spur that had developed during the healing process - but he felt that the surgery would leave my finger just as stiff as it already was. I accepted that the middle finger would continue to be in a socially incorrect gesture for a life-time.

Since I went to the doctor for a work-time injury, I had to fill out an accident report. The doctor's verdict went to the insurance carrier, who submitted a disability report. Without any effort on my part, the state paid me a reimbursement for permanent disability of a stiff finger – I think it was about $200.

My wife and I used the money to buy a much-needed washing machine, as with a pair of little ones under age two years, the production of soiled diapers was a very real issue in our lives. Disposable diapers were way too expensive in those days.

I do not recommend personal injury as a method to increase income. Besides, fully functioning body parts were very necessary in my daily work. Yet, for us, this unexpected windfall was a timely good fortune. I figured an unusable finger - even one that was socially incorrect - wasn't much of a price to pay.

For a while I just accepted the slight inconvenience and possible unintended rude signal sent with that particular finger being as stiff as a Popsicle stick. Even though I am right-handed, since I always did a lot with my hands every day at work, like gripping tools and saw handles, that faulty finger got a daily workout along with the other nine. I never purposely exercised it or followed any plan of therapy – just normal work.

Over a couple of years, the stiffness worked itself out until the finger regained about 90% of its flexibility. This was good. I no longer had to worry about offending anyone inadvertently. I had to mean it if I wanted to flip someone off, just like everybody else.

CHAPTER 28

There were some gray areas in my job, overlapping the work of other unit foresters. Thinning is a sort of crossover between reforestation and timber sales.

The idea in forest thinning is much like vegetable gardening. If too many plants exist in a space too small, all grow slowly and some die, competing for resources. Even over a long time it's possible that none reach a healthy mature state. With thinning, faster growth is promoted, and better health and quality is likely for all still in the ground. Trees can be thinned more than once, but eventually an end product is available for harvest or can be left to grow for a long time, slowly getting larger.

Two types of thinning are common: Pre-commercial is used with young stands of over-stocked trees about ten feet tall, and Commercial is for trees with some marketable value. NWO forest stands selected for thinning were usually young and densely over-stocked, with the trees to be removed being just large enough to have the lowest value at the mill.

Correctly done, thinning a unit of over-stocked forest does remarkable things. Skinny, unhealthy conifers growing within inches of one another change into a beautiful lush young forest within a few months after being released from their confined state.

Older trees on site are not automatically kept – they can harbor problems for the surrounding youngsters. An educated evaluation is important to ensure they will not adversely affect the overall stand. The knowledge needed to decide which trees stay and which go is required, since the purpose is to ensure spacing to promote the long-term good health of the whole stand. Young trees have a lot to overcome without inviting issues for the sake of only a few larger neighbors.

HIDDEN HISTORY FOUND

My crew was working on a thinning project in the most southern part of the district, near a place called Buster Camp. It was the site of an old time, very large railroad logging enterprise. During its hay-day, sometime in the early 1900s, it was really a small town rather than a camp. The workers and their families lived their lives while trees were available in the general area of the track and engines used to haul the logs out of the woods.

The size of the area logged-over was quite extensive. There was no apparent indication of any effort ever made to reforest. Consequently, nature had taken on the job. Without a systematic plan, the re-grown forests in the area were kind of hit and miss. In places, there were very dense stands of naturally seeded stands located next to open grassland that somehow had been skipped over in the spontaneous regeneration process. Nature is inconsistent and usually pretty slow in its long-term regrowth activities. Not so good for future forest production, but much favored by the elk herds thereabouts.

Roosevelt Elk are abundant in the Northwest Oregon Area.
Photo courtesy of CC Dickerson

There were many people that knew of the location of the former camp. Weekend treasure seekers were common, but during workdays we were alone in the woods. If attention was paid, old trash heaps and outhouse sites with lots of relics like tin cans and patent medicine bottles could be found amongst the young trees. Apparently early camp residents would go to the John, carrying their medicine with them. If the container was emptied along the way, the bottle would often go into the pit.

The old logging camp was interesting and I scrounged up some very old small glass bottles.

The reason I recall that place was because of something else, though. I was helping the South Timber Sale crew with marking and cruising trees for a thinning sale, with the goal of removing excess trees from one of the nearby areas that had regenerated with more success that others. In fact, it had grown back too well, and was badly over stocked. Trees that were decades old were only 8 to 12 inches in diameter. Almost anywhere else in Oregon 2/3 of the trees would have been chocked to death for lack of water and or nutrients.

The Tally Man (keeper of our written survey notes and measurements) on this day kept the cards we used safe and dry. They were special Rite in The Rain water-resistant type, designed to record information about cruised trees for later use to calculate board foot volume for the thinning sale. All were tucked into an aluminum Tatum, a sort of clipboard/box with an aluminum cover and sized just big enough to fit about a two-inch pile of 5x8" cards.

Late in the rainy afternoon we all gathered at the two pickups that were to carry us back to the office. I think there were six of us taking off our rain gear and boots, eating what was left of our lunches before traveling the twenty miles or so back to HQ.

A Bald Eagle soars in the Astoria District. Nesting sites and habitat were part of
an active and balanced forest management program in the district.
Courtesy of ODF Fire History Museum

By the way, rain gear is a necessary part of work clothes in that northwest area, as well as most everywhere else on the Oregon coast. It does keep off the rain, but forget about keeping dry while working. Unless it's mid-winter and freezing out, at the end of the work day a guy's clothes are just about soaked with sweat. The gear is just as effective in keeping perspiration from drying off, as it is in keeping rain from soaking through. The body odor that permeates everybody's rain gear is always pretty strong, so the gear is usually stripped off and stashed in the workbox carried in the pick-up bed when traveling. That way everyone can breathe a little easier.

Anyway, upon arrival back at headquarters, as we were putting our gear away, our designated Tally Man discovered that the Tatum with all the cards was missing. A thorough search of both vehicles and everyone's cruiser vests did not turn up the missing Tatum or cards. Further discussion about the missing Tatum led to its keeper to recall setting it, with cards enclosed, on the bumper of one of the trucks as he took off his boots in the woods. He thought he might have forgotten to pick it up before we left, but was unsure.

The cards represented several hours of work by a six-man crew, so the next day as we made another trip back to the site, everyone looked carefully along the access road going to the thinning area. No one wanted to repeat the work from the day before, so we were a pretty alert bunch. No Tatum was spotted.

When the visual search yielded nothing, it was decided to try a scientific approach. We decided to see how far a Tatum might ride on the bumper before it fell off. Starting at the same spot as the previous day, we placed an identical Tatum on the back bumper and drove the same logging road at about the same speed as the day before. The card-keeper volunteered to act as lookout, riding in the bed of the truck, watching to see when the Tatum fell.

About two miles down the road off it went. A very comprehensive foot search of about a half-mile section of the road commenced. This included poking around in dozens of mud puddles. Still nothing. With no other ideas about where to search, the crew reluctantly gave up. the search.

With no hope of finding the data from our earlier day's work, we'd have to re-cruise as best we could. We had to retrace our movements from the day before as best we remembered, plus repeat the cruise of all the trees we'd marked for removal.

A while later I spent one day in the company of the South Unit Forester. He was an older local of Swedish descent, busy in the field doing contract supervision on some timber sales. After checking a couple of sales, we stopped at an amazing place in an opening in the woods. It was where a cabin had been built by hand by some early Swedish emigrants.

This was no ordinary cabin. First, it was constructed entirely of Western red cedar. It was made in the log cabin style where the log corners were notched to fit into the logs on the adjoining side. Instead of round logs, each piece had been hand-sawed to produce planks about 4 or 5 inches thick and as wide as the original log would allow. Some were as wide as a full yard or more. The edges were smoothed down so perfectly they fit tightly against the adjacent log-board. Little, if any, calking between was needed to avoid any cracks.

The roof was made of planks that ran from the peak to the eaves, with the seams between planks covered by another plank. Rain coming off the eaves was caught in carved gutters made from long small-diameter hollowed out cedar logs that ran the length of the house. The whole thing was nearly weather tight and beautifully done.

Outside were three outbuildings: an outhouse, a sauna, and a cookhouse. Apparently, in the summer time, cooking was done entirely outside of the main house to keep the heat out. All outbuildings were also made of cedar and sided with split cedar shakes.

A couple of years later, a group of people with a local Swedish society purchased rights to the buildings. They carefully dismantled every thing while marking each piece. They moved it all to another site for re-construction, to make a wonderful historic display of this excellent example of Swedish cabin construction.

Around that country you never knew what would be found in the woods. A thinning project on the slopes above the Columbia River, near Westport, yielded a history lesson for me.

In a younger stand of very dense Douglas fir, several deep ruts contoured around the hillsides and descending at a gentle slope. The trees we were marking and cruising were growing in the ruts, out of the berms on each side, and generally all around. The trees were in sore need of thinning, but were large enough to have significant commercial value, more than forty to fifty years of age.

The ruts were huge! Easily six to eight feet across and three to four feet deep from the surrounding ground level. The bottoms were gently rounded, so they resembled something like a kind of irrigation ditch more than wheel tracks. The odd thing was, they were single ditches, not doubles and not parallel.

One of my technicians, a life-long local, shared that the grooves were made by old time Bull-Teams hauling logs out of the woods and down to the river. He figured they'd been gouged out sometime from the years 1870 to 1930. The span of dates put the time they were made as either when the area was originally logged or maybe a second cutting. Trees in that part of the state grow at an astonishing rate, so their size wasn't much help figuring accurate years to estimate dates.

He said teams of at least two and up to six or even more oxen were yoked head-to-tail and hitched to one or sometimes two very large logs also chained together in single file order. The logs were pulled at a gentle angle around and down the slopes to get to the riverbank. Once near the water, they were unhitched and rolled into the river using manpower and long levers to then float downstream. They'd be pulled to shore for milling and use in the early building efforts at downstream settlements.

CHAPTER 29

*A*storia is surrounded by sites that are historically rich. Early reports of a west coast access (the Columbia River) leading to the fabled but mythical Northwest Passage go back as far as explorer Sir Francis Drake in the 1500s.

Captain Robert Gray was the first American to sail up the mighty Columbia River in the late 1700s. He set up trade with the local Indian tribes, who were tired of the heavy-handed administration of the Hudson Bay Company.

The first organized American fur trading post built in the territory was named Forts Astoria, named for the trade company's owner John Jacob Astor. Located in the same general area as Gray's exploration, it evolved over time into the city called Astoria.

The site of Fort Clatsop – the wintering location for the Lewis and Clark Expedition of the early1800s – is just across Youngs River from the Astoria townsite. Its name came from the local Indian tribe. The guide for that early exploration was the famous Native American girl, Sacajawea, member of a tribe located in the Rocky Mountains.

Historical relics were in the woods everywhere, over-grown and hidden away.

OUR NEW VERY OLD HOUSE

The monthly rent on the acreage and house next to the slough where we first lived near Astoria, was killing our budget. It was pulling about a third of my net income. Now with a toddler and a new baby, my paycheck just wasn't enough to cover expenses. If my wife began working, child-care costs would wipe out any gain, so that avenue was simply impractical. We were on alert to find almost any means to balance our budget.

Almost exactly on the first year's anniversary of our initial arrival in northwest Oregon, we got wind of a terrific deal to rent a three-bedroom house for only $20 per month - total. Even back in 1968 at that price, there had to be a catch involved.

Bottom line - we were desperate. We followed up on the lead, and soon had a chance to examine the over-aged house.

It was old and looked it, built about the turn of the nineteenth century. Originally it had been very remote, accessible only by boat. Now a lightly used paved road and bridge built sometime over the years allowed us to drive up nearly to the back door. The location was more than twenty miles away from our rental house, about eight miles out the opposite side of town.

The body of water the old house faced was Youngs River, just above where it empties into Youngs Bay barely above tidewater. It was several miles upstream from where the ODF Astoria Unit Office looked over the same bay, but from the opposite side.

The house was in poor condition with warped walls and springy floors. It belonged to the huge Crown-Zellerbach Corporation. There was a dependable oil heater and we were assured the roof was okay. The water supply was gravity fed from a spring-filled cistern far up a nearby hill. The house had no real foundation and the three old chimneys were disintegrating. Also, even though there was an indoor bath and toilet, there was no septic tank. All pipes drained, complete with toilet wastes, into a ditch about forty feet away from the house. A large woodshed and kind of garage/workshop were on the same property.

There were no close neighbors to this rustic house, except for some relatives of the former residents. Their house was across the county road, and down a heavily wooded embankment. Both out of sight and hearing. Going the opposite direction, Crown Zee had a parking area for log trucks about a quarter mile further up the same narrow canyon. This was also well hidden by thick forest, but, at times very noisy. About 5 AM on working days, all those diesel engines would fire up in warming mode, making a huge den that echoed all the way to the old house.

When we went to look it over, the house didn't seem too bad. The moss-covered buildings were in a lush grove of ancient trees, about 1½ acres all together. A gigantic cedar stood within arm's length of the back-bedroom wall and a cherry tree as big around as a Volkswagen was just outside the small partially fenced yard. The location was almost silent as the many historic trees absorbed almost all sound. There was a hushed roar of falling water in the distance, but it couldn't be heard inside the house.

The low monthly rent would free up more than 20% of our income, a huge incentive to move in ASAP. We did just that in late August.

In some ways I hated to leave the other property, especially because of the great crappie fishing and crayfish trapping in the slough. I soon learned that while I had lost the good crappie fishing, I had gained some really great salmon fishing from Youngs River that ran at the foot of the small bluff where the house stood.

In those years, the entire area of the northwest corner of Oregon was something of a sportsman's paradise. Hunting fowl and game, ocean and fresh water fishing, crabbing and clamming were available in their respective seasons. I'd relished hunting and fishing since childhood, and took advantage of the area so rich with opportunities to enjoy these outdoor sports. The northwest woods were pretty wild country, but as long as one dressed correctly and understood the inherent dangers, for me it was no worse than going to work every day.

Fall was just around the corner as we settled in. Soon the Coho Salmon were running and goodly numbers came up Youngs Bay into Youngs River. The free-flowing section of river above tidewater was only a half-mile long before it was blocked by an impassable waterfall that stopped all upstream fish migration. The Youngs River Falls was about a 50-foot shear drop to a large pool below. This natural feature, source of the falling water sound we noticed, was across the road about 200 yards from our kitchen door.

The fish of the fall-run would back up below the falls looking for a place to spawn. I could leave the house at daylight and have my line wet in the last riffles below the falls in about ten minutes. If I did not get a bump in about the first five casts and drifts, I would pull out my line and head home. If the fish were there and biting, I could catch my limit of salmon, be home and have them all cleaned in about a half hour. This left plenty of time to clean up and dress for work, leaving easily by 7:30 AM.

There was wonderful salmon and Steelhead fishing in all directions. Whether it was ocean, beach, jetty, or stream fishing, it was great. For stream fishing, the nearby Klatskanine River that ran into the bay only three miles to the east of our house, was one for the record books. The only problem was that about ten thousand fishermen from metropolitan Portland knew this too. Sometimes it seemed that every one of them would brave the ninety-mile drive to the coast just to throw a line in the water. It could get extremely crowded on weekends.

Our move brought us closer to the ocean. It was now only about ten miles to the west. Over the rugged hills that held our fresh spring-water supply, was the best Razor clam digging in the Pacific Northwest. This was an activity that I participated in as much as possible, usually alone. I enjoying both the dig near the surf and a treat of fresh clams for dinner. I'd try to hit the beach just at dawn a little bit before an early morning low tide, dig my limit and drop off a sack of clams at the house before going to work. The only real problem was my wife tended to react in a somewhat sour way when greeted with a couple dozen clams needing about two hours to be cleaned as her first morning chore.

Our move from one house to another brought with it a number of big logistical problems. Our only vehicle available when we made the sudden decision to move was our two-door Dodge coupe. We bought it (with a loan with a huge interest rate - 9% I believe) to replace the dilapidated car that barely held together through the past year.

It was a good thing we didn't own much furniture then, and were able to relay piece by piece over the twenty-some miles between the two houses. Even at that it took most of a week for us to get everything ferried. There was one very major problem moving our other belongings. We owned two horses.

Our parents had delivered the equine pair to us the previous year not too long after we arrived. My wife's horse was an easy-going, five-year-old, dark brown gelding, and mine was a young stallion colt just over two. My young palomino was gentle enough, but with all the time pressures on my plate, I'd only gotten as far as green-breaking him to ride.

We had no way to move the two of them twenty plus miles between the two properties. We could hardly afford the gas to take our other stuff; to rent a trailer to do the job with the horses was just not possible. We did not have a vehicle adequate to pull a horse trailer anyway. We thought that riding the horses to their new home all the way around the peninsula through town was way too far, and very risky with a spooky colt.

I put some investigation into our dilemma, using maps and aerial photos at work. A possible solution was found, that with a little cross-country riding, I could make use of some logging roads behind the farmhouse to cut down the distance. It would only be about ten miles to ride to the new place that way, traveling over the top of the Astoria peninsula through the wild hills and the forest-filled canyons to the southeast of town. That way I'd be the only one in harm's way, leaving the city folks out of our problem.

This was probably a semi-crazy idea to even consider as both horses were not shod, and one just a green-broke youngster. But I had grown up riding all kind of stock at my parents' home place. I spent almost every day at work in unknown rough country, and besides there really wasn't any other choice. It was just one more risk and taking risks was part of my daily life.

On one more of a thousand cool and cloudy NWO Saturday mornings I saddled up. Both animals had bridles on, and our only saddle was on the older, stronger horse. When on the two-year old stud, I rode bareback to save weight on his young back.

The two horses and I went through the backfield at the farmhouse and into the woods behind the old barn. I had to be very careful for the first half mile, as there was no trail or road through the thick brush. Being herd animals, horses don't care for brushy country. The steady gelding seemed eager to see new places and stepped out well, with the high-stepping colt following behind.

The thick over-growth eventually cleared some. We still numbered three as we hit one of the several forest-roads I had mapped out. I would ride one horse, leading the other for only about a mile or so, then shift to the other. I kept the pace at a slow walk, talking and acting as calm as possible. It was my plan to try to be on the older, steadier Snickers and leading Sinbad who was antsy, through the toughest parts of the chosen route.

After the first woodsy section, I only had one other place where there was no well-defined road. It was about a third of the total way, where a creek-crossing had washed out years earlier and had never been rebuilt. There was a steep slope to go down to the running stream. Then the overgrown bank dropped about two feet to the water, and another three or four feet of wading in knee-deep running water was needed to reach the other side.

Up until this water crossing things had gone well. From the stream bank above, I studied the lay-out a bit. I dismounted and tied Sinbad to a tree with a neck-rope, then led Snickers down and across the water and tying him on the other side of the running water.

Going back for Sinbad to repeat the process, I saw the young stud was dancing at the rope. I figured he would be eager to get back beside Snickers. Instead, I was unprepared when the colt first balked at the water's edge. With some gentle persuasion, he took a tentative step. With front feet in the steam, he made a sudden lunge forward - but too fast!

I wasn't set and my footing was not sure. I stumbled into the water with a small splash. I think the movement and water spray scared the young horse. When he reared-up I tried to hold onto him, but I was still out of balance. Rope and reins slid through my hand. I made a looping grab to gather in the now loose rope, but my own quick movement just frightened the horse more. It also put me on the verge of falling. I had to let go of reins and rope to use my out-stretched arms to regain my footing to avoid landing on my face in the water.

The young stud reacted in a predictable way. He shied away. Quickly he returned to the bank he'd just left. Up he climbed and off he went at a full gallop heading back the way we had come.

I whistled and called, but he was so frightened that he didn't respond at all. As soon as he reached the top of the slope he was out of my sight. I could hear his hooves pounding as he ran farther away on the road above. I know I uttered several choice words as I splashed my way across the water where the steady gelding stood, ears perked and watching the scene unfold. I pulled the slip knot that kept him tied, and immediately was back in the saddle.

Making a spray in every direction, Snickers and I were across the water and up the bank at a scramble. After we'd reached the top, all we could do was follow the colt and hope for the best. At a lope, Snickers took me back about a half-mile on the upper road, over-grown and hardly more than a wide pathway.

Snicker's head came up as we both saw a flash of golden hide through the brush ahead, and then Sinbad appeared coming back toward us. He was still at a full gallop, but slowed to a trot as he neared us, full of happy whinnying and snorts as he came within arm's reach. I guess he realized he was alone in the strange woods and wanted his older, stronger buddy.

I collected dangling ropes and reins, getting us all together and organized. Snickers rumbled a friendly "Hello" to his pal deep in his chest. Pats and soft words calmed everyone down some. A few minutes later we were turned around to try again.

Going back to the stream, this time I decided to ride Snickers across with Sinbad tightly in tow. I snubbed the colt's head up against my leg with his neck rope wrapped around the saddle-horn, and his reins in my extra hand as we wadded across. The colt's head was almost in my lap, but he seemed happy enough to be close to the gelding. We safely reached the far bank of the stream still as a threesome.

I loosened the rope on the snubbed colt and gave that steady gelding a grateful pat on the neck. When we were ready, I tapped Snickers in the ribs with my heels, and again we were on our way to our new home. There was another six miles or maybe a bit more yet to go. Soon we turned onto a graveled road as we approached civilization.

No other real problems befell us, but both horses soon became very tired. It was a long time yet before we would arrive at our destination. The horses had spent the summer largely un-ridden and getting fat. Being barefoot, they were soon getting foot-sore walking in the gravel. Before long, it was a growing effort for me to urge them onward. To help their feet, I began walking about one-third of the time, and rode each of the horses for about another one-third. This was not very comfortable in pants wet to the knees and squishy boots.

We finally got to the new place after about four or maybe five hours from when we first left the farm. The gray day was beginning to darken, so it wasn't any too soon. All three of us were really pooped out. I had organized the roomy woodshed as a cozy stable for the horses, where they got a nice dinner upon arrival. It was good to be home, where my wife had a warm meal waiting for me too.

Our move could have been seen as a retreat from mainstream living – a common thing amongst young people in the late 1960s. When my dad and father-in-law arrived with a very useful gift, we even joked a little about the Hippie movement that seemed to be all the rage.

The two dads had put their heads together, each contributing a few dollars and bought me a 1951 five-window pickup. They delivered it to me around Thanksgiving, with Dad driving the truck and my wife's dad driving his car as their ride back south. The Chevy ran pretty well, but had a paint job that looked like some hippie's drug-induced dream. No hearts and flowers, just primer and paint splatters in four different colors. Having a second set of wheels meant there was a vehicle available for my wife's use while I was at work. This added a little to my peace of mind in case of any emergency.

The old Chevy originated from a Hugo neighbor well known to me – a past hunting chum of my dad's. He'd done some swapping around of some parts from the old truck that changed the rear springs and differential. The replacement parts had affected the load capacity and screwed up the speedometer reading by about 33%. This meant that the reading was off by about 15 mph. I had to mark the glass cover on the dash with a grease pencil to give a more accurate reading to avoid a passel of tickets.

For us, living rough was taken on as a means to reduce our living expenses. Unlike the Hippie-types, absolutely no spiritualism was involved. There were many problems involved that we would have gladly avoided. For instance, someone who was seeking a back-to-nature experience would have cherished our so-called pristine spring-fed water supply. It was a big bother.

A spring far up the canyon wall created a steady water flow downhill, with the pressure in the pipes driven by gravity. The idea of spring-fed drinking-water isn't the same as the reality. Unless the spring comes straight from rock, there will be dirt involved.

Someone who had tried to cope with the dirt issue designed the system. They had scooped up several small earthen dams in the inclined streambed to create pools where silt could settle before the water flowed into a wooden cistern box. The box was a cube shape built of heavy cedar, about five-foot square on each edge. The water fed in through an opening about two feet from the top, and the out-flow, going to the house, was via a smaller diameter hose that went out about two feet from the bottom. This allowed more silt to settle, as the flow would quiet down inside the box.

The plastic hose carrying our water ran beside the stream for a distance of about five hundred feet to the old house below. The distance downhill was mostly steep, but there were a few dips and rises. When there was an especially hard rainfall, water continued to be delivered by the system, but tended to be roily (silt filled), needing to be treated before cooking or drinking. Also, if the system were closed off for any length of time (like when we were away for a day or two), the silt would build up in the low spots of the hose slowing or shutting off the water supply.

Also, any trees or brush over the open water-flow dropped leaves, needles and other debris. Alder leaves in the fall were especially bad, discoloring the water to the color of weak tea. We chose to ignore the obvious presence of various wildlife that may also befoul the water, as there wasn't much that could be done for prevention in that regard.

The process to flush the system from silt and leaves was rather elaborate. We learned to simply leave water running in the sink or bathtub whenever we were away, to postpone build up as long as possible. Even so, periodic clearing of the silt was necessary, and took a full day of hard work to accomplish.

It didn't take long after we settled in before we discovered the most serious and very distasteful problem with our derelict house. Wood rats surrounded us. They lived in the shed, in the attic and inside the house walls.

These ugly creatures are about the half the size of a house cat. Their body is squirrel-like; the tail is less full, but having more hair than a Norwegian wharf rat. In nature they build nests of heaped up collections of sticks and twigs in or next to the crotch of trees. They love to make off with shinny things like bottle caps and gum wrappers.

With two little kids, having this kind of an infestation was not a positive situation. On the plus side – the rats had yet to breach the inside walls of the house. But they sure tried! When we moved in, our bedroom seemed to be the focus of their attempts to storm the building.

It is not restful to lie in bed at night and listen to a very large rodent chew on the other side of the wall a couple of feet away. We tried to sic our pet cat on them, but I think he was out-matched – certainly he was out-numbered. When I forced him into the attic, he thumped around a bit but the next morning we found him sitting outside in the rain, howling a forlorn wail for entrance to the house. We've never figured exactly how he got out of the attic. Probably the same way the rats got in.

The rat trying to get into our bedroom was a keen-witted critter, as the sound of any movement in the room by us would bring a halt to the gnawing sounds, then a long pause before the crunch-crunch sounds would start up again. I took to leaving my .22 rife on the floor under our bed. By using the chewing noises as a guide, I lined up the sights on the baseboard where I thought the rat was at work, then went to bed. When awakened later by the gnawing sounds, I silently reached down and pulled the trigger. HA! No more chewing in the walls. It either killed or at least scared the creature away for good. Scared the dickens out of my sleeping wife too.

Thus, began the period of The Great Wood Rat Hunting Expeditions. Trips were taken, with flashlight and my .22 rifle, into the dark corners of the shed and the wild unseen recesses of the attic. Overall, I was successful, lining up several nasty furry bodies for disposal in the thick woods. I also managed to frighten my older child, then not yet three years old, while she was sitting on the potty in the bathroom. The access to the attic was located above the bathroom sink. When I dropped a dead rat down, and then climbed out of the ceiling access hole she reacted with a yelp, and took off wanting Mommy. To this day many decades later, she can relate the incident in great detail. I guess it was kind of unique – funny the things kids remember.

After about three very weird weeks of hunting under our own roof, the rats conceded ground, but never really left. I'm sure they returned within hours when we moved out about two years later.

It was a good thing that both my wife and I came from parents that taught their kids some 19th century survival skills. Obviously hunting came in handy as a means to keep the family fed. Fishing helped with this big chore too. Still, we had to learn some different ways of keeping the freezer full, plus trying out new foods, like fried squirrel and bear roast.

Hunting and fishing opportunities in NWO were so exceptional, I found it was strange that deer hunting there was just plain terrible. The thick brush and other vegetation growth from the continual rain was way too thick to see through. Moving around in rain gear makes too much noise to do a successful stalk. About all I ever saw of deer were hooves and legs below the brush line.

On the other hand, the grouse hunting was terrific. I would take the wife and kids on these outings, driving the old pickup. Deer season and grouse season were open at the same time so I prepared for both options. We would select a likely logging road for our hunt. My wife took the wheel, driving slowly down the road with the little girls on the seat beside her.

I would sit on the front fender or stand in back, carrying my 12 ga. pump shotgun with one shotgun shell (filled with a slug) in the barrel and two shells of birdshot in the magazine. If I were to see a deer (I never did), the slug would take care of it. If I saw a grouse, I would signal for the truck to stop. With a quick pump to put one of the birdshot shells into the chamber, I could lower the boom on the grouse. I quickly learned to hold the barrel just a little high, taking the heads off the birds with no lead shot in the body. Our team approach let us almost always limit on grouse.

We tried to grow a vegetable garden, but living in the deep canyon combined with the summertime rainy weather made our effort pretty much useless. Not enough sunshine. Although we were able to grow green beans and carrots pretty well, heat and sun-loving squash and tomatoes rotted away. Still my wife had many opportunities to exercise her canning skills and also kept the freezer well stocked with nice things like asparagus and blackberries. Our deep and narrow canyon where the forest was old and thick just didn't get enough sun. We kept a watch out for neglected roadside fruit trees or old abandoned orchards I stumbled over in the woods. All in all, we ate pretty well, stayed dry and survived nicely, thank you.

We most definitely would have preferred a more mainstream style of living with the conveniences and ease it would offer our little children and ourselves. It was neither a spiritual nor particularly pleasant time for us, but under the circumstances, it was practical and maybe even necessary. Living that way was by our choice for certain, but for a very selfish purpose. A nice home for our family was the goal, and we didn't want to go deeply into debt

Over two years was spent living as cheaply as possible in the old shack. After a couple of years, we had saved enough money to buy a new 12 x 60, two-bedroom mobile home with new kitchen appliances included. A privately-owned trailer pad, located next to the Experiment Station behind the ODF Office, became available to rent. It even included a fenced five-acre space for the horses. After our mobile arrived and we moved in, I was able to walk down and past the access road and into the back door of the ODF Office – a nice 200-yard walk to get to work each morning for the final six to eight months before I was reassigned and we left the district.

It was the last week of November 1970 when we left the old house. As usual it was pouring rain. I had the flu, so my wife did most of the work. She was very motivated. Water that was drinkable from the faucet. Real flush toilets that were actually connected to a sewer. No more wood rats storming the walls as we slept! It felt like we had moved into a palace.

Our bank account was almost empty again. It was worth it to live like civilized people again, and it was dandy to also be out of debt.

CHAPTER 30

*A*part of the National Disaster Plan designated the Astoria Oregon Department of Forestry Office **as the lead agency for Search and Rescue operations in that district.** The Sheriff's Office handled the coordination, but ODF did the work on the ground. This made sense, as our personnel worked in the backwoods every day. We were very familiar with the lay of the land. All the ODF people had proper dress for the rugged terrain and our own communications equipment.

SEARCHES - FIRES - RESCUES

There were a few fires and a couple situations that called out the entire Astoria crew while I worked there. The first of these incidents came on an early spring day after we'd moved into the Youngs River house. The sky was overcast and the temperature on the cooler side as was most common in that place at that time of year. Almost the entire ODF office roster was recruited just about the time we were leaving work to go home. Our total number was between fifteen and twenty, all guys.

A small boy, about age 6 or so was visiting relatives with his family when he was reported lost in the woods.

The driving time from the office to where the boy was last seen was easily a half hour. It was near dark when we arrived at the site. We were told that the boy had been missing for a few hours, with family members using the time before the report trying to find him.

The child we were seeking had been playing with another boy near one of the multitudes of small creeks and streams in the district. They had been told to stay away from the nearby water, but as kids do, had gone there anyway. The now missing boy had fallen into the shallows of the creek. With his wet clothes spilling the beans about his misbehavior, he apparently feared punishment. The second boy reported that the littler one had run off to hide in the thick forest surrounding the property across the small creek, rather than return home soaked. A family dog was also missing.

As our guys arrived, a command center led by the Sheriff's Department was getting organized. The searchers were split into a couple of large groups and assigned areas to cover. The decreasing daylight was a problem as careful sweeps were made along the opposite side of the creek. While the men moved through the thick brush, the boy's name was called over and over. Flashlight beams were soon everywhere along the creek as the darkness became deeper.

Special care was taken to check every inch of the banks of the small creek. It wasn't very deep, but was in strong spring flow with a pushy current in spots. Many of us feared the worst, thinking that the boy may have tried to wade back across the creek and been swept into an unseen pool downstream.

When we had thoroughly scrutinized most of the nearby ground, it was fully dark. A few of us (me included) paired up in pickup trucks and started slowly driving the many logging roads nearby that accessed the hillside above the creek. In the woods, we all knew that lost folks tend to work uphill, so the slope seemed like a good place to check out. We hoped that the boy may have come upon any one of the many roads over there and just followed the track instead of going overland.

My partner and I drove slowly and stopped often to sound our pickup horn. We would honk once or twice, listen and call the boy's name. We didn't hear many of our fellow searchers because the thick woods and brush seemed to swallow all sounds. After a few more hours with no success, those using the trucks began to report back in at the command center near the relatives' home

The County Sheriff himself had arrived at the command center. By now it was raining, and in that part of Oregon, rain is often vicious. Since sundown the temperature was getting colder by the minute. We all worried about the now hungry little boy lost in the dark in wet clothes. We were dressed for the woods and rain, but felt the chill. None of us had seen food since lunch, easily ten to twelve hours before.

The teams coming into the command center joined a discussion of some length about the situation, referring to maps and the newest reports from those searchers coming in. In the darkness it was very difficult to determine if any likely areas might have been overlooked.

The sheriff felt we should suspend the search until daylight. Most of us did not agree. If we quit for the night, it would leave the child exposed to some really dangerous outdoor conditions for at least six or eight more hours overnight.

One of our guys knew this landscape particularly well because he lived nearby. He was sure there was a section where a thorough search had not occurred. He wanted to give that spot one more going-over before we quit for the night. There were several of us that agreed to go with him.

After more map checks and redistribution of radios to keep everyone in contact, the smaller group crossed the creek and moved through the indicated area. The search was resumed, albeit with a much smaller number of participants. On the hillside we tried to keep sight of the next searcher's flashlight beam.

After about an hour, our group leader radioed along the line of searchers that he thought he had heard a dog bark in the distance and was going to try to investigate the sound. A while later, another call came. He had found the dog, with the boy huddled against a big tree trunk. They were wet and cold, but otherwise okay.

The little guy was returned to his family. We were all pleased that the search had been successful. Giving up the search for the night would have been difficult if we'd been forced to leave the boy in the forest. This one felt good.

It was pretty uncommon for the whole office to turnout for something. Truly emergency incidents weren't all that common. Maybe because fires were kind of rare, most of our staff took-on a modest sized fire burning in the sand dunes not too far from the breaking surf.

The fuels were mostly thick shore pines and low-level saw grass. That particular species of pine tends to ooze sap, so the fire had the potential to become pretty hot if it got into the trees.

The location was on the fence-line near Camp Rileya, an Oregon National Guard training facility on the beach a few miles west of Astoria. The fire was fast moving, but with so many folks on hand, it was controlled quickly with only a few acres burned. Since all ODF staff are trained in hand-trail technique, the only limiting factors for the crew were the people in less than great physical condition, or maybe the older ages of some of the guys.

What made this fire notable was that the National Guard had a training session going on in their camp at the same time. Some of the vehicles we used to transport our personnel were parked a distance from the fire, near the camp's perimeter. As the ODF folks were doing what needed to be done, a few of the off-duty Guards grabbed a Sherman Tank and came out to offer some help.

I do not know exactly what their intension was, as their machine was in no way equipped for fire fighting. Maybe by going fairly fast and making quick turns they would be able to dig up some grass and make something of a fire trail? Otherwise the tank was pretty useless except for transporting a very small handful of personnel.

Anyway, the one thing the Guards did accomplish with the tank was to run over the front corner of our engineers' Chevy Suburban that was parked along one of the access roads. Needless to say, it made a real mess out of the Chevy.

When the damage was reported, the guardsmen using that tank weren't really popular with our engineering crew. A long list of summer work awaited those guys during the next couple of months, as the real gully-washer type storms didn't usually hit until late fall. The vehicle to haul their expensive equipment plus crew was out of commission for several weeks. They were a very grumble-ly bunch for some time.

Another Search and Rescue situation called most of our people out in late fall during Elk Hunting Season. Again, ODF was notified in late afternoon and again it was overcast and downright cold.

An elk hunter was reported missing and there was a mixed-up report that he may be ill or wounded. The location given was about 30 miles southeast of Astoria. A command center was in the process of set-up in the woods south of Highway 26 (a.k.a. Sunset Highway), the most heavily used roadway between Portland and the coast.

Before our group left the office, we gathered maps and aerial photos of the reported area where the man was missing. Again, nearly all the district personnel, about twenty ODF employees, pulled out their rain gear and corks for a probably wet search in the rainy woods. When we arrived at the command center, we were briefed.

Earlier that day in mid-morning, two teenaged boys also out hunting, had literally stumbled over a hunter in the woods. It was confirmed that the man was alive but wounded, and not very coherent. The kids recalled the location was near a stream. In our district, this information was pretty indistinct.

The boys were so troubled when they first found the man, and eager to find help, that they had run downhill next to the stream until they came to a paved road. They continued a short way downhill on the roadway and came upon a telephone or power company employee in a truck. They told their tale with worried excitement, and the utility man accompanied them into the woods to locate and get the hunter out to safety. Even though the utility truck had a radio, they did not call to report the incident at that time.

After trying to retrace their steps, the kids were unable to locate the spot where the hunter was laying. Coming back to the road the three luckily met up with a State Police officer, who was likely doing Game Warden duties. A call from the state trooper went out to the county sheriff, who had then initiated the callout to ODF.

Again, and with the OSP trooper in tow, the boys and utility driver searched unsuccessfully for the missing hunter. This had all taken several hours.

After hearing this background information, someone in our group asked if the boys were available to answer questions. We were informed that they had been flown out with the Coast Guard helicopter to see if they could spot anything familiar from the air before darkness fell. We thought a helpful coincidence was that the son of the missing hunter was present at the command center. The two had been hunting together, but had become separated.

In reality, the wounded hunter's son was very distraught and offered little real information. He stating that the boys must have shot his dad. He was in his early twenties and shared that his dad was over fifty, but in good condition.

Finally, the boys were returned to the command center. We laid out our maps and aerial photos in an area away from the hubbub surrounding the lost hunter's son. We took turns asking the kids questions. They'd quieted down a lot, and now were giving a pretty clear narrative. Using our materials, we tried to get some sense of where the hunter might be located.

The kids told us that they had been moving through heavy brush together, looking for elk sign. Hearing a shot, maybe ½ mile from them, they changed direction to go toward the sound. These kids had hunted before, and knew that experienced elk hunters will often go toward shots because elk, being herd animals, will run in mass away from the sound. Moving toward a place where shots were fired, there is a good chance of encountering the herd moving across your path.

While in heavy brush, as they followed the sound, one of the kids actually tripped over the hunter on the ground. They agreed that the man had spoken to them, but they said he didn't seem totally aware of what had happened. When we pressed for details about the terrain, they discussed the description between them. It became clear that the injured guy was located atop a small rise between two small convergent streams. We asked about anything else they might have seen in the immediate area, such as fences or cruiser marks on trees. They said that they had noticed several blue plastic flagging strips tied to the brush along the route they were following just before they first found the hunter. Notes had been taken. All the information available was discussed.

We knew that blue flagging was commonly used to mark property lines, and we could tell from the photos and maps, there was a property line in the area. We believed it to be close to the hunter's location.

A two-prong approach to the search was decided on. Team leaders were selected from those who had most recently worked the woods in this area. One of our timber team leaders would take about a third of the searchers plus the two boys with him, and I took the rest with me.

The other group would start from the road and try to retrace their steps back to the hunter. My group took the remaining two-thirds of the available manpower plus the man's son, who was almost frantic wanting to help. Our job was to locate the supposed property line and start a sweep search back and forth from that line until we either found the man or met with the smaller group going cross-country. Hand-held radios went to each group leader to keep all searchers up-to-date about everybody's whereabouts.

My group headed out to set up our grid search using the property line as a base locater. We were now working in full dark, plus a steady rain was falling. Armed with strong flashlights we soon found the marked line. We lined up at right angles to this line and moved very slowly forward. The last guys at each end of the search line hung flagging (not blue), so we could follow the outside edge of our search area back to the starting point. After we believed we had gone about a mile, everyone was called to one end of the line. We offset and repeated our search pattern, only on the opposite side of the reference point.

We were covering about a 300-foot wide strip with each sweep. Each pass took about an hour to complete. It was rough terrain so when we were tired, we'd take a short break and then proceed. This tedious and tiring work continued for well over six hours, finding nothing. The time was now well after midnight.

Suddenly there was a gunshot, making everyone jump with surprise. The sound seemed close, and in a north-northeast direction from us. I knew none of the searchers were carrying a firearm, so at first, I thought that the hunter may have roused himself to consciousness and fired a signal shot.

Our group quickly gathered around me and the hand-held. When everyone was accounted for, I radioed the other group to see if they had also heard the shot. I thought that maybe together we could fix a better direction to go toward the place of origin.

With the call back from the other searchers my plan faded away. They had found the man dead where the boys had first stumbled on him. For some reason their radio would not transmit, although it received just fine. Their leader had fired the shot using the lost hunter's rifle hoping we would call them. The man's son, part of my team and standing at my side, over-heard the report of his father's death. He immediately became greatly agitated; maybe even slightly unhinged.

I was having a lot of trouble following the message coming over the radio what with the yelling and wild movements of the young man with us. The other group was asking me to try contacting the sheriff at the command center. When I finally figured out the message, I did as I'd been asked. It still took three tries, as it appeared the rough ground was interfering with our radio's sending ability too.

The sheriff advised that our group should hike cross-country to join with the other search group. He wanted everyone together. Everyone was to wait for the county coroner to hike in. Also, I was to relay a request to the other group to immediately send a couple of men to the road to mark a trail and then guide the sheriff's team back to their site. I followed directions as given.

My team took some time to comfort and calm down the man's son. Eventually our group slowly headed in the supposed direction to where the other team was waiting. It was a lot farther than it seemed from the sound of the rifle shot. We traveled down a long slope to another stream and then climbed to the top of second low ridge and down again to the next stream drainage before we got there.

It was about 2 AM when my group met up with the other group of searchers. Directions from the sheriff over the radio had everyone briefly looking over the scene so all could make a statement if an inquiry was necessary. We left the dead man untouched, except for placing his hat over his face.

They'd sent the two kids out with those selected as guides to meet up with the sheriff, giving that new group the poorly functioning radio. For the next five hours or so, twenty guys, give or take, sat around waiting for the sheriff and the coroner to make the trek. The dead man lay where he'd fallen about twenty feet away.

Our long wait was spent trying to ignore our hunger, think as little as possible about the dead hunter and trying to warm up. Several attempts were made to light a fire. I was strongly reminded of the Jack London short-story "To Build a Fire". Like the main character, we had very little success with any of our efforts to get anything to burn. At least we didn't have to deal with snow as in the story – just relentless rain. All available fuels were at best, very damp and at worst, soaking wet.

You would think a bunch of woodsy-types whose regular workday element was in the rainy northwest forest, would do a better job at fire building. We were hard pressed to scrape together a small pile of semi-damp materials to use for kindling. From pawing under deadfalls and digging around protected rocky places in the surrounding area, a damp heap of forest duff was gathered.

Using the driest of fuels we could muster, plus all the surplus paper from every pocket amongst us, we finally got a light – or maybe a "smolder" would be more correct. Those nearly one hundred inches of annual rain mostly won the contest of flame versus fizzle.

Eventually a big smoke was going, but not exactly a fire. By standing right in the smoke as close as possible to the really pitiful flames, there was some small amount of warmth to be had. No one could stay in that spot for very long, as the smoke was choking. To breathe clean air, it was necessary to step away into the wet chill. At least the move let someone else have a turn in the semi-warm smoke.

In every possible way, it was one of the longest and most miserable nights I can ever recall. No one slept. The man's son continued to loudly grieve and accuse, being certain that the two boys were somehow the culprits in his father's death. The unfortunate dead hunter lay off to the side, ignored as best we could, but not forgotten by anybody.

We had nothing with which to cover the body, except respectfully placing his own hat over his face to keep the drizzle off. This somehow seemed wrong, but everyone needed their rain gear to prevent hypothermia.

Just at early light, the sheriff and coroner arrived. When asked, the two group leaders from the night before helped the coroner with his on-site examination of the body. It was not a pleasant task – one I never want to repeat.

The over-view of the body was not real thorough, but I suppose adequate for the situation. The coroner stated that the man had been shot in the back on one side below the ribs and from a low angle. The bullet had traveled slightly upward, exiting above the lowest rib in front on the opposite side from the entry wound. The tentative cause of death was that the man had bled-out internally.

The sheriff's group had brought along a stretcher. After the coroner was finished, we loaded the body, being careful again to cover his face with his hat. Two or three of our ODF people cut the trail with machete's and two others carried the stretcher. We each took turns with these jobs getting back out to the road. Again, more waiting as some folks returned to the command center to bring back transportation.

At long last, we were on our way home by around 8 AM. We were all starved but no one wanted to stop and eat. Getting safely home seemed to be very important to everyone that morning. Only one clerical staff member manned the ODF office that day.

Some six months later the investigation result of the hunter's death became public. The son had completed a tour in Viet Nam and returned home just before the shooting. Under hypnosis he told authorities that he and his dad were hunting up that drainage on opposite sides of the stream and had become separated. The father had apparently, for unknown reasons, turned back downstream. The son heard the crash of brush or limbs breaking and instinctively turned and fired without thought, as he would have in the jungles of Viet

Nam. He had not checked his target, firing only at sound. He didn't even realize he'd fired at all. He was never charged with a crime.

There was one other, much less spectacular recovery that happened while I was working out of Astoria. It only involved a helping hand to a friend, but maybe saved his life. I'm not sure that "rescue" is the correct word to describe what happened.

The Viet Nam War was a very big issue in those years I was assigned to the Astoria District. I was slightly older than most of the guys that were called up, but many who were the same age as my wife and brother were drafted. Between us, we can easily name a dozen or more who were either seriously wounded or killed.

Back in my last year at OSU, four former ODF fire fighters, all at least a couple of years younger than me, made use of two empty upstairs rooms in the house my wife, baby, and I rented in downtown Corvallis. The seven of us shared downstairs living space and the kitchen for several months, with expenses divided between us.

One of our roomies had endured a lengthy go-around with the draft board. He suffered from bad knees, and was seriously color blind. His name was on a list of guys with minor physical problems. He'd been called up at least twice, then rejected from the draft at the physical. When the criteria changed, the Army scooped him up again, and he was eventually sent to Viet Nam. My wife and I had worried a great deal about this friend, and many other young guys we knew too.

In the fall of 1970, I got a letter from this soft-spoken young man. He wrote to me from Nam with a request. The military had an "Early Out" provision for draftees, allowing personnel who were near the end of their tour of service to be released early. The main requirement was that they must have a legitimate job-offer in hand, and the offer was of a nature that could not be held over until a later time. If I could find a suitable winter job for him, he might be released up to six months early and get to come home.

It was fall, a time of year when I was busily getting my winter reforestation and rehab projects planned. Filling out the correct forms that had been provided, I mailed him a written job offer as a tree planter to start in January 1971.

He ran all the paperwork through the necessary channels. Our combined efforts were successful and his early release was granted. Just a few days after Christmas we picked our friend up in Portland at the downtown bus terminal.

He'd flown straight from Nam to Hawaii, then into Fort Lewis near Tacoma, Washington. From there he immediately caught a Greyhound bus going south. He'd not slept from the time he'd boarded the first transport plane in Viet Nam, afraid he'd get bounced anywhere on the long trek and sent back.

Dressed in a much wrinkled and soiled Hawaiian shirt and looking like he was coming off a five-day bender, his appearance was pretty rough even for the dismal neighborhood in Portland where the bus terminal was located. We hardly recognized his haggard face. It didn't help his image in that he carried a dysfunctional Chinese rifle with his meager luggage.

As I said, he had always been a very quiet kind of guy. For several days after his return to Oregon he was unbelievably jumpy and had serious problems sleeping. His eyes were hollow and he often seemed confused by simple questions. He obviously over-reacted to loud noises, and needed all the lights on while sleeping.

He lived with us, using our hide-a-bed couch for about six to eight weeks until he'd found a suitable and inexpensive apartment.

From the first, almost every night in the wee hours, our younger daughter, then barely three years of age, would leave her own bed. Bringing her much-loved Blankie, she'd crawl into bed with our friend on the living-room couch. Oddly in his nervous state, she apparently didn't disturb his sleep. Rather like a puppy, she curled up snuggling next to him. It seemed to give him some comfort, seeming to somehow soothe his inner demons. They became very close in the weeks he stayed with us.

Slowly day-by-day a little bit of our old quiet and gentle-natured friend returned. When I transferred to a different district in early June 1971 he stayed on a few more months in Astoria for summer work, then returned home to southern Oregon. He married my sister a couple of years later.

CHAPTER 31

The generally rocky Oregon Coast is a place known for its rainy climate. It's famous for growing tall, beautiful conifers at a pretty phenomenal rate. Astoria, at the far northwestern corner, has the most severe weather and can produce timber fifteen to eighteen inches in diameter on average every fifty to sixty years – if no contradicting factors slow things down.

South down the coastline, annual rainfall is less. After about 150 miles, the Coos River empties into the Pacific Ocean, following a huge "S" shaped course for the final handful of miles. Forested land belonging to the State of Oregon in that area, known as the Elliott State Forest, receives around sixty inches of rain per year. The reduction in rainfall slows the tree-growth rotation (for a 15 to 18-inch growth diameter) to around seventy years on average. This compares to the eighty to ninety years needed to grow the same sized tree inland on the scattered state land properties of the SWO District. Water and average temperature is the key.

SURPRISE, SURPRISE – THEN MOVING ON

Living in the Astoria area was an interesting experience. The weather was certainly different from my home stomping grounds and the strong marine influence in the forested areas sure affected my job. The international mix of local residents led my family to experience new and interesting cultures and customs. Other office-sponsored social activities like pie socials, flag football games and city league basketball were also enjoyed.

I'd handled almost four years at the reforestation job when, in the first part of 1971, the job description was re-evaluated through the state office. The total amount of work, responsibility, and supervisory load was examined as compared to other similar positions in ODF offices around Oregon. As a result, I was informed my work was now upgraded from Forester 1 to Forester 2. With the reclassification, I was automatically promoted into the new position without interview, and at an increase in pay.

The Astoria area was a satisfactory place to live, except for the one big thing - the weather. I will concede it was a really depressing concern for people like my wife and I. We enjoyed a long list of outdoor activities and all the other benefits of warmer, dryer places. Also, both my wife and I missed our families. The more than seven-hour drive with two small children aboard, removed us from any casual contact with those people who were most special to us. The distance was a barrier to our girls having grandparents and other relatives, as significant people in their lives. We talked about the problem often, but could find no easy solution within our direct control.

And then, just a few weeks after my promotion, an unknown and unexpected visitor arrived at my office door. This guy had the gift of gab. He was about fifteen years my senior in age, wearing ODF suntans and a friendly grin.

He said he was had been at the Forest Grove office visiting with the Area Director and decided to come on up north to Astoria to see me. He'd recently been named as the new District Manager of the Elliott State Forest outside of Coos Bay. His Reforestation Forester had just transferred away, so the purpose of the visit was to pick my brain for any new perspective.

For about an hour we discussed reforestation and rehab particulars. The seedling tree growth in the Coos Bay area was a little less sure than ours in Astoria. They had a serious backlog of weed, brush and alder encroachment issues that needed to be addressed to allow younger trees more growth success. We talked about how NWO was dealing with those and other similar problems.

Then he asked me an astonishing question. Might I consider taking on the Coos reforestation challenges with a transfer to his staff? That stopped the conversation cold. I was totally unprepared for such an offer. I realized I just sat through a very in-depth job interview, without a clue it was happening.

My mind went into over-drive. It had taken a little over a year for me to get the Astoria reforestation job under control and now, three years later, I was definitely ready to take on something a little different. The temptation was strong to accept the offer on the spot, but this wasn't just my decision to make. I asked him to give me a few days for me to consider his offer.

After my visitor left, I could hardly contain myself until going home that evening. With genuine delight I shared my tale of the day with my sweet wife. Within minutes we concluded this offering out of the blue was exactly what we had been waiting for. The next morning, I turned in my notice at Astoria and called Coos Bay accepting the offer.

Before we left, Astoria had one more very big surprise for us.

Just a few weeks later, everything was set up for our move to Coos Bay in early June. We had used the long Memorial Day weekend to visit our families in Grants Pass and nail down our moving details with our folks. With our two girls, we had arrived back in Astoria late on Monday afternoon of the holiday.

After all the miserable weather in NWO for four years, the sun was brightly shining with a spectacular sunset. The western sky was brilliant with hues ranging from bright orange to deep purple. We had missed one of the few nice weekends Astoria so seldom enjoyed. We paused at our mailbox to retrieve letters delivered during our absence. I drove the car up the long driveway to our mobile home at the top of the hill, glad the long drive was over.

My wife began opening the mail. Suddenly she yelped for me to stop the car. With a halting lurch the car stopped, and in a shaking and excited voice she read aloud a letter we had received. Apparently when renewing our subscription to the Reader's Digest back in December, an entry was automatically submitted into their sweepstakes contest. We'd won a second prize of $3000 cash!

I started work in the Elliott State Forest on June 15,1971. Moving our mobile home to the new district hadn't been too horrible, and the state paid all the costs. I suffered through some traveling issues driving the old Chevy pick-up such a long way, but all problems were solved and my family and I began to settle into the new location and job.

In Coos, I had one person on my staff, a Forest Technician. He was a bred and born Coos area local. I spent much of the first week or two with him traveling the roads in the Elliott to get a feel for the land and what situations were to be faced in reforestation. Not too long after, another young fellow joined our team. A few years into the future he would replace me there, and would much later become ODF State Personnel Director working out of Salem. Our three-man team worked very hard getting the local reforestation program into shape in the Coos Bay District.

Every time I went out into the forest for the first month I was there, I spotted a black bear. This seemed very unusual to me, as I had seen only a few bears in the wild up until then. I guess we'd moved to Bear Country, or at least this part of the Coastal Range had a particularly large bear population.

ODF management was relatively new to the Elliott, having been initiated only fifteen years earlier in 1955. That is less than half the time in a short-term tree-growth rotation. Just as the District boss had shared back in Astoria, Coos did have a serious backlog of brush control work to be accomplished before successful reforestation might happen.

I also soon discovered a clerical problem that, for me, needed urgent and immediate revision. After my first review of the site files, I found that while the record system in use was accurate, it was very cumbersome. I was using too much time trying to navigate the office filing system to pull needed information so I could make timely assessments.

Coos Forest Protective Association Office in Coos Bay. Oregon Department of Fish and Wildlife shared office space with CFPA and Elliott State Forest management personnel.
Courtesy of ODF Fire History Museum

Like Astoria, each reforestation unit file included the facts in detail that were needed for analysis. The clerical problem in Coos was that the units were given chronological file numbers. On a large map of the forest, each number was placed to indicate the location. This worked well enough for someone familiar with the landscape, but was a challenge for those just coming into the area like me. My solution was to spend a bit of time adding to the file, a name and unique identification number that included the township, range, and section followed by a letter: A, B, C, and so on. In combination, now the full title would denote its chronological addition of the site to the file, its specific legal location and name, and relative age without reference to a map or necessary file search.

Groundwork or whenever going into the field with the Elliott was difficult. Most of the ground was very steep or brushy – often both. The access roads were primarily on the ridge tops, which avoided casting excess road building dirt onto the steep gradients, as would be the case with mid-slope roads. With severe inclines, roadside casting is bad news. The loose dirt is unstable and generally dangerous and stays that way a long time.

Some of the people at the Coos ODF office called any fieldwork "going into the pit or into the hole", since it mostly required parking vehicles on a ridge top and a slip-slide hike downhill, at times hugging each tree on the way. The return going back uphill was too often a scrambling crawl, again possibly from tree to tree.

With this personal experience in the Elliott for the next five years, imagine my astonishment when, thirty years later the Governor of Oregon (an out-of-state transplant living essentially in Portland), announced retirement of the Elliott State Forest from active management, to make it a recreation preserve. Hiking or camping, and even hunting in the Elliot would certainly be an interesting experience for the public on much of the ground, though not very enjoyable unless someone was half mountain goat. Those of us who worked there seldom saw anyone "recreating" anywhere away from the roads in the Elliott for obvious reasons. Politicians!

Also, today's modern world puts unbelievable pressure onto all forested lands. Like it or not, humans are part of the equation. Wise forest management is a better choice than simply turning our backs and thinking everything will be just fine. Harvesting (e.g. logging) is just one more tool in a complex mixture of applications used to keep the forest healthy. It also provides an income to pay to get the work done.

Active management of the Elliott was closed down in 2017. Up until then, almost all logging in the forest was done with some type of cable system, either high lead or skyline, except in a few of the less severely sloped areas. Logging in the Elliot was very dangerous simply because of the terrain. During my five years of experience in that forest, I all but witnessed the death of two loggers. An additional third man died within months after we moved from the area. All three were young and healthy guys with their whole lives ahead of them. All went to work one morning and never went home again. This doesn't even address those who were injured but survived. The Elliott is a dangerous place.

I vividly remember when that first logger died over forty years ago. I was driving up to the main ridge road and encountered another pick-up coming toward me in a hurry. I stopped and the driver, a guy likely in his late teens or early 20's, excitedly asked if I had any communication – he desperately needed to radio out.

Apparently at the landing where he had been working, they were unable to get outside with their radio call. I said I could reach our HQ Office. He asked that I have them send an ambulance to their work site immediately. I followed his directions on the spot without any questions.

The logger then explained that a choker setter had not gotten clear when the turn started into the landing. A log had hit a stump and swung sideways, hitting the man on the leg and literally knocking it off. Other crewmen had gotten to him quickly and since he was not bleeding much, they put him in the stretcher kept with their emergency stuff to haul him to the landing. The guy I was with went to find help as they worked to get their buddy up the hill.

It wasn't until we returned together to the landing that we learned the injured man had died. The gaping wound to the mangled leg had opened during the move up the mountain. The choker setter had bled out before they could get him to the top. A simple tourniquet applied immediately may have saved his life, though unlikely.

The second logging accident about a year later involved a mobile yarder-loader. These are smaller and more easily moved machines used in small timber, usually for thinning operations. When used as a yarder, they have two guy-lines running back each to an anchor stump at about 45 degrees from the angle of the mainline.

The fellow in charge had made a temporary replacement of the guy-lines with used mainline. Mainline is smaller in diameter and has less strength than what is specified for guy-lines.

When the yarder engineer was bringing in a turn of logs, one got hung up on the pull. The lighter-weight substitute anchor lines snapped under the strain of the hung-up log, causing the yarder to literally leap off the landing. It landed about fifty feet down the very steep mountainside on its top. The engineer in the cab, who was not belted in, hit the top of the yarder cabin with his head. An exposed nut and bolt-end securing the roof to the cabin was driven right into his skull. It killed him instantly. No hard hat, no seatbelt, unsuitable lightweight cable – one dead operator.

Both these accidents were due to improper procedures. Both companies were fined heavily.

The third fatality was a friend. Five years later, only a few months after I transferred away from Coos Bay, we received word that one of the fellows I knew well and played sports with had died. He was a very skilled lead timber faller. On the day he died, he was training two novices in this very dangerous occupation. One of the newbies had started working on a difficult tree. My friend assessed the tree and told the trainee to stop his cut due to the hazardous lean. He stepped in to finish the job himself. Then everything went bad with the tree. The partially cut tree broke off the stump prematurely, twisting around striking my friend, killing him instantly. He was very good at his profession, yet an unexpected circumstance killed him in the woods just doing his daily job.

This was something of a shock to me. My friend was my age, less than thirty, also with a young family. How many trees have I dropped over the years? Why him and not me? He'd hand-made a beautiful Myrtlewood clock for us as a going-away gift when we moved. His hair was flaming red, he had a huge, friendly grin. He was full of life. So sad.

Logging and most any other work in the woods are jobs with many potentially dangerous moments. Much of the Elliott is very steep, and in a place where bad weather is pretty frequent – adding even more dangerous conditions.

Most people outside forest industries see only the beauty and quiet tranquility of the woods. Those who work there also enjoy that environment greatly. In fact, they cherish it more than is commonly realized. So often I've found that casual woodland visitors seem to have a difficult time comprehending, and often even deny, just how dangerous the forest can be … most especially on the Oregon Coast. The breath-taking beauty seems to be a distraction. When warned, a remarkable number take offense, rather than realize the advice is being shared because of much pain and sadness learned through experience.

Forests are not a place for goofing off or for novices to go wandering around unprepared and unknowing. I encourage people to enjoy the forest, but to use developed areas … and take some time to learn the very real and dangerous hazards.

CHAPTER 32

The field projects in Reforestation and Rehab I directed in the Coos area were most often aerial spraying, pre-commercial thinning, aerial seeding, and scarification – that is brush removal and piling with dozers.

Getting young tree seedlings planted on lands under ODF stewardship was accomplished with contract crews hired for the whole planting season. Until 1985 the hiring of planting crews was done directly by each unit staff, so I developed the ability to interview scores of job candidates and crew supervisors, then selected those that seemed best suited. Later we began contracting most tree planting and other labor-intensive work – a wonderful relief that saved me a lot of time. Even so, on smaller plots, my regular crew and I often did all the work.

WINTER WORK ON THE COAST

Mostly my five years in the Coos area was uneventful, but there was some excitement occasionally. Once an aerial spray program was in progress on a nearly clear and quiet morning. My technician and I were observing the helicopter pilot at work on the unit below the road where we stood. There was no wind and only thin wisps of fog that ribboned through the tiptops of the conifers here and there.

I have always been in awe of the skill of spray helicopter pilots as they wield their machines in acrobatic sweeps. They look almost like birds as they use their copter to follow the contours of the hillsides without any apparent effort.

A helicopter working on a Spray Project. Aerial spraying is a very cost -effective method for even application of fertilizer or chemicals on large forest tracts.
Photo courtesy of CC Dickerson

Like most of these pilots, the guy we watched was very experienced and capable. He made a spray pass near the unit boundary where young, shorter trees sided up with the tall mature growth just over the perimeter line. We heard a loud POP, POP, POP that sounded a lot like a toy cap-gun.

Immediately we observed a thin shower of Douglas fir needles and twigs flying all over around the copter still in the air.

The pilot urgently radioed us on the landing, and asked if we heard the noises – we answered affirmative. Within moments he landed the copter at our location. He made a minute detailed inspection over the whole machine.

When finished, he explained to us that he'd misjudged the space available at the edge of the unit, and had just barely clipped the small upper limbs of the adjacent trees with the main rotor. This could have been a disaster, but he had been fortunate to just brush the foliage. No real damage was caused to the chopper. Another few inches and he and copter would have fallen like a stone to the steep hillside below. A grim scenario to picture.

Another time during my first winter in the Elliott tree planting, there also was a bit of excitement. Our planters were working a very steep unit. Being February or March on the coast, it was no surprise that it started raining early in the workday. The rain kept increasing its intensity and soon was coming down in translucent sheets. On the coast, workdays continue despite the weather pretty much year-round. Even after a few hours in the downpour, the planters were still out in the unit getting the job done.

There was no warning. First a small section of soil and debris began to move. Then other places, together making a sudden deep throated roar. The slides took some very large trees down more than one nearby draw. All let go almost simultaneously, so that so much ground was moving around us that it was both spectacular and downright scary! For a time, the slides roared down through that unit and out the bottom into a creek bed far below. Fortunately, no crewmembers were in the path of any of the moving ground, but still everyone was pretty shaken up.

I don't know if anyone has actually figured a way to accurately predict these kinds of landslides. Geology is not my field of study. Some slides could be related to disturbed ground, or heavy rains. There must be other factors involved as well. Many slides I've personally observed appear to have little relation to ground disturbance or even rain. I've watched the ground shift on undisturbed, relatively gentle slopes. In other places steep hillsides defy any slippage on inclines that would measure easily sixty percent incline.

A non-fire or logging incident gave me a scary reminder of the facts about dangers in the forest, particularly in the winter. I think it was sometime also in February or March. The southwestern part of Oregon was drenched with an unusually violent rainstorm accompanied with strong winds. It was a stubborn storm that sat on top of the area and hammered everything for at least twenty-four hours straight. Most storms have lulls and gusts, but this one was just a big long slam for hour after hour.

The wind caused trees to rock back and forth loosening already wet soils, which in turn probably contributed to especially violent slides on steeper slopes. Since most of the Elliott stands on edge, landslides are not uncommon, but this storm was really pushing the situation beyond what people who lived in the area considered normal.

Fairly late in the evening of that storm, my boss called me at home. He directed me to go investigate a possible problem on state land. At that time, I was supervisor of a timber sale team. A slide had likely originated on a road built under contract for ODF to provide access to one of our sales. Although the slide has missed their house, the people who lived on the land below where the slide came down were understandably concerned. They had called ODF asking if more debris might yet move and endanger their home. They wondered should they evacuate until the storm subsided.

Dressed in my ODF uniform, I went to the office and took one of our 4x4 trucks out to the house in question. The rain and wind were still at it, making it almost impossible to drive. The windshield wipers could not deal with that much water.

When I arrived at their doorstep, I introduced myself and asked to see where the slide had come through. They showed me a small, steep stream between their house and a shed nearby, or maybe it was a garage building. Mud and small to medium sized debris had come down that hillside stream and settled out just below their house.

I said that I could not really advise them as to whether they should evacuate or not. That would have to be their choice. I would drive to the area up the slope and see if I could determine what had happened to cause the slide. It would take awhile, but I'd report back to them after a bit.

Oregon Department of Forestry uniform patch – Half Tree emblem adopted about 1971. This logo was not popular among employees.

Photo courtesy of CC Dickerson

Off I went to the forest access road in that area and up into the mountains above.

The active timber sale that we had in the area had required some road construction going out a prominent ridge well above the slide. I had inspected the project about a week earlier and had noticed nothing unusual. I was thinking that maybe I should have looked closer, although the vigor of the storm hadn't yet been a contributing factor and additional work had been done.

As I drove toward the road construction area, it was very scary with water tumbling down and across the road. The roadside ditches were all running over. The large trees along the roadside were waving limbs back and forth like the arms of crazed and wild dancers. My truck was bucking at every wind gust. As I went further up slope, the violence of the trees in the wind increased to the extent that I expected some of them to come down across the road any minute. If one did fall and hit my truck, it could all be over really quick. It was not a feel-good situation.

When I reached the edge of the new road construction, I stopped. I did not want to drive on the new raw, water-saturated surface, as that would cause even more damage than the storm. I set out on foot, struggling against the wind and ever mindful of the roadside trees. Mud grabbed at my boots, building up with each step. After hiking about a half mile on the new roadway leaning into the wind, I came to a place where about a hundred feet of the outside road edge slumped away, having slid out of sight down the hill. In the storm and darkness, I could not see for sure how far or where the slide went. I feared to get too close to the deep cracks in the fresh soil. The map I was using showed I was about seven hundred to a thousand feet uphill from where I had started at the debris field near the house below. With the map flapping around in the darkness, I really couldn't swear the slump here was connected or not.

With my flashlight, I could see that the slide material was loose side-cast dirt that was supposed to have been end-hauled to a safe deposit area and not pushed to the side on this steep ground at all. There had also been scattered and inter-mingled wood debris remaining at the top. This added to the instability and indicated the ground had not been adequately cleared before the road excavation in the side-hill had begun.

It didn't much matter if this hillside had slipped all the way down to the house, the potential was there. The longer I observed the situation, the more scared I became, realizing that the entire rain-soaked area could take off under my feet at any time. If it went, I would not have a pleasant trip down the hill. I decided that getting off the side of the mountain and leaving the area PDQ was a really good option that I should take.

Doing a quick about-face, I hiked double-time back to my waiting truck, very relieved to see that it was still there. Every step was beginning to feel like walking in partially set pudding. I didn't even scrape the gooey mud off my boots, but immediately climbed in the cab of my truck, rain gear and all, and got the heck out of there. Trying to be as cautious but also a fast a possible, I went back down to the house the slide had by-passed. I described the unstable ground I'd seen. I told the owner that visibility up-hill was very poor. My report to the owner was inconclusive. I did say if it was my house, I would find someplace else to stay for a few days, or at least until the storm was over.

Driving back to town, I reported what I'd told the home-owner to my boss. The following morning at the office, it took only a very short time for me to contact the rep for the company that had purchased the timber sale. He was on the receiving end of some pretty sharp words as I told him about the shortcomings in the road construction that I'd observed. I made it clear the company would be required to fix the problems PDQ, and at his company's expense. Damage liability was now their problem.

I was not aware that the same night I was out in that rotten weather in the Elliot, several miles away that same storm did a number on a hillside near Canyonville (inland about fifty miles). A telephone company crew of six men was working on a damaged line just south of town along Canyon Creek that ran next to I-5. A large chunk of the mountain above the crew let go and came sliding down upon them and into the creek below. No logging, no road building or any earth disturbance of any kind was involved. Just rain.

All but one man perished in the slide. The lone survivor had just walked way from their tent shelter to go to his truck to get a thermos of coffee. Five men died. One body has never been found.

CHAPTER 33

Overall, any forest is a hugely complex and dynamic environment. Taken as a whole, the State of Oregon contains four major Forest Types, each with their own soil types, indigenous tree species, predominant weather, various elevations, and native wildlife. All the factors interact within their own sphere while being impacted by an amalgamate of parts from the others. Knowing how they all function together takes more than casual contact. To further complicate things, human demands on these places may be similar but always different, and often conflicting as well.

I came to know three of the four Oregon forest types well, and could probably hold my own within most scientific groups in regard to the fourth type (the high desert).

No single individual could possibly be expert in all parts of Forest Management, as it is so vast a science to begin with. Also, every square inch is in a constant state of change. My career as a professional Management Forester was spent, primarily as a "generalist". Working with "specialists" was a daily occurrence.

Management Timber Sales Teams in the various districts of ODF were responsible for handling the harvesting part of the forest growth cycle. As with all applications, harvesting actions are site specific. Those in charge for ODF lands are guided in their job by the governing laws, the mission of the department to promote healthy forests, and up-to-date forest science knowledge. No action is lightly taken.

TIMBER SALE TEAM LEADER

After the move from Astoria, I had settled into my Coos Bay reforestations job pretty quickly. The biggest challenge was getting to know the new landscape. The job itself was essentially the same as in Astoria with slightly different ingredients. Within a few months I was fairly comfortable settled in at work. At home it took longer.

With a drive of only two hours duration, many more visits were now taken inland to Hugo for sharing time with our extended families. Our oldest girl began kindergarten and the younger daughter was off to preschool four mornings every week. Also, once again we were expecting a child, but home-life was anything but settled.

Our living arrangements weren't ideal or even close. We were living on a tiny trailer pad not much larger than the total size of our mobile home – barely 700 square feet. It was a huge change from the near un-tamed forest surrounding the derelict house on Youngs River. Neither my wife nor I were city types. For me, it wasn't long before I was looking for activities away from our cramped quarters. Overall, changes would soon be needed for the whole family, with the girls growing fast and the new baby's arrival approaching.

I made several new friends from connections through people at the office. Although I went fishing and clamming pretty often, I needed more activities. Not long after moving and looking for recreation opportunities away from work, I joined the Bay Area Jaycees. Mainly, I chose that group because they had a city league basketball team. This newest association led to more and more participation in other Jaycee programs for self-improvement and volunteer community service projects.

The local Jaycees chapter was well known for their less than temperate beer consumption at their meetings and work projects. They also had so many activities available with built-in recreation; soon I was gone from home a lot on weekends and evenings. The conflict between my family and my volunteering and recreation activities began to escalate without me really being aware.

At the same time, my wife was tying to cope with a pregnancy that was a lot less comfortable than the previous two. She suffered from severe nausea off and on for the first four months. Her spare time went into delivering our little ones to their schools and seeking out alternate Real Estate possibilities.

We knew our very limited living space would soon be bursting at the seams. At best, our family of four was currently way too snug in the two-bedroom mobile. The crowded location of the mobile was a big issue. None of us much liked where we were placed at all.

We began looking around, hoping to find a house we could afford to buy before the new baby came. In spite of the prize money we'd banked, every property we looked at was either beyond our means or still too small. We wanted rural, but couldn't afford even a small city lot.

The fifth member of our family arrived in mid-May. We now were the proud parents of two beautiful girls and a handsome baby boy. Overnight our two-bedroom mobile became impossibly small, with hardly space to move around. We endured this problem for three months, when pieces seemed to fall into place for our family to move to larger quarters.

We came upon a very snug, but neat three-bedroom house eastward across the water from the City of Coos Bay. It was close to my office and, most importantly, had both a front and back yard and a small garage.

But the asking price was still too high for us. Both our budget and the house would qualify for a loan, but only if the seller reduced the price a bit and made a couple of minor changes. The owner seemed eager to sell, as everything to meet the requirements was done in record time. The price was dropped to just barely within our means.

When we were talking to the realtor putting the deal together, we needed nearly all the cash we had in the bank to make the down payment. It was perhaps four blocks to the bank from the realtor's office. I walked down the street to get the money as my wife waited with the children.

The bank teller counted out nearly $3,000 in $100 bills, telling me that a little old lady had just come in that morning and deposited 500 of these crisp bills. She must have been stashing those bills away for some time. It doesn't seem like so much now, but then it was a whole lot of money, especially to those who were perpetually broke, like my little family. I recall feeling kind of funny walking down the street back to the agent's office with $3,000.00 cash filling my pockets.

Once more our savings account was nearly bare. But shortly after we sold the mobile and recaptured a few hundred dollars in equity. At least our housing strain was now somewhat improved.

After a couple of years working as the Coos Reforestation Forester 2, I applied for and was able to take a lateral transfer into an opening as the leader of the Tenmile Area Timber Sale Team. Tenmile was one of the three timber sub-units of the Elliot. There was no salary increase, but the job change was new and interesting. I turned my focus from getting young trees into the ground, to getting mature trees in the form of logs, coming out of the forest.

This rounded out my practical education of the total lifecycle of the forest. When mastered, my Forest Management know-how for Oregon to the west of the Cascade mountains was pretty much complete. The change meant that again I had a lot to learn in a short time, but this time much information was over-lapping, taking most of the confusion and urgency out of the learning curve.

Now my year-round crew included two technicians and two Forester I's. We also usually had a summer trainee or two who worked to gain experience while on summer break from college studies in forestry.

While I worked in Coos Bay, I continued to have various fire assignments, mostly as Sector Boss, Dozer Boss or Division Supervisor. Most of the fires were pretty much the norm of long hours, lots of dirt and ash, designing strategy then directing crews to carry out the line building. I still felt the exhausted but very satisfied personal feeling of defeating the fire.

I particularly remember on fire came in early-summer 1973. Four or five Coos District employees, including me, were sent to help Grants Pass ODF. They were over-loaded with fires across their district. Mostly from lightning starts, I think. I ended up at a fire of moderate size on Murphy Hill located east of Williams Hwy and on the north side of the Applegate River.

Back in 1965 I had been on a fire with my Hotshot crew I think almost in the exact same place. That earlier fire had been on the west side of the hill. This fire, eight years later, was mostly on the east side. The fuels and conditions provided much more potential to grow.

My '65 crew had been all the way to the top of the hill mopping up after the fire was contained. It had been steep, hot and tedious. We thought we were done with it, but a day or two later the public called in a smoke visible from the roadway below. The smoke was believed to be from a slow-burning snag that would need to be felled and dry mopped.

Even back when I was a super-fit kid fighting fire for wages, I did not relish the idea of packing a chainsaw and necessary fuel to the top of a steep ridge in hot weather. Handing the trek to the guys on my Hotshot crew didn't seem too fair, as I was the regular saw guy. So, I hatched an alternate plan.

I'd gone into the GP HQ compound warehouse on 12th Street and dug around for a while. After a search into dusty corners, I finally found exactly what I was looking for - a six-foot Misery Whip (cross-cut hand saw). I did a little filing to touch up the edge on the saw, and away I went to rustle up the Hotshot crew.

When my good '65 crew saw the vintage tool, they immediately bought into the adventure and novelty of my idea. We tied the handles together, forming the saw blade into a big loop for ease in carrying over the shoulder. We took off with the oversized hand tool, along with an axe or two, a couple of wedges, Hazel hoes and shovels. I drove the Hotshots to the base of Murphy Hill without much urgency and we hiked the steep slope to the top in a rather casual way, as the fire in the snag really had nowhere to go.

Hiking burned over ground, even after it cools isn't really very fun. It is dirty, and the ash in the dust isn't easy on the lungs. Even so, there was no trouble finding the offending smoke. It took a little work felling the snag, as our technique with the old saw probably wasn't all that great. But it was easier than one man (me) hauling the much heavier chainsaw plus fuel, wedges and oil up there alone. Probably safer too.

Different crewmembers wanted a turn with the old crosscut, dividing up the actual work. A little mop-up on the downed snag and we were heading back to HQ.

While traveling to the fire in 1973, I remembered the earlier excursion well with pleasant feelings. This time I was working on the ground helping direct a helicopter. We were dealing with water drops on a fire trail that was in the process of being built on the fire's flank. A hand trail crew nearby was making headway when a call came to send our copter immediately to the command center.

The chopper was needed for an emergency medical transport, something that always trumped the urgency of fire-line needs. This kind of message always traveled down the line in record time, as on fires serious injuries are always a possibility and big news when they happen. The emergency nature of the call meant the copter was in the air, without the bucket, within minutes.

The injury was pretty bizarre. It was later learned that the fire IC had been eating a box lunch at the command center. He took a bite of a ham sandwich and didn't notice a yellow jacket wasp land on his food at the most inopportune moment. The result was a mouthful of angry insect that stung him on the tongue. This was serious business and he was in distress almost immediately.

The Unit Forester was called at HQ about the same time the copter left our line. From different directions, the aerial E-vac with the IC aboard and the unit boss all met up at the hospital at the same time.

The Unit Forester was striding alongside as the IC was wheeled in to the emergency room. Swollen lips and tongue were obvious and the IC was wheezing heavily. The admitting nurse, as they seem to do, started asking all kinds of questions.

The Unit Forester was not about to allow time to be wasted. He exploded, telling her to get his man some help, and "Your damn questions will get answered later!"

Very quickly medical attention was on the spot. In that the injury could easily have cost the IC his life, it would seem that the angry demand for immediate help was appropriate.

That evening when our Coos team was released from the fire at the shift-change to travel back into Grants Pass, we found a place in Murphy for dinner that was new to me. I hadn't lived in the area for seven years and this establishment was something I didn't know about. The new restaurant had the best, coldest draft beer in a big icy stein with a green olive at the bottom. I never liked green olives, but this was really good. I'm not a beer-buff, but that little added salty-olive taste really set-off the earthy flavor of the beer.

It took a few days for the local crews and out-of-district help to get the fiery results of that lightning bust under control. When our Coos group was released to go home, I rode with a CFPA guy (Coos Forest Protection Association) on his engine for the 2-hour trip back home on the coast.

Driving home about dusk, our rig climbed over the shoulder of my old friend, Mt. Sexton. Our drive continued through the up-down section of hills and valleys before the turn-off going toward the ocean. We came over Stage Coach Pass north of Wolf Creek and were heading down toward the Glendale exit (#80) on I-5. There is a left turn that requires traffic to slow-down in order to handle it safely. We were in the left lane about halfway around the nearly blind turn when we encountered a Volkswagen Beetle upside down in our lane. A couple of very flustered young women were standing with their backs against the inside guardrail. The accident apparently had just occurred with dust still flying through the air.

With some fancy steering and braking, we managed to get stopped PDQ and off to the outside right shoulder without slamming into anything. My cohort herded the upset and crying twenty-somethings out of the middle of the road, and I grabbed some road flares. Back up the hill I ran to warn on-coming traffic of the accident and disabled car in the middle of the road.

Despite putting about six brightly lit flares out, I still had to jump the center guardrail a couple of times myself to avoid getting hit by cars coming way too fast and two abreast. I mumbled bad words to myself about them ignoring the flares and hoped no one on the downhill would get hurt.

In a few minutes a State Trooper arrived and got things under control. Since we'd not witnessed the accident, he allowed us to continue our way home to Coos.

There was another fire around that time; a local burn on the Elliott. A group of Coos management employees worked the incident, I think in the fall. It must have been an escaped slash burn, or CFPA would have handled it. There were maybe eight or ten of us, all from the ranks of permanent staff and all recruited in the HQ parking lot just as we were climbing into our cars to go home for the day. Suddenly we were a fire crew.

Our mixed pick-up crew worked through the early evening, then into the late night, building hand fire trail to contain the fire. It was a challenging fire, but for a whole crew of people who did other woodsy non-fire stuff, we did a pretty decent job getting it into the corral. We had one young woman with us, a forest technician working on the Engineering crew. She wasn't a big girl, but she worked as hard as anybody. Now she was suddenly a wildland firefighter – welcome to ODF.

Author working night shift on a fire as Division Supervisor.
Photo courtesy of CC Dickerson

Considering when and how we came to be a fire crew, there was no food and only little water available. These small details came back to haunt me in particular just a few hours later, reminding me that several years had passed since I regularly worked a hard physical sixteen or eighteen-hour day on the line. I wasn't quite thirty and actually in pretty decent shape, but certainly not in the same tip-top condition I'd been in a few years earlier when on the Hotshots.

We kept at the job until the fire was contained. It was long after midnight when our impromptu crew headed home. For several of the folks coming off that fire, it was closer to go straight to their homes in town than drive all the way through to the office on the south side. We stopped long enough for everyone to shuffle around to share rides, with the drivers simply taking the ODF rigs home. It was expected they would bring the vehicles into the HQ the next day, and then switch to their own vehicles.

Of the group, only our young female technician and I lived beyond the office. We two took one truck and continued on to switch to our own vehicles at HQ to go home. At HQ after parking the ODF rig, I stepped out of the truck when, WAM! I almost went to the ground.

Some really horrible muscle cramps and spasms in my legs struck me like a bolt of lightning. I could hardly keep to my feet let alone walk, and couldn't help but groan in agony through clenched teeth as I lay across the hood of the truck, trying to stretch out cramped-up muscles.

Bless that girl's heart, she stayed with me until the cramps passed, even though there was nothing to do but offer moral support. After what seemed like hours - maybe five minutes total, the pain eased a little and I was able to hobble to my own truck to go home. I felt like I was that girl's grandfather, all bent and crippled up that way. Thankfully it was only a short drive to home. I was able to gut my way safely to my destination.

Unfortunately, leg cramps have been something I have been plagued with most any time I am involved with long-duration, hard physical labor or strenuous sports efforts. Sufficient water helps, but does not always prevent the cramps. With trial and error, I eventually found that eating bananas; taking potassium tablets and swigging straight vinegar helps somewhat. That night none of these aids were on hand, so I just had to suffer through. How embarrassing!

CHAPTER 34

Within most states in the western part of our nation, vast tracts of land of shockingly large size are under control of the US Forest Service, the National Park Service and the Bureau of **Land Management.** These lands should not be confused with county or state lands, and are administered by agencies based in Washington DC.

Wildland fires take no notice of property lines on a map or which agency might have authority over the landscape. When larger fires occur in the west, fire fighters at every level from line crews to top tier administration may be called to assist. Their ability to cooperate is essential to dealing positively with what is essentially a shared emergency.

Much difference is apparent in how various organizations handle wildland fire. Basic philosophy of attack is notable and has been an issue for decades. Some folks want to down-play this on-going problem. It's something that should be addressed straight on and ended.

MY FIRST OUT-OF-STATE FIRE

In 1974, I was one of several ODF employees dispatched to an unusually big project fire in northeast California. It was near the small towns of Bieber and Nubieber. A liaison was named from ODF, who was on the job before we arrived at the fire. His job was to provide as the communication link between the various ODF personnel sent and the two larger agencies already working the fire, the CDF (California Department of Forestry) and the USFS.

This was my first out-of-state fire and was also the largest fire that I'd ever been assigned up to that time. At the close, it was just short of 100,000 acres (97,000). That is equal to well over 150 square miles. We left Interstate-5 at Mt. Shasta not far south of the Oregon/California border, and headed east over the Sierra Nevada Mountains.

The guys with me were as shocked as I was as we started down the east side and the view began to open up. As soon as there was a clear panorama down to the flatter lands below the mountains, we could see a gigantic smoke plume.

To me the column of smoke looked very much like photographs I had seen of the mushroom cloud from atomic explosions over Japan in World War II. It rose up thousands of feet into the sky with occasional bolts of lightning visible through the thick brown smoke. The hair on the back my neck rose in excitement and maybe fear too. This was one ugly sucker!

We arrived at the fire camp and checked in explaining who we were and where we were from. Before our trip of several hundred miles, we'd been told we would be acting as either Division Supervisors or Dozer Bosses. All involved were seasoned fire veterans.

It was only mid-morning, with almost a full Day Shift still available. The people there at Check-in were very casual, maybe even flippant, when telling us that they did not have assignments for us at that time. With an indifferent wave they sent us back to Bieber and told us to hang out at a location there until needed. This was an odd reaction, in that we knew much conversation had occurred between our Salem HQ and those actively recruiting resources for the fire. Also, close to eighteen hours had gone by since the night before when their initial request for help had been delivered.

Everyone on our team was well experienced with wildland fire. All were antsy without much to do and fell to discussing the reception we'd experienced. The reaction at Check-in didn't sit really well with any of our group. As we sat cooling our heels at Bieber a short discussion between us resulted in contact to our designated liaison. He was out in the field, so a message was relayed to him about what had transpired at the Check-in station.

Apparently immediately after our call ended, the liaison received our message, got on a phone and started talking with various ODF people at our Salem HQ. The communication must have been successful, as he called us back quite soon. We were told to return to Fire Camp Check-in.

There didn't seem to be much change in the attitude when we returned, but this time the Check-in people at least had assignments for us. We took our personal stuff to a safe place and separated to our different jobs. I was detailed as a Dozer Boss.

Since we'd divided our people between two vehicles for travel, several of us – me included – now had no transportation of our own. I was given over to a National Guard soldier with a military style jeep. He was strictly business, offering no conversation at all. His body language clearly said he did not want to be there. Period. He stoically drove me to the location indicated. I was to meet up with my dozer equipment at that spot.

As I climbed from the Jeep, the guardsman abruptly left without so much as a wave of the hand. Now I not only had no personal transportation, I also had no means of communication. The only ODF radios were attached to our vehicles – which of course I didn't have. The Oregon people had already discovered that even the radios we brought with us from Oregon were useless. None of our radios were on frequencies being used on the fire. With no handsets issued at the Check-in, I felt like I was in a dark room without even a match.

With a quick look around where I now stood, I discovered there also was no equipment anywhere in sight. I stood alone at a remote road junction in a barren and rather dismal high-desert landscape pretty much in the middle of nowhere.

I'd never been on a fire without radio communications. The entire time on this fire the lack of integrated communications was a major problem. CDF had their radio frequencies and USFS had theirs, but they could not talk to each other. I do not know about the Forest Service, but the CDF could not even communicate between their own folks that arrived from different parts of that large state. Most certainly, no one could talk with those of us with ODF recently arriving from Oregon.

If any emergency arose where I now stood, I couldn't even make an SOS type call. None of us had even considered there would be no radios available. It was like firefighting conditions before crews had two-way radios available – decades past.

(After fire note: Advise future crews assisting on out-of-state fires to bring their own communication equipment to maintain contact at least with other ODF personnel in attendance. You won't know you might need your own most basic equipment until you arrive!)

Here I was, on a huge fire with no communication at all. I did not know and could not find out what was going on. I didn't even know who I might contact, as there was no one at that site to ask. The promised equipment (dozers) were missing. I didn't even have a shovel, so an attempt for any action at all was useless. The only positive was that at least it was a relatively safe spot.

I am not known for having an excessive amount of patience, but I managed to keep a lid on it for a while, looking around at the rather dry and empty landscape and trying to decide what to do. The more I ran the scenario through my mind, however, the more frustrated I became.

After sitting on my thumbs for about an hour I was wondering if I should just say "What the Heck" and start hiking.

I was pretty hot around the collar when a CDF station wagon rolled up in a cloud of dust. It first appeared the driver was just going to pass me by, but having spied me standing there alone in suntans and white (Overhead) hardhat, the car screeched to a stop. The two or three long antennas attached to the car were whipping around importantly as he stopped.

Being in the mood I was, I thought with some sarcasm, "This guy must be of great relevance with all those radios!"

Maybe I was just jealous, or was I supposed to kneel or something? Still, I managed to hold my temper and keep control of my mouth, but just barely.

He stepped out importantly from his car and asked pleasantly who I was and what I was doing here alone. I politely explained my situation as best I could. He told me they were evacuating the lines in that area and regrouping. He indicated that I should be OK where I was.

DUH! I could see for myself that there was almost nothing to burn at that location. A terse answer was on my tongue, but I kept mum.

He said he would go find the equipment I was supposed to be commanding and would return soon. My opinion of him immediately became much more positive. At least he was trying to help.

Zoom! Off he went in a cloud of dust.

I waited what seemed like another impatient hour. Nothing! Grrrrr.

Another of our ODF folks, a younger guy from Coos that I now remember only by the name Dave, showed up hoofing it up the road.

Dave indicated that he had been told to come and assist me. Well, I wasn't really sure how we two might do anything, but okay. At least I now had someone to talk too.

We two waited a little more and watched as a finger of fire topped a small hill and burned on past us several hundred yards off to the east, with no crews in sight.

I kept thinking the same idea over and over in disgust, "This is a really rotten way to run a fire!"

Finally, that same CDF guy drove up again. With a relieved smile he said two dozers were on their way and upon their arrival, I should take them further to the east a short distance. There I would find another road. The fire would be to our southeast. We should start a dozer line at that point running to the east until we found a railroad right-of-way in another two or three miles and tie into it with a line being built there.

With dust flying everywhere, in a rush he was gone again. I began to sympathize with the guy, as apparently, he was being used as a kind of communications runner. In view of the situation, what a rotten job!

Our wait was much shorter this time. The dust from the CDF car has just settled, and I could hardly believe it when in only a few minutes, a D-6 and a D-7 dozer huffed and clanked into the area where Dave and I awaited. Following the verbal directions given, we each climbed aboard a dozer with the operators, went where told and started the machines building line. Ours was a pretty meager crew, but at least we were at work at last.

I had the D-6 take the lead, as it was faster but not quite as strong as the D-7. The smaller dozer would clear the way for the D-7, which would clean up, widen and strengthen our built line. With no hand support, it was important to use the terrain contours to aid as much as possible, and we would have to keep a very sharp lookout for slop-over problems.

Visibility on this eastside high desert landscape was excellent. Before we stared working our line, I noticed a trail being built in the opposite direction from where we were going. They were moving up a not too steep ridge with fully six dozers, and had hand trail crew support as well. The dozers were placed side-by-side, but slightly offset like harvesters in a wheat field. That crew was actually building line that was six blade-widths wide. The hand crew people were strung out along the line obviously waiting for the fire to approach this mega-line.

I was not familiar with this particular approach to using dozers and hand crews, and watched for a bit to make sure I understood what was happening. Since we didn't have the crews, I couldn't use the same method anyway, but I was always interested in learning new ways of fire attack.

For us, I used methods that fit with what assets we had available and I knew from past experience that, if we were lucky, would be effective. This obviously was a very nasty fire and my crew was badly outmatched. We couldn't afford to take risks.

We had built maybe about ¼ mile of line when a twenty-man hand crew came hiking up the access road. They had been told to find and work for a specific person – but it wasn't me. They'd been wandering around for a while unable to find the right guy.

The hand crew had the same problem we had – no transport, no radio and no way to check anything with anybody. I told their crew boss, if he agreed, that until someone corrected the situation, they were very welcome to stay and work with us. We really needed the hand trail support, for sure.

With relief and a big grin, the crew boss gave the okay. I knew just exactly how he felt. Finally! We were in business.

The fire was now within sight, burning vigorously through 4-foot tall brush and loosely scattered 30-foot trees. It appeared to be traveling straight for us.

According to the way I'd been trained and from past experience, I directed the hand trail boss to spread his crew along our built dozer line well behind the dozers for safety of the men on foot and also the machines. I told him to start using his Fusies (quick ignition sticks similar to highway flares) to start up a burnout at our line's edge toward the face of the fire. I emphasized that they should light no more than they absolutely knew they could control. I left Dave with them to help direct their efforts, as I wasn't sure the crew boss totally understood what I wanted. English obviously wasn't their language of choice. I stuck with the dozers, watching their back.

All went well and we only had one real threat. A large pine snag next to the outside line began to smoke from radiant heat as the main fire drew near. About the same time the snag burst into flames, I quickly got the attention of the D-7's operator. He came back, got on the backside of the snag and pushed it over and into the approaching fire.

At the end of the shift at early evening, we had accomplished our objective, reaching the rail line. The hand crew we'd picked up was very fast and effective. With that skilled crew backing up the dozers, when the head of the fire-line arrived back at the site, every inch of our line had held. We all felt pretty good about this, as most all other lines in our area, including the six-blade wide super-duper fire line I'd watched under construction, had been over-run by the fire. Those crews were now chasing the fire trying to find a defensible spot to make another stand.

The CDF boss with the antennas came by once more as we were being relieved around 6 PM. He asked me, as he sat in his car, how things had gone. I told him about poaching the wandering hand crew and how, with their excellent help, our lines were holding against the fire.

I was surprised when he parked his car and got out to look around some, with obvious curiosity. He seemed somewhat baffled that our part of the line had held when every other section nearby had been overrun. He carefully examined our construction asking how we had accomplished secure lines with so few assets. I told him what we did, and showed how it worked. It was pretty standard stuff, learned during my Hotshot days from years before. This guy seemed very interested in the process, which appeared to be all new to him. He was quite pleased with the result.

I guess he didn't share the info or maybe he wasn't so important after all, as the next day when I went back on the line in a different location, I noticed that the crews were applying the same tactics I'd witnessed as before. Once more a super-wide dozer-built line with hand crew was awaiting the flames, rather than attacking with a burnout when given the opportunity. There wasn't even line refinement by the hand crews. So, it was no surprise to me that at the end of the second day, they were having exactly the same lack of positive results as the day before. Just as before, the line was breached and the crews were falling back.

There are always some mix-ups and confusion at the beginning of any fire, and big fires can be the worst. Most certainly the communication issue was a really big part of the problem on this incident. Considering the size, everyone was very lucky that some "lost" crew didn't get trapped. This fire was easily the most chaotic one I've ever witnessed. I do not recall many specific details except the name was the Scar Face Fire. What a mess!

For a couple of summers, my periodic trips off to some big fire outside the Coos District interrupted my timber team schedule at work. When home, my growing time commitment to volunteer activities had pretty well eliminated my participation in family life.

There were some benefits with my volunteering activities that carried over to my job and helped build some personal skills. The service organization I'd joined taught know-how needed to accomplish big projects. They also promoted public speaking skills. Learning about the political process and influencing public opinion were other goals. It was pretty inclusive, probably even admirable and I was having a lot of fun. Yet the huge amount of my personal time required in the participation with community service definitely did not promote marriage compatibility. At least not in my marriage. My personal-time commitment grew larger over time, and maybe the fun-factor made it too easy to get more involved than necessary or than I really wanted.

I was not interested in becoming a chapter officer, but, over time, I did chair several important projects, such as an on-going Annual Logger's Competition at the city Salmon Festival, which I also helped initiate. There were public park clean-ups and renovation of a Little League Baseball Field. I did run for and was elected as one of two directors for the chapter. My participation came to occupy much of my time, most especially the sports activities. I played basketball and softball, even a couple of charity tackle foot-ball games, all during our time in Coos Bay, usually going out for a beer with the team after all the practices and games. While in Astoria my smaller, younger family attended many of these same types of activities with me, but in Coos Bay there were more formal events, much more frequent. The logistics of bringing a new baby plus two school-aged children to such activities was usually a big bother. Once in a while, my wife would accompany me to a dinner or party, but most functions were not really designed for families. My non-work time at home shrank in favor of organization events where I went alone.

Altogether I gave very little time or thought about the lack of activities with my wife and kids. Anything beyond an occasional weekend, or even a few hours after dinner were infrequent. I was happy enough with my activities, but my wife was not pleased. If any consideration was made, I thought my wife and kids probably felt a little left-out with me going off alone so often. Without me realizing it, the reverse was a lot more accurate.

The lives of my wife and kids had settled into a fairly predictable rhythm that mostly revolved around the school calendar. I was the one on the outside, missing a lot of the accomplishments and important events of my young children. Beyond work, my life more closely followed scheduled activities of the service club. In combination, my involvements, including summer fires, took me out and away from my family a lot – a lapse that now seems akin to my early collegiate study habits. I didn't get it.

A kind of turning point arrived not quite a year after our son was born. Just as spring arrived, my dad passed away after having a stroke while in surgery. I felt his absence even at a distance. He had always been there – even when I wanted to be master of my life. There was a hole that couldn't be filled.

A very big problem that came with Dad's passing, was that my mom was pretty much alone on the family farm back in Hugo. My younger brother and sister had grown and left home, and Mom soon scaled back most of the livestock on the farm. Her teaching job provided a good income, but she had no intention to move away from the family home.

The author mowing hay on the old family farm in late May 1976
Photo courtesy of CC Dickerson

The first year, the approaching annual hay harvest after my dad died was a pressing issue. I used most of my annual leave (vacation time) to go to Hugo to put in the hay crop that year, and then the following two years as well. Like the fire calls, there really wasn't much other choice. I mostly maintained the service club schedule as well. Altogether, these commitments didn't help me at home with my family. I think someone was trying to get my attention without much success.

Then the ante went up. It was about this time that the health of our younger girl took a decided turn. The evolution of her illness took some time, but became a genuine crisis over the following months. It seemed like her every sniffle that next fall and winter turned into a severe cold. In turn, asthmatic reactions would then develop into repeated pneumonias. During this very scary year and a half, our active, robust six-year old turned into a very thin, hollow eyed and sickly waif. By her seventh birthday our little girl was spending more days at home sick than days in school. My wife was on a first-name basis with the hospital emergency nurses.

First one, and another, then also the third pediatrician at the local clinic teamed up to work on the case. Many sleepless nights and trips to the emergency room of the hospital ensued. My wife handled most of the medical contacts; any patience she still had for my many volunteer activities drained away. She became very quiet. We didn't argue. We just existed.

Symptoms suggested Cystic Fibrosis – at that time an almost a sure death sentence during the teen years of the afflicted child. Fortunately, further very lengthy tests revealed a different problem. Our child was allergic to many things, including several common mold spores and even some of the viruses causing the common cold. Various treatments were initiated without any change. A tentative recommendation by the most senior doctor on the case, with no guarantees of success, was to permanently get our child away from the damp coastal weather.

Prompted by the health issues of our little girl, we started preparations to sell our house and move to a drier place. We began these improvements around Halloween of 1975. Fresh paint throughout, new kitchen cabinets and a repaired roof graced the small house before the next spring.

I had no inland job nailed down – things were very iffy! A couple of unsuccessful job interviews ensued, with each failure met with great disappointment. Meanwhile, we dealt with a very sick little girl and kept collective fingers crossed that she would survive.

I learned there was a possible job opening at the ODF office at Grants Pass. I would have to take a voluntary demotion to work this transfer. The job would be a step backward in what was until then a career with soaring promise – but I didn't care. The doctors treating our daughter had provided written confirmation of the reasons behind my transfer request. The Grants Pass Unit Forester offered the job to me if I wanted it - and I took it. I would be back in Reforestation as a Forester 1.

It was time to go home to Hugo.

PART THREE

*Forest Management back in
Southwestern Oregon*

CHAPTER 35

Over nearly four decades in time, I was assigned to several different positions in three ODF districts while in the employ of that state agency.** These jobs were all within slightly different structures at each posting, put in place according to the local forest needs and traits. All were also under the statewide guidance of the Board of Forestry for the health, safety and renewal of Oregon's forestlands. Fire Protection is only part of a large range of issues.

Today, wildland fire protection is provided by ODF for a bit under 16 million acres of Oregon owned or administered by private, city, county, state and federal entities. This equals to about half of the total forested land in the state. Oregon Department of Forestry should not be confused with the US Forest Service, the Bureau of Land Management, the National Park Service, or any other forest management agency

In the 1960s the Astoria Office focused on Forest Management, as the area is heavily forested. Most personnel work on Engineering, Timber Sales, and Reforestation teams in the Clatsop State Forest. Personnel with prime responsibilities in Forest Protection (fire) were few. The few holding that role divided time with duties that supported the other needs of the district.

In Coos Bay, the Coos Forest Protective Association (CFPA) handled protection issues in the district by contract with ODF, sharing office space with the state wildlife (ODF&W) and ODF forest management personnel. Like Astoria, Engineering, Timber Sales and Reforestation teams managed the dense forest under their stewardship, mostly on Common School Lands in the Elliott State Forest.

The Grants Pass office maintained a large Protection group of personnel, and a much smaller Management Unit than the other two districts. The large number of protection people reflected the district's record for most annual wildland fires in Oregon each summer. Only three or four permanent employees addressed the smaller acreage under Management care. No Engineers were assigned to the office. Usually at least two people switched between Management needs to jobs in Protection each summer months of fire season.

REFORESTATION AGAIN

My first day as a permanent SWO employee was July 15, 1976. I moved my personal equipment into the space dedicated for use by forest management personnel – my immediate supervisor and myself - in the basement of the old 12th Street Grants Pass HQ. In so many ways, it was as if time had stopped for the nine years since I'd been a whelp of a summer fire fighter working out of the same building.

But things weren't the same. Thankfully I was pretty comfortable with the demands of the reforestation position I'd transferred into, after so many years of successfully handling the same job on the coast. Compared to my first posting in reforestation, at first, the time at work in GP was somewhat peaceful. I knew exactly what to do to get the job done. Compared to the demands of my private life at that time, where the stress level had jumped into over-drive, I felt the reforestation assignment was very much under control. This was good, as the other, senior management guy, transferred out in the fall.

Away from the office, my family had no home. That situation would not change until my wife and I, and all the other folks who helped us, physically brought it to an end. To stretch our modest savings as far as possible, we'd decided to construct our new house ourselves. We'd made the commitment to build a house rather than buying, back in March, when we came into ownership of just over ten acres of bare ground. The location was the farthest northwest corner of my parent's Hugo farm; a gift from my Mom.

Between the time I accepted the job, but before we moved from Coos Bay, my wife and I had traveled to Hugo nearly every weekend for a few months. We cleared brush, leveled ground, and did other preparation work to get utilities and other necessities in place on our small property. Once more we were a strong team, working in tandem on a big project.

In mid-May I took almost a month off between our move and starting work to put up my mom's hay and do the heavier ground work for the new house. This included leveling the grade, marking the layout and building the driveway and the septic drain field, and digging a ditch for the foundation footing. Just days before I began back at ODF, we poured concrete for the footing and laid the block foundation. We had a long way yet to go.

A moving company did the transfer of our belongings. They packed up absolutely everything (even stuff I would have tossed into the trash), and stashed it in safe storage our parents had arranged. Once we arrived in Hugo permanently, the children were spread between the two households of their grandparents. My wife and I moved into a tent next to the construction site. We were hoping the length of time for this arrangement would be just till late fall. In fact, our family of five didn't come to live under one roof again for eight more months.

During the summer, the house construction was complicated by weather that was very uncharacteristic to the area. A long parade of thunderstorms, each with down-pouring rains, filed through the district between June and October. The squalls at least kept the fire danger down, reducing call-outs a bunch, but were very inconvenient to our urgent building project. Delays due to weather were frequent.

Then the cold weather arrived. We were weeks behind schedule. By mid-November we were dealing with sustained temperatures in the teens – another oddity in SWO. When the cold became more than we could handle, we borrowed a small travel trailer from my brother-in-law. Around Christmas we finally got the roof on the new house and all the windows in place. The gaping hole for the fireplace and chimney was finally bricked-in the day before the holiday. This allowed our bed to be moved inside the half-finished house.

The bank deadline for completion loomed over us like a black cloud. My wife suffered from nightmares almost every night. I just tried to keep plodding forward on the huge project we'd undertaken. Almost all my time away from the office went toward work on the house unless I was asleep. It seemed to never end.

About a year before I transferred back to SWO, a new Unit Forester boss had come into his position at the Grants Pass Office. He was a kind of guy who was ready with a joke and first to lead the troops out for a beer after work was done. When I joined the GP permanent staff, I came to like him as a person and a boss. There were some things, had I been in his shoes, I may have done differently, but his way as a boss suited me almost all the time. I was fortunate to have a boss just then that was a very up-front guy – something I try to also be.

The district as a whole was about to enter into a sort of limbo period for several years. The prime issue was the urban location and limited size of the SWO HQ compound. The slow wheels of state government were grinding toward a solution. The process of finding a more appropriate office site, getting the necessary structures built and actually getting everything safely moved had landed on the desk of the unit boss. The budget for this huge project was nil.

There were a few sticky issues also floating around at work that more or less inter-mixed making the lives of many people more complicated. It was my misfortune to become part of this group. As a result, my stress level multiplied.

The unit boss was dealing with the long over-due issue of the location of the office. Larger quarters in a better, more rural locale were sorely needed. The biggest barrier to such a move was the lack of money in the Unit budget. My new boss had decided the Grants Pass staff (sometimes with a bit of help from the Medford personnel too) could and would put out the effort and personal time to design and build a completely new Grants Pass Headquarters. His enthusiasm for the project was infectious.

An appropriate piece of land was found and acquired through both property trades and creative means to purchase. This first step took several years to negotiate, and I arrived just as the first contract was signed. It took a lot more time for the final ownership to be completed.

Next, permanent personnel sat in many meetings where everyone shared their own wants, needs and dreams at the table, developing a workable set of building plans. Much more was still needed on a limited budget, so unashamed begging from local loggers, mills and building supply outlets was done to help obtain building materials.

At work the knowledge and talents of personnel were put to work. Our dozer operator graded the new compound site. I did the grade surveying for the driveways and site placement of buildings. Later I even planted various landscape choices. Our summer and winter crews volunteered to pour concrete and pound nails. The physical move came in increments, dependent on inspections from the county Planning Department, and which in-house departments were packed and ready to relocate. The parallels to my own long-drawn-out building project were obvious.

The new Monument Drive compound slowly became the Unit HQ during the winter of 1979-80.

The new Grants Pass Unit Office on Monument Drive, near Merlin. The groundwork, compound, offices and landscaping were largely completed by district personnel, with all moved from in town by early 1980. Photo courtesy of EE Witaker

I had worked out of the old compound for five years in the early 1960s. The move to a new site was close to twenty years later, and the old GP office was a kind of second home for me. With many good memories, the place held a spot in my heart. As the plans and actions for the big move became more definite, I was one of only two or three old-timers on the staff – even with my nine-year mid-term absence. I certainly felt some sadness as that important landmark from my youth was decommissioned.

The Unit Forester recognized my attachment and made a special effort to address my torn allegiance. I really appreciated the individual time he took. His interest came at a particularly difficult time for me in all parts of my life. He fulfilled my expectations of a good boss in nearly every way, offering an understanding ear. I particularly want to thank him for the excellent job he did in regard to the relocation for the Grants Pass ODF office. Well done!

My personal upheaval at work had come at about this same time period. Late in my first summer back in Grants Pass (1976) things began to unravel. My problems had little to do with the actual skills needed to get my job done. I was unable to do much except swallow a lot of dissatisfaction and ride it out.

It was very complicated.

Adjustments at several other ODF districts came into being, tweaking my situation each time. This continued all winter, the entire following year and more. I was up to my knees trying desperately to get our house to a point so our kids could come home. Big issues from a totally different source at work were most unwelcome.

Essentially a rash of job shuffling in ODF locally and across the state that fall were because of a budget shortfall. The first change came when the SWO Management Forester job opened up. This was because of the transfer of my immediate management supervisor. The opening was essentially the same job at the same level I'd left in Coos Bay. That demotion, just a few months previous, had been at my request. When I'd been in that supervision role, I thought I'd done well - also in the reforestation position in Astoria before. My unit bosses had been happy with my work. Upon learning of the pending opening at GPHQ, I was at first quite hopeful about regaining my earlier rank.

The Department could have offered the opening to me, but didn't. This action confused me, and hurt more than a little too. Even worse and counter to the normal process, no applications were taken and no interviews were held for the now open job.

Instead, the Area Director in Roseburg decided to use the empty position to solve a problem he had with a job elsewhere in the Southern Oregon area that was about to lose funding. The odd-man-out was currently at a Forester I level in Roseburg, and he had no forest management experience.

I was surprised, even shocked when the fellow was promoted into the GP Unit Forester 2 Management job with none of the usual promotional process occurring. More than most people, I was well aware of the complexities of Forest Management positions. I had put much time and effort into learning the specific background support information for both the Clatsop and Elliott State Forests to be able to handle the management needs that the job required. Even back here in SWO, kind of my own backyard, there was a conglomerate of issues that had demanded a purposeful educational approach to just the reforestation assignment.

The poor guy newly selected to fill the Forester 2 job did not have any supporting experience at all. Unless he was Superman, he was going to be in way over his head for a year or two. There was a serious, very large job to get done in SWO. For the sake of the district's forests, someone with management knowledge would have to guide the new guy in a crash-course for a job that was difficult at even the most basic level. I did know there were a couple of local, in-district forest technicians that held dual assignments, sharing time with protection duties. They would probably give the new fellow some help.

At this point, I was disappointed and had some very hurt feelings. It took a while before I felt genuine sympathy for the new guy.

Things were going to get worse. Within a very short time, just weeks, both of the local part-time management technicians that could have helped out the new guy, transferred to open fire-related jobs in other districts. At that point, all the top tier supervision people in the SWO District offices were strictly fire guys too. There was no one to provide any of the vital forest management know-how and guidance to the newly assigned head of the Management Unit ... with one exception. There was me.

The Area Director in Roseburg had accidentally set up a very difficult circumstance. Fortunately, the local GP Unit Forester was an honest and genuine kind of guy – his words and attitude were good examples. I approve and admire people who gather information and try to come to a clear, unbiased decision without a lot of drama. Just as he dealt with the challenge of the physical change of location for the district HQ, he shared ideas up front to help me and the other fellow in this mess, without hidden agendas or any manipulation or attempts to shilly-shally around behind the backs of others. I gladly accepted and appreciated this. Such people are kind of rare, complete with warts of temper or whatever, and do not pretend to cater any special audience.

So now I was in the really odd situation of holding a lower rated job position and doing that job, while also unofficially advising and assisting (with no authority whatsoever) my supposed direct supervisor in forest management. There was important work to be done, which coincidently, would help the newbie to hold his job.

We three continued in this very strange setup for about a year and a half. I came to realize I had no choice in the matter, except maybe resignation. That was out of the question. Mostly I was left on my own to figure out the particulars of how to deal with the obvious conflict of the relationship at work. Not very happy, but driven by my own standards, I did my very best helping the new fellow learn, plan out and execute the forest needs and run the overall Forest Management Unit, as well as to carry out my very demanding reforestation piece of the stewardship job as well. I was busy with this unsatisfactory duel-role, finding it as stressful as my out-of-work home life.

Eventually the new fellow sought a transfer out of the SWO District. Shortly after that transfer, he left ODF for a job with Weyerhaeuser. A couple of years later, downsizing by the giant timber corporation eliminated the position he held there. I lost track of him after that. In retrospect, he definitely got the worst end of the whole mess.

I was pretty peeved when the same Forester 2 position once more was vacant in 1978. This time the job was posted according to the normal process, and I applied through the regular channels for the again empty SWO Unit Management position. I figured I would easily fulfill, probably far exceed, whatever job requirements that could be included in the job description.

I interviewed successfully for the job. Without much fanfare, there I was, back to the Forester 2 rank I'd held in Coos Bay almost two years previous. I was a bit banged up by office politics that were well outside my sphere, and also coping with the really big responsibilities at home that had hammered my family all at the same time … but I was still functioning.

At least during that difficult time, I'd been lucky enough to know how to successfully accomplish all the forestry work that had to be done. In addition, I had the benefit of a strong family holding the fort on the home-side.

There was a vitally important bright spot. The thing that set off my unwilling progression through all these difficult circumstances, our little girl's poor health, had improved greatly. After we moved into the new house, she suffered through one bad asthmatic bout that went to pneumonia. After that, no more. Thank God.

After all the dust settled, my marriage was still intact and all three kids were now healthy. We also had a new, albeit not quite completed house located pretty close to where we'd always wanted to live. It could have been much, much worse.

One day about then I found myself stumbling over the doorsill of the entrance into a classroom filled with little kids. They were all somewhere around age six; most of them didn't even top out at my waist.

Smokey the Bear visits first grade schoolrooms with Fire Prevention messages.
Courtesy of ODF Grants Pass Unit

I had figuratively lost a coin toss to determine who at the office had to dress up in the very heavy, uncomfortable Smoky Bear suit for an elementary school Fire Prevention presentation.

I was too tall for the suit, so I had to slouch the whole time. It was also hot and itchy, and I couldn't see well. One of my co-workers was my helper to make sure I didn't trip over desks, or worse, children. I wasn't supposed to say anything, just wave and make motions.

We'd finished the prescribed script for the visit, and were working our way through the crush of short bodies toward the door to leave. I felt a small hand on the furry suit at my arm.

I struggled to see who was trying to get my attention. A pair of enormous deep-blue eyes and a thatch of untidy white-blond hair was scarcely within my very limited line of sight, but immediately I recognized him

His soft voice came to my ears as my son said, "Hi Dad." The quiet message showed he didn't want to spoil the illusion for his classmates.

There was no fooling my kid! His warm childish smile showed that he'd recognized his old man in spite of the disguise. A very special secret message was passed to me from my little boy. It was something to treasure. It might have been lost.

The moment reminded me that the efforts my wife and I had put into the difficult move from my Coos job to our home back in Hugo were justified. I had learned a very valuable lesson from that trying time. I realized that when I chose to protect and nurture my family, that decision had become the definition of who I was as a person – because any loss in that part of my life would have been unbearable. The volunteer work in Coos had needed to be cut-back. My job, though important, would always be second to my wife and children. I may have to accept certain conditions because of this choice, but in the larger scheme of things, I would never regret that decision.

I was working alone in the management office mid-morning one day not too long after the promotion, when the Unit Forester came in. There had been a lightning storm the evening before, so it had been a busy summer day for the fire crews, with much coming and going all around the office.

The boss was sending me on a tricky fire located along the Rogue River downstream a bit from the Hellgate Canyon formation toward Galice. The familiar landscape in that canyon when moving away from the river flow is pretty barren, and this fire was currently burning in light fuels with short grass, scattered brush and clumps of runty trees. The soils are so poor there, that the canyon will not support much vegetation. I have often remarked that in places like this and others in SWO with serpentine influenced soils, more vegetation of any kind simply will not grow unless something else on the site dies first.

The lightning caused fire had started on the south hillside just above the river and bridge approach. If this fire got into the heavier fuels upslope (such as conifers and thick brush), the potential was there to become a very serious problem. Mostly because access was so difficult. Also, just over the top of the ridge, a trackless wildland filled with explosive fuels continued for several miles. The outlook for a big fire in a remote location was very bad.

The county road from Merlin to Galice rises up to higher on the hillside going toward the viewpoint for Hellgate Canyon. Then the road descends to a point that is about 150 to 200 feet above the river's actual water flow. The roadway stays nearly level onto the new bridge (built after the 1964 flood), crossing the river not far upstream from the ever-popular county-owned Indian Mary Park.

The boss told me to take charge of this incident – that is, acting as Incident Commander (IC). I remember it particularly well because it was a really nice change for me to be IC in the daylight. That he was showing confidence in me with this assignment was gratifying.

The man had many years of protection experience under his belt and any advice he had to share was worth listening to. Before I left HQ, he told me what resources I had available, and to focus especially on a helicopter bucket operation.

There were ground crews already on the fire, but in limited number because of so many incident commitments elsewhere. Because of the serious potential, I had two large and one medium sized helicopter at my disposal. Such riches of resources also made this fire special for me. With the river literally a stone's throw away, there was an unlimited amount of water available as well. The boss's last comment to me was that he expected me to direct the copters to "wash the fire off the mountain".

One end of the over-view turnout north of the river had become the Command Post (CP). There was very little room for considerable distance along the narrow roadway for parking space on either side. Since there was no access off-road to the fire for the engines, and distance from the road was not practical for even a long hose lay to reach, the engine crews that had been called out left their trucks and joined the hand crews.

There was only one really big problem that almost immediately became obvious on this fire, even before I arrived on the scene. It was approaching mid-summer, also most aptly known as "The Tourist Season". It seemed like half the population of Josephine County had decided to take a drive out to Galice that afternoon. The influx of heavy traffic was apparent to me just driving to the fire.

A medium sized helicopter makes a water drop on a fire. Helicopter attack on wildland fire is very effective especially with a water supply close by.
Courtesy of Oregon Department of Forestry

I usually get an initial reaction when coming to an incident. As I drove near my destination, my first feeling about this fire was very positive. Terrific resources, adequate manpower and a dayshift IC role – for once a great fire assignment. It kind of belied the serious potential the boss man had conveyed. As I looked for a place to leave my rig, a good feeling of knowing my job and how to successfully get it done softly settled over me.

The larger helicopters we had that day could carry about 500 gallons of water each, and the medium one could haul about 150 – 200 gallons. All were able to draw water from any deeper spot in a river or pond. In this case the choppers would take on water from two moderately calm river pools, one just above and the other just below the bridge.

Whenever copters are used on a fire, emergency landing areas need to be established, as a remarkable number of dangerous conditions can occur especially in a narrow canyon like this one.

There were two wide turnouts on the county road shoulder upstream from the bridge that could serve well as emergency landing spots for the choppers while they dipped at the upper pool. If they ran into any problems lifting out of the river, these spots would be nearly level or just down hill from any place from the fire itself. The other fill-area below the bridge also had a nearby escape landing spot at a rough but usable place on the lower sandy bank of the river located below the road.

The two big turnouts were quickly emptied, with vital command vehicles safely moved to one side. The space was designated as emergency landing for the copters.

As soon as space was cleared, it seemed that all the lookie-loos out for a drive felt these were irresistible vacant-looking spaces designated just for tourists to stop and gawk at the fire and the interesting work of the helicopters.

It was obvious within moments that the mass of on-lookers was limiting needed copter activities. A potential catastrophe coming from this chaos was in the making unless something was done.

I made a brief review of the fire suppression work, which was going quite well. I recruited a couple of our bigger, more imposing young men from the crews on the hillside to patrol the landing areas and make sure the two emergency copter sites stayed totally clear of vehicles. I also sent word to HQ to find some traffic control signs in the warehouse there, and asked that they be ferried the twelve to fifteen miles out to the fire for posting along the roadway. These much-needed supplies arrived in record time.

Soon the poor guys I had put onto landing patrol work were about worn to a frazzle, maybe even putting out more physical effort than those building hand lines on the fire. Not a moment went by when they weren't kept busy having to chase away some new car wanting to get a good look at the fire or the copters or both. It would seem that many of those drivers simply were unable to read a simple sign that said "NO Stopping", "NO Parking", or "Keep Back". Because of the excess of traffic, we sent a message to Dispatch to contact the local radio stations with the plea, asking people to stay away. Yet nothing seemed to help much.

The work on the fire was going smoothly, but seeing my hardworking traffic patrol guys over-whelmed a couple of times, I even helped them run cars off to keep the landings clear. The message to the persistent drivers - that if one of the helicopters had an emergency, it was possible it might just land right on top of their car - was effective, but had to be delivered over and over. When it penetrated through the fascination with the operation, interest in all that was going on seemed to wane quickly enough. Many drivers would nod in surprise then drive away, still looking back with interest as they left.

Really quick results getting the cars out of there came about when the copters would come down off the hill and were just hovering when filling and lifting their loaded buckets up out of the river. The big rotors would scream as they would create a very strong downdraft sending dirt and gravel flying all over, striking cars, chipping paint and glass, and even making small dents in hoods and side doors. It was kind of rough on those of us on foot trying to direct traffic too. This happened a lot, as the copters were very busy. When the rotors' roar would start up, drivers mostly would exit very quickly on their own without a word from us.

Later in the afternoon, people seemed to finally get the idea about keeping the emergency landing areas clear. Fewer cars turned in, so less energy was needed by those patrolling the site to keep the areas empty.

The fire died down pretty much as the daylight faded. I've heard arguments that you can't control a hot fire without hand crews, but in this particular case that is pretty much what happened. With the hand crews hard put to quickly build defensive line, we worked the helicopters hard most of the day. Still the encircling line was essential. Eventually the fire stopped spreading up the hill or to the sides. That fire was controlled primarily with water.

*A Heli-Tack Crew training. This method to deploy crews is a newer innovation. Crews
repel down lines to the ground to quickly access fires in remote locations.*
Courtesy of ODF Grants Pass Unit

CHAPTER 36

*S*ometimes people seem to forget that trees are living things that age and die. Older trees do not visually change much, giving an impression that they will continue in a certain state indefinitely. The term Old Growth is not so much an indication of age as it is more a description of a certain stage of life and stand structure. Trees cannot continue indefinitely at any stage of life anymore than kittens, elephants, or people. Living things that are old have issues.

Many of the more isolated parcels under ODF management were at that ending life stage. The norm with these sites was excessively mature stands in poor health. Most were over-stocked with trees where the quality was deteriorating throughout. My team coped with a lot of this, doing quality work bringing the out-laying units into good production as mandated by the mission of the department.

In some cases, earlier partial cuts had encouraged slower growing, but more prolific species (brush and hardwoods) now over-populated the stands. These situations were also lending to the deterioration of the larger conifers. Available water was sucked up near the surface before the deeper roots of the bigger trees could receive it.

About fifteen months or so after I initially reported for management work at SWO, I promoted into the Unit Management Forester position. By then the time I spent with the Reforestation and Rehab area brought the files much more up-to-date. I directed my small management team to select the out-laying land parcels on the wide-spaced edges of the unit for our main focus. On several of these complex sites, we spent a longer than average span of time.

The extra care was needed because my review of the files showed these locations had seen little management activity for so long. They were also some of the most diverse and complicated parcels to analyze in the district.

A BIGGER SHOVEL

There is an old saying about when a person discovers they are in a big hole they should stop digging. After our move from Coos Bay, either I wasn't smart enough to recognize that all my time was already pretty much committed, or I just didn't think things were really that busy. It seems that around then I went looking for a bigger shovel (more things to do) – and kept digging away.

Back in Coos Bay, after we'd decided to move to Hugo but before the house construction and weird shake-up at the ODF office, my mom approached me about taking on the farming responsibilities on her property. At that time, taking on the farm work seemed a very appealing and realistic idea. Then our house construction got into the way of most of the farm work for some time.

It was in mid-winter of 1976 that we first chose to run a cow and calf to help use up some of the hay harvested off the old farm. My mom had sold off all of Dad's livestock, except that one cow/calf pair. I bought the pregnant cow, thinking my growing family could use a source of cheaper meat. I wasn't about to get tied down to milking twice a day, but the cow could raise calves for locker meat. Besides, the continual interruptions to the many demands on our time by people wanting to buy only one or two bales of hay had become a major annoyance. Having the cow eat the hay was supposed to make things go smoother. It didn't quite work that way.

Well, actually in some ways it was easier, but only when things went right. People who deal with cows will tell anyone who will listen that for every time things go right with cattle, there are a whole lot more times that they do not – usually with much drama and bother. Cattle, even quiet and tame ones, are much like cats – they do their own thing unless forced to do otherwise – and forcing a half-ton cow is a whole lot more difficult that forcing a house cat.

In early spring the next year, our mama cow produced twin heifer calves, and then another heifer the following year. I don't like to use heifers for meat, so asked a friend to act in my place, and buy some steer-calves for us at the Medford Livestock Auction to fatten. He misunderstood, bringing back four more heifers.

At the same time our girls joined 4-H. (As did the boy when he was old enough.) They all chose Market Beef Cattle projects. The girls' two steers were purchased with money borrowed from savings accounts set up by their grandma when each was born. When both girls made a nice profit that summer after their project calves were sold and expenses paid, both were able to buy another steer plus their own heifers too. In just three years we were unexpectedly and heavily involved in the cow-calf business. Altogether the herd we had on the land was producing up to a dozen baby calves each spring.

Ah, for the carefree days of my youth. I thought I was over-worked on the farm back then. Little did I know! My wife and all three kids helped as they could, but since I never could be at the farm full-time, we played an on-going game of catch-up. The kids usually accompanied me to the barn twice per day to feed. Other smaller daily chores were divvied between children and wife making the very demanding life-style do-able. Except that no one in the family had much free time. Similar to my childhood, our kids roamed the less used areas of their grandmother's farm. They enjoyed the same encounters with flora and fauna as I had, resulting in moments of wonder and the occasional scarped knee or broken bone.

Originally, we operated the farm on a business basis with my mom, where annual rent plus all expenses were paid to her, and we assumed all profit (not much) and loss (a lot). I thought the situation was different than what my dad had faced on the same property. In the ways that really count, it was pretty similar. Little income, little time, limited help.

I came to realize that some pretty sizable pieces of my Dad's personality had somehow slyly been hidden inside me. Now I was the slave-driver Dad. As a kid it had confused me that my Dad seemed to seek out extra work. Here I was working fulltime at a very challenging job, and playing both carpenter and farmer in the evenings and on weekends. And I had no nearly full-sized teenaged boys able to do major farm chores or work with the animals. Our little guy had just started kindergarten and our older girl was barely eleven. Today, our family has a long and lively list of family tales involving our escapades with on the farm and with the cattle through those years.

I never missed the Jaycee activities I'd left behind in Coos Bay, but then I had no downtime to miss anything. I actually enjoyed the farm lifestyle, felt pride in accomplishing the house construction, and gained much satisfaction from doing my ODF job well. Eventually I even returned to playing city-league basketball again. After a few years, my long-limbed growing son joined me.

Over time the arrangement for use of the farmland with my mom drained us so much, both in time and expense, that my mom and I sought out a solution. We reorganized a different way to remit for use of the land. Along with much needed household and medical help coming to my mom from my brother and sister, and with me keeping the land productive, our mom was able to stay in her much-cherished home on the farm in spite of failing health. She died in her own bed several years later.

Time-wise the farm responsibilities took about twenty extra hours per week out of my schedule. Every spring there was a period of dawn to dusk work for about two weeks at a stretch, devoted to harvesting the hay crop. From my perspective now, forty years in the future, once again I think I was nuts.

But, most importantly, my family was back together, working at a common task. In Hugo grandparents, aunts and uncles, and life-long friends were just down the road – a gift of an unusually close community for our children to experience in the modern busy world where such things were pretty rare.

There were many small things with our house that remained unfinished for years – just from lack of time for finishing. These didn't seem very important. Our lives took on an annual rhythm that was heavily connected to the seasons of the year and school calendar. As usual, we were strapped for cash.

My wife's contribution to finally solve our ongoing financial dilemma, was to return to college and earn a teaching degree. She had always followed a plan for this, taking tiny steps toward her goal over many years. When our youngest began school, the time had come to put all her time and energy into getting the plan fulfilled. It took her two years to finish the degree requirements. Immediately after her college graduation, my wife began working as a substitute teacher for the remainder of that school year, then began teaching full-time the next fall.

The huge demands on my wife's time while finishing college meant more adjustments around home. The kids did most of the housework and I began doing stuff like Parent-Teacher Conferences or taking a half-day from work to wait for the washing machine repairman to show up.

When my wife began teaching full-time, it was apparent that the new way of doing things would continue as the norm. Eventually the upheaval after moving to the farm settled into a demanding but predictable family routine. For the next ten to twelve years, seasons and school years followed neatly in a row like railroad cars on a track. We hardly noticed as our kids grew taller and older. We continued to be slightly surprised as each, in their respective time and place, graduated from high school. These rich and wonderful years flew past in the blink of an eye. Between school concerts, extra-curricular sports and showing cattle in 4-H at the summer county fair every year, my wife and I were able to share a great deal of time with our children as they grew into adults.

New patrol engine design about 1978. Note: dual hose reels and red paint.
Courtesy of ODF Grants Pass Unit

My kids sometimes were included into the mix as my management crew and I handled the requirements of the job. My guys were working several spring days on a contract spray-job in the Glendale area. I decided to have the spray helicopter kept over-night in our front pasture (about 3 acres in size). It was quite secure there and it saved a little fuel the next morning by not flying all the way back to the HQ location. Having a genuine helicopter essentially in the front yard was pretty special to all three of my kids. Many questions were asked and answered, with lingering inspections and explorations allowed.

Other things that sort of fell into my lap brought home and worked together while my wife was off at school. Our farm had a weed issue in the same field where the helicopter had been parked. I decided to burn off the problem rather than spray herbicide on three plus acres. The kids helped me trail the site with the tractor and disc, and were given a briefing on why and how we would proceed on the burn. With permits in hand and an ODF engine crew on site, we lit up with a drip torch, burning from the top of the hill down. It was a cool fall day, but the kids were properly impressed with the fast-moving and scary looking grass fire. It took maybe twenty minutes total for the whole field to burn. The children learned the delights of fire mop-up first hand. Soon after, a mid-fall rain and a couple of sunny days, the field turned into an even green carpet.

One of the main fire protection support activities that I became heavily involved with, was that of Aerial Observer for fire spotting following lightning storms. Upon occasion during summer vacations, I would take my young son along when I was aerial spotting for smokes after a lightning bust.

Both my boy and I learned the hard way that unlike his dad, he gets airsick. Also, since babyhood he has had the ability to fall deeply asleep almost instantly, anywhere - including in a small uncomfortable airplane searching for smokes. Needless to say, any emerging potential as a future Aerial Fire-spotter didn't show up in my son.

I also hauled the poor kid along when doing contract administrative chores connected to forest management work. One evening after a long day driving to different logging sites in the woods, my son shared the highlight of his day. I thought it wasn't very important, but at the dinner table he announced a bit of news that made my wife kind of upset.

"Hey Mom," he said with true awe in his voice. "Dad drove his truck over the top of a log deck!"

I didn't think this was such a big deal – my work rig was a 4x4 and the logs that were in the way were only about 12 to 15 inches in diameter. The pile was only a few logs high, but my son apparently was pretty impressed. My wife had ridden many back-woods roads with me. With maybe too much insight into my off-highway driving habits, and more than a little familiarity with the SWO mountains, she did not approve. Especially when our youngest was in the vehicle with me. She made it clear I needed to mend my ways.

With about half our herd of cows belonging to our kids, it was only fair that they take on a good share of the work involved. During the school year the three of them accompanied me to the barn each morning before school and again in the evening before dinner. There were times they were called upon to handle this work by themselves.

Sometimes in the summer the children changed a short stretch of irrigation pipe as well as feeding the livestock. Later when they left home, my wife did the honors. "Manure Happens" was kind of a motto for our family, with the double meaning apparent to all members.

The added income from my wife's teaching job, when combined with my own paycheck, finally removed the financial sword that had hung over our family from the beginning. It was just in time too. When the oldest girl entered high school, we discovered that formal dresses, various sports events, a general expansion in her wardrobe and other teen requirements found a way to put big dents into the household budget. Also, feeding the unending parade of teen-agers that wandered through our house for about a decade, rivaled the cost of the national debt.

My wife and I ended up as 4-H Club leaders, although normally I was pretty tied up during the mid-August County Fair connected to the program. When summer demands of my job kept me busy and absent, everyone seemed to manage.

After all the years of using my personal leave time for the hay harvest, skipping things like family vacations had become something of a habit. The lack of an annual extended trip somewhere never seemed to bother my kids much, as it was simply the way of things in our life.

An excellent example of why summer-time requests for vacation-time away from work just didn't fit our life-style happened one August. Most of the time my job and home-life revolved in different worlds, with only an occasional cross over. Then a summer came about that produced a collision bigger than average. I was my own fault – I shouldn't have asked for the time off.

That year I had arranged my State Lands Management fieldwork so that, for the first time, I could use some personal vacation leave time during the August County Fair. Our 4-H Club was scheduled to show their beef animals at the county fair. Our three kids and a few others from the Merlin/Hugo area were involved.

ODF employees and their families understood that requests for time-off during fire season might not hold-up unless truly urgent personnel needs occurred. Fire calls pretty well took precedence.

Our kids had invested in breeding stock, as did a couple of our other 4-H club members. The club was small in membership and large in animal count. Also, that spring our family's small purebred herd had welcomed its first registered bull calf and we decided to show him in Open Class. By then our girls were showing both cattle and sheep in their high school FFA program. With animals in three different shows, a busy fair week was ahead.

We'd all spent the weekend before opening day of fair getting ready. This included several trips from Hugo to the fairgrounds in south Grants Pass, cleaning barn space, building and decorating display areas, moving equipment and feed.

On my first requested day off – the Monday prior to opening of the fair the next morning, we started loading animals at first light, around 5 AM. After making three round trips to the fairgrounds, loading and unloading, setting up our stalls and tack areas, and finally bedding down the animals, we had just arrived back home at about 10 PM at night.

The kids were zonked and would be immediately sent to bed, with another early morning wake-up call set for the next exciting day. My wife and I had at least another hour of gathering show clothes and other small necessities before going to bed as well. The telephone began to ring as soon as we walked through the kitchen door.

It was the newest Grants Pass Unit Forester. He was calling with a fire assignment for me. A very large fire in the Northeastern area of Oregon was going great-guns. He told me that I was to be at HQ at 2 AM, ready to travel to Wallowa with three others fellows from Grants Pass ODF.

With much experience from previous call-outs, my wife gathered and packed my fire gear. As she worked, I lay down for a short nap trying to get at least a little rest. Mostly I worried about how she and the kids would deal with the responsibilities of the fair, plus chores with the animals left home as well.

My traveling companions were three guys from my management crew who were switched over to protection in the summer months. We would take two vehicles, one of which was assigned to my State Lands program. It was a brand-new Ford ¾ ton 4x4, still showing glue on the windshield from the temporary license.

The ODF people met up at HQ at the proper time, pairing up in the two trucks. Traveling in tandem and by the shortest route we could, off we went into the wicked hours of the night, driving across the state to Wallowa, almost on the eastern border. As the crow flies, the distance is nearly 500 miles. In Oregon there aren't many roads that provide a straight shot anywhere.

None of our team expected a Sunday tour type of drive, but it turned out to be a more brutal trip than any of us imagined. Not only had all the other guys worked a full eight hours in the field that same day, but after my hardworking weekend, plus a 17-hour day of fair prep, I was just about useless.

Our whole group was having a lot of trouble staying awake, even with trading off driving chores. We tried everything - driving with the windows down and frequent stops. Nothing seemed to help much. We even stopped a few times where cold streams were near the road, splashing icy water on our faces and running laps around the trucks.

Before we'd left, we agreed that each of us would take the wheel for about two hours before changing drivers. This allotted driving time got shorter and shorter with each change as we all became more and more tired. None of us could keep our eyes open longer than a few minutes. The whole drive took about twelve hours.

We finally arrived in Wallowa at about mid-afternoon on Tuesday. We were still alive, but not exactly at the top of our game. Our first task was reporting in at the Resources desk at Fire Camp. We were told to get some rest, (Wonderful!) and report for briefing at 5 PM to go onto night shift. (Are you kidding?) Talk about the Walking Dead.

The Fire Camp was for a "complex", or in other words, there were several fires being managed out of this same Fire Camp that was located at Wallowa High School. We were all on the night shift, but split up between various incidents. I was given a Division Supervisor role, assigned to the largest of the fires, the Wildcat Canyon Fire.

There was a need for a 4x4 pickup for deliveries and other overland jobs, so my program's brand-new rig was switched ASAP for something else in the camp car pool. I ended up being assigned a 4x4 Chevy Suburban that I shared with a day shift guy, also the Division Supervisor for the same section of the fire I worked.

We had been told that we could bed down in either the school gym or the Weight Room. As is with every facility like these I've ever been in, it was impossible to get any good rest especially during the day. With lots of foot traffic in and out of the building and the camp noise seeping in from outdoors, it was a nightmare of massive proportions. Both rooms echoed every sound, and the crashing of heavy doors opening and closing throughout the school building was downright horrible, sounding like bombs dropping at every opening and closing. A loud "crack" was heard as the panic bar released the latch, then BOOM as the heavy door would swing closed. Crack – BOOM! Crack – BOOM! It went on all day.

Nearing the shift change that first day, my sleep deprived body stumbled from my sleeping-bag in the gym to the pre-shift briefing. That noisy gym didn't promote languishing abed anyhow.

The following first night's twelve-hour shift was just plain awful! I was working in an almost stuporous state, and do not know how I stayed awake during the full tour. Driving back to camp from the fire to attend the next morning's 5 AM briefing would have been interesting to observe. Suffice to say somehow, I arrived back at Fire Camp alive, not rolled up in a completely mashed up vehicle at the bottom of some mountain canyon. Frankly, my own memory of the drive from home and the first day is hazy at best. The briefing of the following morning is completely wiped from my memory. I think I may have been asleep with my eyes open. I hope I at least looked awake.

The second night in the gym brought only the worst kind of sleep, if any.

Only absolute and totally consuming fatigue made things any better, but still inadequate. Sometime in there, though, I hit my second-wind.

There must have been a lot of complaints about lack of quiet and available rest, because the next night, the third, many of the Overhead guys were provided rooms at the local motel. That is capital T-H-E motel.

The night shift guys, like me, were "Hot Bedding" it with day shift people. Never a real positive situation. Kudos to the motel staff of that small town. They managed to get clean sheets on the beds between shift changes. Well done, and much appreciated.

In the darkened motel-room it was possible to get some good sleep – but awakening at the right time was more than a small challenge. Clean sheets and quiet rooms tended to encourage over-sleeping. Of course, with the day shift guy shaking your shoulder wanting you out of the sack so the sheets could be changed and he could take over the bed, lying around was kind of hard.

In spite of those first ugly nights sort-of half dozing in the school gym, I was up and around a little early before my third shift. I wanted to see the area in the daylight to kind of get my bearings. That day the cool morning air was brisk and helping me become more alert at least for a little bit.

I was looking around the operations center trying to come to full wakefulness, when someone said that the IC was looking for me. After I tracked him down, he asked if I could spend about an hour to recon the fire by air. (This experience would have been listed on my personnel sheet.) I was assigned a helicopter and was told to report back as to what seemed the best course of action to try for containment on my assigned fire of the complex.

One of the biggest issues with that particular fire, was that Wildcat Canyon neatly divided the burning area, from north to south, in two equal parts. The fire was progressing upstream traveling to the south. The canyon had extremely steep sidewalls with a shallow waterway in the bottom. Currently that topography was working against the suppression efforts. There weren't any access roads that crossed from one side of the canyon to the other without a long drive way out and around to the south. Several times resources from one shift were reassigned to the other side of the fire for the next shift. This made it difficult for replacing operators on equipment, or for me and the other Division Supervisors to even find and line out our resources to begin work after each shift change.

A nice chilly copter ride was just what I needed to get my tired brain back on function mode. I quickly went to the copter pad and found the aircraft warmed up and waiting for me. We took off immediately. After circling the perimeter of the fire, I had the pilot fly as slowly as possible up the canyon. I could see where several attempts had been made to put trails down the canyon walls on either side. In each case the fire had always escaped the line.

Although probably not apparent from the ground, from the air it was easy to see the reasons for the repeated escapes. The control lines had not met up at the bottom, but were offset by 50 to 100 feet. The steepness of the slopes allowed a lot of fairly large burning material to roll downhill with such force that debris would bounce across the small stream in the bottom and over to the other side. The burning litter would sometimes be landing outside the trailed area, on unburned and tinder-dry ground. Quickly the fire would catch hold and race up the other slope to the top. This seesaw had been repeated several times as the fire progressed up the canyon, frustrating current control efforts. There was a need to amend strategies.

Moving further up the canyon I saw an area where, if we moved the control lines about 200 yards upstream, we could put the trails on incoming side-ridges that actually met at the canyon bottom. By using this advantage of terrain configuration, the change in slope face would be an advantage. If any burning stuff did roll down and bounce across the stream it would still be inside the fire lines.

Keeping this vision of strategy in my mind, I indicated to the pilot for us to quickly return to the copter pad. I reported back to the IC and the Line Chief about what I saw, described the landscape and shared my recommendations. I also suggested that we try to install a pump and hose lays in the streambed near the place where the fire lines would meet at the bottom. Using the ready water supply there would help make sure that we had no more escapes near the streambed. It was a bit risky for the guys at the bottom, so lookouts would be necessary.

The set-up was easy to describe but more of a challenge to build. Nevertheless, the suggestions were implemented over the next shift and we achieved containment and control on that fire in another couple of days.

When mop-up began, more than a week had passed since I'd left home. When I was released I went looking for my "new" State Lands rig. I would be driving home alone because the other three guys I'd come with were remaining on their respective fires they'd been assigned to. For at least a few more days they would stay, riding home together in the second truck to SWO.

It took awhile to find the new pickup. For one thing, it didn't look so new anymore. It had been thoroughly trashed, was filthy inside and out and would hardly run because the air filter was so plugged with dust and ash. It was also in need of an oil and filter change. The local ODF shop took care of the maintenance issues, but I had to handle the washing and cleaning out the inside myself. Even after the clean up it smelled like a giant burned marshmallow on the long drive home. I was very tired, so took much care on the long drive home alone.

There was an unusual result that came out of our Wallowa assignment – at least new for me. I filed my summary Fire Report, and turned it in as expected. Normally that is the end of an incident for mid-tier guys like me, but a little more occurred this time. I'd mentioned in my report the fatigued condition of my traveling companions and me when first arriving at the Fire Camp, plus the various sleep issues following.

An outcome from that complex fire was that Resources at Check-in after that were required to ask new people when they checked in at Fire Camp what was the last time they had sufficient sleep? That way people would not be put in the same dangerous situation that our group had been, being assigned on the line with little or no rest. This consequence may have come from any one of several other origins, but at least I felt that somebody was reading the submitted summaries.

I think that I got back home on a Tuesday or Wednesday, over a week after leaving. I learned that the newest unit boss at the GP office, (infamous by all who knew him as a champion in unawareness and being forgetful), had called my home the day or two before on Monday, asking why I was not at work that day? It seems he thought I'd been on vacation all the previous week, having no memory about calling me out the previous Monday night.

The fair had closed the previous Saturday night. All day Sunday my family had handled the reverse of the set-up chores, breaking down displays and moving animals back home. My wife, after the exhaustive fair week, was in no mood to coddle my spacey boss.

After close to twenty years of marriage, she was well aware that it was within the Unit Forester's prerogative to call out any and all ODF personnel during Fire Season. This time though, she was pretty offended that this boss had sent me off to a big out-of-district fire and forgotten completely about it. She gave him a terse ear-full, essentially saying "You should know where he is since you, personally, sent him there!" The remark was 100% on the mark.

With the new boss, this kind of stuff happened too often, but the guy seemed totally unaware of his problem. It is my opinion that my wife let him off easy. The dispatch people were always excellent about notifying families and keeping track of people – why hadn't he talked with them? His ability to "shine-off" just about anything that didn't slam into his face was remarkable. He never seemed to learn to take notes or use any other means to jog his bad memory – and was continually baffled by the numerous problems it caused for other people.

During my absence the boss had also taken a telephone call from a lady landowner whose property abutted an access road to a state timber sale. She was rightfully upset about the dust issue caused by trucks hauling logs past her house. Normally this type of issue would have been mine to handle, but of course I had been sent out of town. My boss promised the lady that he'd contact the sale buyer about the issue, then promptly dismissed the problem. His lack of action after the complaint made a really big mess for me to fix when I returned two weeks later. That lady was much angrier after being ignored for another couple of weeks. The irate taxpayer roasted my ear over the telephone, while the boss man was unscathed.

As for my wife, she is a quiet and patient person. I doubt it ever even crossed the new boss's mind what Fire-wives might have to contend with, usually without complaint, when husbands just kind of disappear. Even with the very best scenario, people are gone sometimes for several weeks, then arrive home with a pile of laundry stinking of smoke and dead tired. My family had endured a really rough week without my help. The legendary ability of that particular supervisor to just ignore such stuff had touched an open sore with my wife that put him in the cross hairs. She never did warm up to him while he was assigned to the GPHQ.

I didn't mind being called-out for fires - it was just the way things were, and in August very likely. My absence during the county fair had produced a handful of difficult problems that my wife and kids handled. I learned the whole story over time. I suffered some pangs of guilt as a result. That my too often space-case boss had been brought up short for thinking it was all trivial, actually gave me some comfort.

Between 1984 to 1990 our kids all graduated from high school. The nearly two decades when our children were in school had been very busy and structured. Year-round things were predicable, even organized. In retrospect, especially the 1980s seemed to disappear in a rush of busy days.

At the time, I didn't think my family was much affected by my job. If so, only from a distance. Over many years, the up-close connections seemed to be few, but must have had some impact. My kids know a whole lot about my job - more than I ever realized.

CHAPTER 37

When I came to the SWO Reforestation job I knew exactly what my first efforts would be. Having done this twice before, I needed to make sure I was well versed about all the lands that were my responsibility. Since the location was where I'd grown up and I'd fought fire all over the district for five years, I was pretty well informed about the landscape involved. This was good.

I was aware that the specifics of each block of ownership would require that I spend time on the ground checking for details. Thankfully the total number of acres was considerably less than in my earlier assignments. On the negative side, the district was large, but each parcel of the SWO lands was (and still are) generally small in size. But they are also located all over the map, with almost half just barely beyond the district boundaries. Another complicating factor was the great diversity of the district. Many disciplines related to forestry came into play with this new posting, requiring a more general approach to successfully manage the lands under my responsibility.

The few consolidated parcels of land I first wanted to inspect were long distances from the office. Much of the management activities from previous years had been in the larger, closer blocks. When I came on the scene, it was a challenge to simply find the ODF sites among the patchwork of ownerships in the district. The goal was to apply sustainable forest management that met the Plan for the whole district. Daily transportation to and from some locations for everyday fieldwork was not always a simple thing.

I decided to aggressively face the problem. I directed my very small crew to actively seek out the most remote SWO locations, at least for a look-see. I also chartered light aircraft so I could fly-over most parcels and take up-to-date photographs.

BUG BATTLES AND LONG DRIVES

While my children were growing up and my wife now dealing with her own professional career, I was coping with the challenges and changes in the SWO forest management unit. From the beginning, spending time in the field brought peace of mind and satisfaction to me. I'm an outdoor type.

After leaving Coos, there were a few projects that had been left undone when the first forester left the management position in Grants Pass. Most of these prescribed actions were thoroughly planned, but not yet completed. We had some fieldwork on a timber sale to finish near the top of McCullough Creek, west of Glendale about thirty miles north of the GP HQ office. The site is the second largest tract of SWO ODF ownership in the district. It contains about 1900 acres.

This was soon after my family moved from Coos, so things were tough all around at that time. It was good for my general out-look to get out into the wilds as much as possible. Sometimes I think a good bit of mental health when adversity enters our lives, is to take a step-back from the situation and keep a sense of humor.

This particular day was one when seeing the funny side was badly needed. My hoped-for time for peace and renewal didn't pan out.

It was mid-summer 1977; another very bad year for yellow jackets in SWO. Such summers seem to be cyclic, loosely connected to heavy rains and high/low temperatures at just the right times. Once more the much-despised wildland summertime wasps seemed to be everywhere in large numbers.

Bald Hornets have a bad reputation, but by comparison to the yellow jackets they are the nice guys. With Bald Hornets the bottom line is you simply leave them alone. Their distinctive balloon-like above-ground paper nests are often built high up in trees or shrubs. By being on the lookout and somewhat careful when in the woods, the nests can be seen and avoided. It becomes second nature to those working in SWO wildland sites to maintain such a watchful eye.

On the other hand, yellow jackets favor nesting in hidden lairs underground or in old rotten logs and stumps. It's easy to be caught unawares when moving through brushy country. You are walking along minding your own business, when suddenly, without really knowing where or how you disturbed them, several dozen of the small, evil-tempered buzzing biters surround you, doing their best to make you immediately miserable. The only solution is to run out of their protected area ASAP, trying to slap them away as you go. Knowing which way to run can be a tough choice.

Yellow jackets are extremely protective of their nests. They spend most of their time patrolling and looking to get after anything that moves in their chosen territory. Not being a bee, but a type of wasp, they can sting multiple times. Strong and sharp pincher type jaws let them bite as many times as they want. The bites hurt as bad as the sting, often drawing blood, just without the venom. Add to all this, these critters actually seem to go around trying to seek out victims.

These nasty little guys don't mess around when upset – they are tenacious and easily sting through lightweight clothing. They are so persistent that they will give more than a good college try to their protection efforts. I've seen them make repeated efforts to sting through a steel-plate covering on a warm bulldozer engine.

Our newly put together management crew that summer had already spent some time marking and cruising for a sale on Little Bull Run Creek, a tributary of Quines Creek on the northeast side of the Cow Creek valley. We'd encountered a lot of the yellow-stripped critters there, so were on the lookout.

The bug-alert situation continued on up to the higher elevation of McCullough Creek across the valley to the southwest – but it didn't help much that we were now on the watch for the much-despised tiny biters with stinger reinforcement. That I remember this very clearly forty years later gives a hint to how severe the problem was.

On that day, it seemed like every few minutes someone on our crew of about five would let out a howl and take off running in one direction or another. Usually the paint gun and Biltmore stick that was carried along, was tossed to the ground so as to swat more effectively while running. The problem then was, once away from the nest site with the wasps slapped off, it remained for each guy to sneak back carefully, hoping the little beasties had calmed down enough so the dropped tools could be quietly retrieved. If, by chance work was interrupted in mid-assessment, before paint markings were completed or all cruise data was recorded, even more caution was needed. That's because then it was necessary to return and stay long enough to finish cruising the last tree (or more) within the wasp patrol area. True dedication to the job was necessary.

The whole thing was kind of funny, but only to somebody watching from a distance well away from the angry wasps, or maybe remembering back in time. Picture a group of scruffy looking guys spread out on the hillside each in various stages of being chased off ... then sneaking back to where they'd been.

It may have appeared to be some kind of game, but it was no laughing matter to those of us under attack. For one thing, the stings inflicted by these flying pests can be very dangerous. Many people have allergic reactions to the venom and have even died when not treated quickly. Fortunately taking an antihistamine immediately can help considerably until medical attention can be obtained. Carrying a few allergy pills during summer work in the woods is a pretty good precaution.

As it was, all we could do was try to avoid the offensive little devils, do our job and lick our wounds.

About eighteen months later things were better in the office, but I still tried to get out into the field whenever opportunities were available. One of the more remote parcels of state ownership in the district had no current inventory records that I could find in the office files. It was a full section of Common School Land in eastern Curry County named Raspberry Mountain. (A Section of land is a square parcel that measures one mile on each side, and contains about 640 acres.) No one of our small team had ever been to that site, so I decided that a visit to the property was needed to look around.

A young guy I'd known from Coos had transferred to GP a short time after I'd moved. He'd been on my Coos team, and now filled a Forest Technician slot on my GP crew. We were pretty good friends. Our goal was to first find the parcel, then give the tract a quick once-over to see what might be needed there. What little information we had indicated that the parcel might contain some older timber. Just a good windstorm or fire could have changed that overnight. Eyes on the ground are best.

We loaded up our gear and lunches in a 4x4 pickup and took off on the route that seemed most direct. Up over Galice Creek to Bear Camp, and down the other side of the Coast Range. If we were lucky, we might be able to find the property before we got back down to the Rogue River, near Shasta Costa Creek.

It was late winter or early spring. As could be expected, we hit ever-deepening snow before we got to the highest ground at Bear Camp. The crusty snowdrifts finally defeated our efforts to drive through, so we decided to turn around and go back to HQ. Such conditions are not unusual in almost daily fieldwork required by jobs in the woods late fall through to spring.

At that time the two of us had about twenty plus years combined management experience within the Coast Range. We were veterans in following maps and finding our way to remote places in the woods. To say the environment is not forgiving is an under statement and we knew it. We still wanted to look over the property, but use of caution was wise. When we hit the snow, for safety sake we decided to try an alternate route the next day.

It's too bad those of us who work in the forest can't seem to convey the need for this type of caution to the general public.

A few years later at this exact same location, also in early winter, an elderly man and his dog became trapped in the snow. He had read a map that showed a road over the Coast Range, much shorter than the most traveled and maintained routes normally used. The man, in poor health and on crutches decided to try out what actually is a glorified logging road from well above Gold Beach to Merlin near Interstate 5. He ignored all the indications that the road was not well traveled and likely blocked by snow at high elevation. Two of my staff in the field that day, and driving a 4-wheel drive pick-up truck, pulled him cold and wet out of the snow. If not for more than a little good luck, the man would have been a winter fatality.

Going in the opposite direction a few years after that, a California family tried to use this same road, following GPS directions. Electronic directions are often deceiving and inaccurate, whether in the city or out in the woods. The excursion of this unfortunate family was also in the winter. The parents chose to venture on an unknown back-woods road. As soon as they saw snow they should have turned around.

They decided to try a short cut to travel from Interstate 5 to the coast from directions on the GPS say-so. They became lost exactly where we turned back that day. With two small children in their car they tried to force their way through. The car became high-centered and was stuck in the snow. There are many Dead-zones in Oregon where there is no cell-phone service. The family was declared missing, with many people risking their lives out searching. Finally, a helicopter spotted the car. Sadly, the father, not well experienced with Oregon's outdoors, attempted to walk out and get help. He became disoriented, likely due to hypothermia, left the roadway he was following and perished. His body was found a few days after his luckier wife and children were rescued at the site where the car was located.

Anyway, after our first unsuccessful attempt to get over the mountains, my tech and I loaded up again the next morning. A second try to find the Raspberry Mountain parcel was about to be attempted. The chosen route this time took us down the Rogue River, past Galice to the Graves Creek Bridge, crossing the Rogue River, then uphill toward Trappers Cabin. To avoid the highest elevations, we continued northwest to Powers (a tiny community in the deep woods) and then swung south again to Agnes on the banks of the lower Rogue River. We knew we could use the bridge at Agnes to get back to the south side of the Rogue, and then turn left to go upstream to Raspberry Mountain.

It turned out to be one l-o-o-n-n-g, time-consuming trip. In fact, we had to stop for lunch before we even reached the river at Agnes. At least there was no snow on this route. We finally did get to the general area where we thought the state property was located. It looked right when compared to our map and aerial photos, so we took enough time to search around in the brush to actually find a survey marker to confirm that we had found the right place. Our search for the monument also gave a good look at the landscape and vegetation.

It was then mid-afternoon, well after 2 PM. It had taken about five or six hours to drive from the GP HQ and we did not relish the thought of back tracking the way we had come. After some discussion, we decided to head back to the river and follow it down to Gold Beach and then go down Hwy 101 to Brookings, then the Smith River dipping into northern California, over to Hwy 199 and through Gasquet and Cave Junction back to Grants Pass.

While still high enough on the mountain for radio contact, we called HQ to report that we'd be late. We were too, by over two hours. Even so it was a little quicker by more than an hour compared to returning using the same approach route we'd come by.

As mentioned before, one of the problems encountered with the State Lands program in SWO was the long travel distances to access some of the parcels. Much of the ODF ownership in SWO took 1 to 1-1/2 hours from the office to the site, far enough for sure. Also, in particular, the Raspberry Mountain site in Curry County and another parcel along Slick Rock Creek in southern Josephine County each took an extraordinary amount of travel time to get to them – sometimes up to a half a workday if conditions were iffy. A third site in the remote northwestern part of the county was Trappers Cabin, also was a very long drive. All of these tracts were owned by the State Land Board and managed under contract by ODF.

Following the inspection of the Raspberry Mountain site, I decided to put the unit at the top of my list for harvest, reforestation and rehab. The old trees there were deteriorating due to age and over-stocking. Many stands needed partial cuts to prolong and improve growth of healthy trees. There were places where final harvest and reforestation was the only practical remedy.

Just how to get the needed prep work done for a timber sale was a challenge in logistics. Raspberry and Slick Rock each took 2 to 2-1/2 hours simply to reach the site. When working at these sites a crew could only get in about 3 to 4 hours effective work each day, with the rest of the time spent in a moving truck. Not good use of time at all.

A couple of strategies were put into play. One was to work four, ten-hour days per week. The limitation there was that such a schedule can only be used in late spring until early fall. In Oregon, late-fall through early spring doesn't give enough daylight for a full outdoor workday. I didn't want to wait until the seasons changed to begin work on these locations. The sooner planned management activities began, the better.

This led to another idea that we tried. Actually, it was my crew that decided to have a campout. We chose summer because of the warm weather and the day-length. We selected a week to camp near the site starting in August 1978.

ODF rented a small travel trailer in order to have cooking and bathroom facilities (of sorts) and also bought the food the crew would need for the five-day/four-night excursion. My wife (plus our 3 kids) went along to handle meal preparation and keep the camp while we were away working. The crew slept outside, as it was quite warm, although our pre-teen girls opted for a tent for privacy. Counting me, we had a crew of five guys – plus one new puppy whose owner couldn't find a dog-sitter. The site selected for the camp itself was near the confluence of Shasta Costa Creek with the Rogue River.

Hunters or maybe rafters from the river had used the undeveloped campsite before us. There was no safe and clean water supply and the area was somewhat trashed, but it was nicely shaded by hardwoods. It was located about 100 feet from Shasta Costa Creek where we could swim or wade in the off hours. From there it took only about a twenty-minute drive to the remote Raspberry parcel where we would be working.

The first morning our crew carried several canteens and large water jugs with us as we drove up the mountain. This became our habit every day to stop at a nice clear spring on the drive from the camping spot to the work site. There we'd stock up on drinking water and load the extra jugs to bring back for camp on our return in the afternoon. The routine sale set-up work went very well, with a lot accomplished each day.

Coming back to camp after Day One, my wife informed us that a black bear had come into the midst of camp in mid-morning, apparently to look over the garbage dump that we had mostly removed upon our arrival. Only she had seen the bear, as the kids had been playing in the creek at the time.

The crew all laughed. They teased her, saying it was more likely a Labrador retriever or other wandering big dog. They didn't know my wife - she knew a bear when she saw it and was insistent about the visiting bruin, and that we make the campsite secure in case it returned. That night she was proved correct.

Around mid-night, the young puppy started yapping and trying to crawl into his owner's sleeping bag. Everyone woke up at the noise. Sure enough, there was a medium sized bear rummaging around. Luckily, we'd packed things safely into the trucks.

As the bear sniffed around the camp equipment, one of the guys sat up in his sleeping bag, clapped his hands and yelled loudly. This seemed to discourage the bear, which left at a fast pace. We didn't see the bear again, but the kids were warned and given instructions about what to do just in case.

The morning of Day Three the crew again stopped at a small stream we had discovered, in order to water up as per our routine. We'd switched from the spring, as its water flow was almost drip-by-drip. As the crew was leaving after filling our water containers, a man's wallet was discovered lying on a rock ledge about three feet above the water flow. It most certainly hadn't been there the day before.

When the wallet was opened, we discovered it held about $400 in cash. Further examination showed an expired Washington State driver's license, a receipt from cashing a $1200 Money Order and a few other folded papers.

Back at camp we tucked the wallet away for safekeeping. Why was the wallet there so far from any well-traveled route? Where was the owner? Had something happened to him?

After our work on the fourth day while heading back to the campsite as usual, our truck radio receiver began to pick up a large number of broken messages. The area we were in was very up and down, with the ridge tops interrupting radio transmissions. Some of what we heard was from HQ and other messages were obviously from people who were somewhere out in our home district. The transmissions were garbled, missing words occasionally. I took one of the trainees along with me, driving to higher ground to get better reception.

In one of the more complete messages, we could hear a voice saying they were in contact with someone else who had three dozers available, and did the other person want them? The answer was that there was an order for ten dozers, so yes, they were wanted.

We were unable to contact HQ from our location and it would be even worse once we arrived back at our camp in the river canyon. After puzzling over the parts of messages that we'd overheard, we decided there must be a significant fire back in the district. An order for ten dozers indicated it was no Rinky-dink affair.

We had planned to return to HQ the next day anyway, so the last night at the campsite was used to pack up, saving time the next morning. Early the next day we made a small caravan going down river to Gold Beach, south on Hwy 101, then left to Hwy 199 at Smith River, and returned to HQ in the early afternoon. It turned out that the radio traffic that we heard in bits and pieces, was about something called the Grave Creek Fire. It was fairly large and most of us ended up working it in one way or another over the next few days.

The little mystery of the wallet took me about a week to solve upon our return to HQ. I eventually contacted a woman from a graduation card found in the wallet with name on the front and phone number written on the back. That led me to her mother, where this guy had roomed for a while. This in turn led to his parents in Reno. They directed me to send the wallet to them, as they said he would call or show up there eventually. Mystery solved – at least my part of it.

Our Raspberry Mountain campout was such a success we decided to try it again at the other most remote location early the following summer. This time the site was at a planned sale on Slick Rock Creek located in extreme southeast Josephine County, near the California border in the Siskiyou Mountains.

This site is a fairly high elevation spot and on north-facing slopes, making it a cool-temperature area even in the hottest late summer weather. It was only mid-June. The whole crew was experienced enough to know the radiant heat from the high elevation sun would mean our hardworking bodies would over-heat on the sunny side and have goose bumps on the parts that were shaded. Coats were required at night.

Along on this trip were three of us from the previous summer, plus one more guy making four management personnel in total. One fellow had only recently married, and his wife was attending summer college classes in Ashland in the valley below. For a night or two she also joined our high-country excursion, driving down to Southern Oregon State College during the day for school. Like before, my family also came along.

Slick Rock Creek itself is a small, snowmelt fed stream. The terrain is quite steep with little flat ground anywhere. Finding a suitable campsite was a trick. About the only place level enough was just a wide spot in the logging road we used for access. The site we chose was very dusty, and immediately after the road crossed the creek. We reasoned the stream water above there should be fairly safe for drinking, as there was no other access to the creek past that point. Camping in the middle of the dead-end roadway wasn't much of an issue, as there was absolutely no traffic the entire time we were there.

Once again, the ODF Management program had rented a small travel trailer to provide cooking and bathroom facilities. Up the stream from the campsite a very short way was a depression in the rock-lined streambed maybe three feet deep and about four feet wide. It would provide a place to bathe after long workdays, but with one serious problem. The new snowmelt water temperature was such that a person would go numb with cold after only a few seconds in the water.

The bathing regimen involved getting wet, then standing out of the water on a rock that afforded a bit of sun and a place to soap down. Up to this point the discomfort was still at a minimum. Next was talking one-self into jumping into the freezing pool of water and immersing completely. It was necessary to rinse off completely as fast as possible. By then the leaping back out of the water was just pure instinct to avoid hypothermia. Boy, that water was cold!

I guess we proved to our own satisfaction that foresters are made of pretty tough stuff. The chill from the coldwater bath lingered for a long time after. These so-called baths were important, as the work site was both dusty and muddy from snow. These were undoubtedly the shortest bath times on record. All of us were uncontrollably shivering to the point of not being able to speak for the chattering of teeth before getting dried off, and for a time afterward as well. Our late-afternoon warming fire at the camp site was a welcome place to gather.

We'd forgotten to bring a pancake turner amongst our kitchen utensils. As missing camping equipment goes, things could have been worse. I found a fairly straight-grained chunk of Chinquapin wood that came from home for the campfire. By splitting this as thin as I could and applying a little jack knife whittling, I made a serviceable turner that we still use in our kitchen to this day forty years later.

The sale preparation went without a hitch and the subsequent contracts and other necessities were completed back in the office after our return. After the unit was sold and a couple of years later when the purchaser began hauling out logs, it was found that the log stringer bridge that crossed the main stream cracked under the heavy log truck traffic.

The bridge had been examined carefully at the time of the sale, but some of the stringers had broken between the check and the act of logging, making it unsafe. The contract was modified to credit the purchaser for hauling in a 65-foot railroad flatcar (with wheels or "trucks" removed) to replace the old structure and serve as a bridge.

Underside view of Slick Rock Sale access bridge. Note the broken (fallen) timbers.
Courtesy of ODF Grants Pass Unit

The ODF ownership at that site is surrounded by Forest Service lands, with the bridge actually located on a sliver of USFS property. Although I'd notified the feds about the temporary nature of the new bridge when it was installed, the harvest on the Slick Rock sale was nearly completed before USFS finally sent someone out to inspect the bridge on their ownership.

Their representative did not like that railroad car as a permanent bridge at all, which it was never intended to be. Finding it totally unacceptable, his objections, while justified, were somewhat over the top. He wanted it replaced, and pretty darn quick too. I sensed a possible unspoken motive may have been to get ODF to build an unnecessary replacement for the aged and now unusable stinger bridge. I had no budget for any sort of construction, and besides – it would be unneeded.

Since traffic on that very secondary road was minimal, I would have probably just left the flatcar bridge across the creek just for everyone's convenience. This was not to be.

I did not intend to interrupt the nearly finished harvest a second time to build a new bridge to be in use less than a couple of weeks. In view of the inspector's objections, I decided to leave the flatcar for now. Truck traffic for the sale was nearly done and the buyer had met all the contract requirements with ODF.

Since the USFS inspector disliked the temporary bridge so much, as soon as the purchaser had moved his equipment out, I had our equipment operator take the district's D-6 to the bridge site on the lowboy. He pulled the railroad car out, loaded it onto the lowboy, and hauled it back 65 miles to the GP HQ. He then returned for his dozer.

I wasn't sure what to expect from the Forest Service. I figured they couldn't complain too much because the original bridge had been built a while earlier through an ODF contract. I never heard another word of any kind from them about the bridge.

Anyway, that flatcar sat in the back of the GP compound for a few months. Later I found a good use for it. I had it hauled to Windy Creek outside Glendale in southern Douglas County. It came in very handy as a <u>permanent</u> replacement for a low water crossing on that important Steelhead and salmon-run stream. The last time I was out there (2016) it was still there and functioning just fine.

Maybe a run-in a couple of years before had left me with a bit of an attitude when dealing with USFS people. One of the earliest BIG fires that I was sent to work on after returning to the SWO district was in Hilt, California. Located near the border between Oregon and California, the USFS was in charge of the fire on the California side and ODF on the Oregon side.

My assignment, as described to me by my supervisor before I left HQ, was to provide aerial recon information to the ODF Overhead directing our people working on Oregon lands. I was to report back fire conditions and potential topographic opportunities. These short and easily understood directions caused me several unproductive days of headaches and frustration trying to fulfill my job.

The helicopter I was to use for recon was under contract with the USFS, and I'd had no hand in the arrangements for its use. The agreement had been through third parties with each agency. The copter was supposedly to be shared with USFS on a cost basis. This seemed like a simple enough compromise to me, but I received a lesson that working with USFS can be difficult under even very simple situations. Many encounters over decades of time has led to my belief that any contact with federal agencies should be approached with caution.

My main problem at the Hilt fire was that every time the copter was available for even a few minutes and I tried to take-off for recon, the USFS air controller would bring a fixed wing aircraft into the operational area. Certainly, I knew the air traffic was busy there, but the federal people didn't seem to experience the same problem when they chose to fly for their recon work.

The presence of the airplane in the air space required the copter to sit down and stay down until the space was cleared. I understood the safety issues, but the lack of flexibility or even an attempt at cooperation was an increasing irritant that continued day after day. I had no alternate avenue to pursue either, as the copter pilot had to comply with the controller's decision or lose his contract work.

I'm unsure if the interference was coincidental, or if the people at the air camp there just couldn't be bothered by someone who wasn't connected to USFS. Whatever it was, my ability to actually recon fire on ODF ground was almost completely stymied. I observed only a small part of the ODF lines.

Reporting back to my superiors several times produced absolutely no change. Eventually I was directed to forego any more recon attempts. I was released from the fire by ODF to return to Grants Pass after two or three days of sitting on my rear and getting more and more frustrated.

Back at work, my management job provided more than enough work to keep me busy year-round. Getting upset about the situation was a waste of much needed energy. When Protection called in the summers, though, I had no alternative except rearrange my schedule and go wherever I was sent.

At home life ran at about the same pace as at work. After we moved into our partly finished house, I think my family just accepted that our days were completely overstuffed. I was in pretty good shape physically, still playing competitive basketball with people half my age and well able to lead my management crew on sustained hikes through rough country in daily fieldwork. Unless things were extremely demanding physically, I did just fine.

Still, I did notice was that during summer fire seasons, when the list of negative factors got too long - when weather was hot, sleep at a premium, and endurance most in demand - it was getting harder to do the fire line jobs that required stamina, like Division Supervisor or other very physical fire line jobs that up until then I was usually assigned to. The muscle stiffness and cramps that had been temporary and only a nuisance before, had become more common and more excruciating in pain.

All my life I coped with leg cramps following demanding and sustained physical activities. The cramps were especially bad when I was careless about getting plenty of water into my system. As I moved into my forties, the leg cramps were becoming much worse. The stamina that I'd once felt pretty proud of, was beginning to become shorter in length. I could still push through, demanding that my body do what I required, but the price in pain afterward was high. Sustaining high physical performance over several days when sleep or even just quality rest were short, was becoming a big problem.

I knew that there were lots of younger and very able people available who wanted to do the middle tier fire line supervision jobs I really enjoyed. I still had a lot of good information to share, and so I decided that I would seek out more training for other fire related Overhead work that might be less physically demanding.

A chance arose to sample something different when a fire complex near Sisters was threatening homes in several of the nearby rural housing developments.

The Fire Camp was set up at the Sisters Rodeo Grounds just on the east side of town toward Bend. At my request I was assigned to work in the Logistics Section. It was totally new to me. Logistics work on fires relates to procurement of all the needed supplies and setting up an organized, well run fire camp as fast as possible.

Since I was the new guy at the Sisters Fire Camp, I spent my first days driving to Bend or Redmond picking up goods and transporting them to Cache at the Fire Camp. Other parts of the job entailed putting up directional signs around the camp to identify areas, and a lot of the lower level time-consuming jobs that are necessary for good organization. None of this work takes a lot of physical effort, or much problem-solving skill either.

At that fire, most of the camp functions, including Logistics, Resources, Planning, and Finance, were set up in a building used for display of chickens and rabbits at fair-like events. At least it was out of the sun with some protection, but in the mid-summer heat the smell was not very pleasant.

I had arrived early in the fire camp set-up process. The first afternoon a Team Roping event was scheduled at the Rodeo Grounds, and well in progress by early evening. That would not have been any problem except that the competition continued long after the projected ending time around sundown - and then some.

During those extra hours more and more fire personnel arrived at the camp. Most were bedding down as soon as twilight fell. At that latitude and elevation, full dark arrived around 10 PM.

As the roping activity went on much later into middle evening and then into the night, it seemed the noise grew louder. Various representatives from the Fire Camp walked over and advised the rodeo organizers a couple of times that firefighters were trying to sleep and get ready for their early morning shift just on the other side of a stand of scattered trees.

There was no apparent change in the event or the noise; the rodeo participants and small but loud audience continued doing their thing. In desperation, finally the Sheriff's Office was called in. Whatever was said was unbelievably effective, as within minutes the place was cleared out completely – horses, steers and all went PHOOF!

This fire was my assignment for several days, and it was an excellent learning experience. As the fire was moved toward mop-up stage, another large fire broke out near La Pine several miles southeast. As the second fire grew in size, most of the camp staff moved off to a new Fire Camp at a more convenient location.

Three of us stayed and were assigned to handle the Sisters Fire Camp demobilization. Our HQ was moved to the Sisters ODF offices – a much more pleasant atmosphere without the strong chicken-rabbit manure smell.

At that point our job was to checkout personnel and resources, making sure that all timecards and other paperwork were complete. We also made sure that everyone had proper transportation and their base HQ was notified of their estimated arrival time home. Lots of paper shuffling and time on the telephone.

Since our fire was not yet completely contained, the checkout process was sporadic over several days. The crews were being relieved from the fire-line as they were no longer necessary to the operations. When the camp completely shut down and our on-site beds were no longer available, we moved into a newly opened motel just west of Sisters. They had a hot tub and swimming pool, which was great. Such luxuries had never been available on any fire I'd been assigned before.

The assignment wore on and the newness wore off. The work was obviously necessary but not hard at all. I had no problems at all fulfilling the requirements of the job. Soon I decided that Logistics simply was not what I was about. People are just suited to different things. Sitting at a desk all day, one following another without much variety, ensuring that proper forms were complete and filed correctly just wasn't me.

Mingling with the other Overhead people for the long term on the Sisters Fire made it apparent to me that I had experiences and knew things about wildland fires that many of them did not.

When we were released from that complex, I decided to pursue more training in the areas of Resources and Planning. I was pretty sure my years of fire-line experience could be of more value in a different place than Logistics. More than many others, I understood first-hand the snafus that might occur in the Planning Section. Such problems in-turn, cause much grief for the Operations Section. From there issues trickle down to the line and can seriously affect what happens to the people directly working the fire.

CHAPTER 38

The SWO District had experienced difficulty with reforestation and rehab for many years. Tree planting survival rates had not been very successful. Many times, re-planting operations were required, and when done, most of these were also less than a complete success.

Not long after I became the Unit Management Forester, the District Forester gave a directive to my Management section. We were to develop a systemic, workable Reforestation Plan for the district. The design would be used as a guide to future applications and treatments, with the ultimate goal being to bring about highest possible survival rates in spite of the difficult demands on the forest by the SWO diversified conditions.

An excellent program was in full swing then under the direction of Oregon State University. Named FIR (Forest Intensified Research), it was available to us for consultation. Armed with a publication from the FIR program entitled "Reforesting Oregon's Forests", a creative approach was utilized to write a plan and set up a program that would fulfill the directive.

SWO FOREST MANAGEMENT PLAN

Even when at its largest, the SWO Forest Management team was always small in number. Still, the members collectively had a lot of practical experience. I was very eager to get to work on the job assigned to us by the District Forester.

I'd already directed the crew to change over to a few practices I'd learned on the coast. With the experiences of the people on our staff at that time, I figured we had several of the answers to the district problems somewhere between us already. All we had to do was for everyone to dig into our group know-how, write down the whole of our knowledge in an organized way, run everything past the OSU FIR program and see what came of the effort. Solutions we needed were just mixed up with other ideas and thoughts, with some kind of distilling process needed to produce workable remedies. I referred to several personal experiences I'd had in Astoria and Coos Bay. I wanted the others on the team to do the same with their own ideas.

We began with a series of brainstorm meetings. First, everything we could think of that might help with tree seedling survival was listed, no matter how impractical. We also noted, for future reference, who offered up an idea.

I wouldn't allow any comments, positive or negative at this point. When everyone ran out of ideas, we went back to the list to gather more details. The person who made each suggestion explained it in much greater detail.

At that point, the rest of the staff was allowed to ask questions and make comments, making sure that everybody had a good clear understanding of every idea.

After all the ideas were completely explored and explained, clearly typed copies were made of the whole business. Everyone was given a copy of the complete list of the ideas and comments to study for a few days. Also included was information taken from the FIR publication, but most material originated from the practical experiences of the people in our group.

When everyone had time to review the material, each was told to independently place every idea into one of four categories:

1. Should be implemented.

2. Should be conditionally implemented (complete with notations telling the specific conditions to add or change).
3. Requires further study or research.
4. Not practical.

The four categorical lists became the basis of our written Reforestation Directive. The final document included the goals listed below.

The main objectives of the Directive were:

- To improve the planning processes for reforestation, to be initiated during timber sale preparation and/or when a rehab project began, and noting potential problems to be addressed.
- To better select seed sources to best match the planting site location (identified by ¼-section, elevation, and aspect).
- To better select seedling types to best match the challenges of each site.
- To increase care, over-all handling and protection of tree seedlings throughout every aspect of every planting project. (This included using refrigerated storage, insulated pickup truck-bed canopy when transporting, and insulated planting bags. In addition, seedling roots were to be dipped in a gel-slurry when loading into planting bags.)
- To expand and improve the gathering and monitoring of results as follow-up after planting, with survival plots and stocking surveys indicating causes of successes and failures.

Our team embraced the written product we had designed. A couple years were needed for our team to implement all the aspects of that Directive, but improvement was noted in survival rates on surveyed sites almost immediately after the first actions were taken. Every success gave more validity to what we'd written. Buy-in was complete.

When the entire plan was fully in place, our data showed the revised Reforestation program to be very successful. Since I retired, there have been a couple of times I've driven into the woods and inspected sites we worked during my years of supervising the management program. I can proudly say they are healthy and doing very well.

One of the now thriving reforested sites gave dramatic proof about the success of our plan. We also stumbled upon an effective product to help control browsing damage by deer. We'd never even heard of the stuff before we gave it a try.

There was a sale set up on the lower end and west of McCullough Creek outside of Glendale. This was the poorest stand in that area with chinquapin and madrone making up most of the stand and a few scattered Douglas fir.

Brush and hardwoods dominated the entire area - a dangerous mix that encouraged more intense fire damage in the future. The soils were fairly good on the slopes facing east and south at the site. These two areas within the parcel were about twenty-six and twenty-four acres respectively. The reproduction of conifers in these two spots was likely the result of clearing by a low-intensity fire, years in the past. They had been allowed to naturally reproduce, so there were issues of both crowding and unwanted open space.

The parcel had no direct access, so we laid out a grade and designed the road into the areas for a sale. The ODF Equipment Operator, built the roads in the late fall and early spring before the sale was auctioned. As I drew up the sale contracts some special additions were made to make reforestation more successful after logging the stand. We required that all hardwoods be felled, with stumps chemically treated. All the larger debris was to be moved to the landings. The purchaser could choose to remove the hardwood logs from the sale area if they wanted.

When harvesting started on the sale, there soon developed huge piles of hardwoods at the landing sites. The operator did indeed choose to remove almost all the hardwoods through a company called "The Wood Man" out of Roseburg. They used a fleet of self-loader trucks, and the decked materials disappeared very quickly.

The purchaser constructed fire trails around both units as was also required under the contract. As that fall moved toward winter, my team decided it would be best to lighten the fuels loads on site by burning any concentrations of logging slash still there. We began the process of setting up a prescribed burn.

At that same time, another sale set-up required my presence for a couple of days several miles across the valley, working with some ODF people from Coos Bay. I sent two of my guys out to the West McCullough sale to check conditions for burning the slash at the original site.

I was returning to HQ at the close of my second day out. Driving on I-5 near Wolf Creek in late afternoon, I saw the ODF D-6 dozer loaded on the lowboy trailer headed north. The driver also recognized my rig in the opposite lane, and within moments he called me on the radio. He told me I needed to turn around and head back north. We had an escape fire at the West McCullough Creek sale.

When I arrived at the site, I found that almost all of Unit #1 had burned up, as well as a small amount of ground between the Units #1 and #2. The fire at that time was moving across Unit #2 from east to west. A small area across the access road was also burning, but just then was heading north.

The dozer was soon off the trailer and immediately put to work. It quickly trailed and contained the fire above the road. I joined my crew working with water and hand tools to prevent the fire in Unit #2 from escaping the trailed unit. This was all successful, and only about six acres of extra ground had burned over what had been originally planned for the slash burn.

After we had the fire down, the two fellows I'd sent to check about fire conditions had time to tell me the fire was their doing, but not their intention.

The account shared went like this: Just as I had directed, the day before they set a small test-fire in some debris at the landing. It had sputtered badly and smoked, with poor flames. The reaction indicated conditions were not good for a burn. Both men were sure the gasping and weak test blaze was put out before they left – but obviously not.

These were two very practiced protection people. Both had several summer fire seasons of experience plus many controlled burns in their past. Even so, they thought that smoky test-fire was dead.

They were wrong – fire can be deceiving and very sneaky. Through the night that little smoker had obviously rebuilt and made a run. Yet this particular escape wasn't too serious. Everything had been pretty well trailed before the thing was even lit. By happy coincidence weather and fuel conditions were both on our side.

The result was two well-prepared reforestation sites ready to go, nearly matching what was in our written plan. The fire turned out to be a very inexpensive slash burn even though a few extra acres of brush and trees had been under-burned (a low temperature fire that leaves large fuels untouched). The cost saving was because we had to do so little to accomplish it. The expense of knocking the fire down cost no more than the intended burn expense. When the numbers were crunched, it was, in fact much cheaper – but certainly not an advised method, with any expectation of a repeat.

When late winter arrived both of the units were planted under the first Tree Planting Contract that had ever been used in the SWO District. (Until then we had always hired our own crews. With the new contract process, all of the peripheral employment bother was no longer in my hands. A welcome part of the workload removed.)

Our plans called for the east facing unit to be planted at 10'x10' spacing using Douglas fir and a few sugar pine seedlings sprinkled in. The south facing unit required 9'x9' spacing with Douglas fir and a few more assorted sugar pine seedlings included. This was because we expected normal mortality on Unit #1 that would result in about 350 – 400 trees per acre (TPA). On unit #2 we expected a few more losses because of the warmer drier south slope.

From the onset we didn't have actual site inventory history to guide restocking choices, so the decisions were educated guesses from other district sales that had similarities. Such historic information is vital for success.

We weren't anywhere near done with this parcel yet.

Three years later, and to the great surprise of the team, the survival survey data was way better than expected on both units. The third-year stocking density was 430 and 510 TPA respectively.

But new problems had developed. The new openings in the previously over-stocked hardwood/conifer cover had now become a favorite deer haven. The area was at the end of a long remote road with a locked gate that denied casual human access. The doe-eyed browsers were mostly left undisturbed. The site was now filled with large amounts of some of the favorite foods available for nibbling deer – succulent new growing tips of young conifers at exactly the right height.

Our baby trees were surviving, but were being severely munched on by deer to the point where they looked like little cultured Bonsai creations. Their average height was about 1.5 to 2 feet tall. Each had a very round bushy appearance but no discernable leader. Almost every one of the trees was being used as part of a bountiful buffet for the local deer herd.

We needed to find some way to protect the seedlings for another year or two until they could outgrow the reach of the deer. I set out to research treatments to stop the deer browsing issue. This quest took some time, but I did find possible answers. One empirical study I found tested several deer repellants applied with various methods to trees in an enclosure. This looked very promising.

The process in the study used an enclosure that had a known population of deer and contained other vegetation such as shrubs and grass. Deer in the wild have a broad menu of available foods. The study chose a site with adequate choices so that the deer would not be forced to browse trees or starve.

A product called "Deer Away" (sold in a powder form) caused no discernable damage to the trees or the deer, and was indicated as being very effective for preventing deer browse on seedlings. (Another formulation in a liquid form did show a little "burn" damage to seedlings.) Our choice, the powder, had to be applied by first moistening the trees with water, then shaking a small amount of the "Deer Away" onto the boughs.

The study included that different actions during application may enhance results. It was found that if a three-foot strip of plastic survey flagging was first tied to an upper lateral branch the effectiveness was increased by about 10 – 20%. No answer was given as to why the flagging increased the way the product worked, and little effect was observed for trees that only had flagging attached. Also, seedlings left untreated in the study were almost 100% browse damaged.

I decided that this product along with the flagging application was a good first start for our deer-browsing problem. We would apply in the spring just as early growth began.

We knew from our survey there were at least twice as many surviving seedlings as needed. I decided that maybe we could do some sort of "thinning by deer browse" by giving repellent treatment to only every other young tree. A plan was hatched where we would use teams of two. One person to carry a backpack sprayer with water to dampen the seedling (except on dewy mornings or when the weather sent a light mist not likely to become rain.) The second person would sprinkle the repellent and tie flagging. We didn't want to have our repellent washed away, so when significant rain was present, we would suspend application. The flagging also did double duty by marking treated seedlings.

A second treatment period was scheduled for the next fall, but just for the previously treated seedlings. A year after the second fall treatment we would again survey the results, with additional follow-up surveys performed as needed.

At survey time, we inspected the young trees with great care. Our Anti-Deer Project was a phenomenal success – well beyond anything expected. The deer, almost without exception, had avoided the treated seedlings. Our investigation revealed only very minor deer browse to untreated trees located on the perimeter next to the forest edge. There was no browsing at all on any of the interior placed seedlings. Also, nearly all tree seedlings had grown three feet plus. This was terrific. The growth of the young trees was enough to put their terminal buds out of reach of the deer.

About two years later, another survey showed there were no problems with these two sites. The trees had done so well, by then there was a need for pre-commercial thinning.

CHAPTER 39

*M*anagement responsibilities didn't just disappear because a lightning bust happened to blow through the valley, or some nut case with matches got his jollies setting arson fires up and down some roadside. Busy fire seasons interrupted management duties, and management jobs had to be wedged between urgent fire call-outs. In my section of the office, there was a continual juggling act every summer between Management and Protection.

Outside of the daily Forest Management issues, over the final twenty-three years of my career I was involved in many fires both near home and far away. At times I also filled protection functions at the District level. These included aerial patrol following lightning storms, and investigating various accidents and firefighting mishaps.

The ODF policy that all employees are on call during every summer fire season meant that a lot of my fire contacts were in-district. My action on any given fire could be anything from Incident Commander directing crews and equipment, to digging line sometimes by myself on a mountain top. With the notorious summer fire history of the SWO district (having the most fire incidents in the state annually) added up to plenty of fires to keep my hand in, no matter what my actual job might be.

JOB ASSORTMENT

The hills north of I-5 between Grants Pass and Rogue River are an area that saw numerous fires during my 38 years with ODF. In this narrative several of these fires are described, but there were many nearly at the same location that not only overlapped some of the same ground but are also blended together in my memory. I can't swear they were exactly in the same place, but they were close.

The chain of command on fires is that the initial response guys are in charge unless or until relieved by someone else assigned to command. I acted as an Incident Commander on countless smaller fires, especially during my early years when on initial response with the Hotshots.

Because of my Management position in the SWO District, I ended up with the night shift Overhead job on one of the multitude of fires on the hills surrounding the City of Rogue River. The command center or command post (CP) on this particular fire was set up at the Rogue River Water Filtration Plant. The fire itself was not a difficult operation, but it eventually grew to about two hundred acres.

The nightshift this time had about five engines and a hand crew on the lines. As so often happens on a fire at night, if there isn't much wind, the fire dies down a lot after darkness falls. This is a result from cooling air and increased humidity, among other factors. When this happens, it is an opportunity to strengthen lines and even attack weak spots especially on the flanks. Nighttime can offer excellent attack opportunities.

White patrol engine, about 1982 in the new Unit compound.
Courtesy of ODF Grants Pass Unit

At the evening shift change at 6 PM I'd laid out my plan for overnight. The crews dispersed to their assignments. Most of the active attack work I had assigned was completed before darkness, around 9 PM. The radio traffic dropped off and not much else was going on in the command center, so I took over some of the dispatch as well as overall direction of the fire operations. This made available a couple more working bodies to go out to the line.

During some of the quiet time I'd directly telephoned home, asking my wife if she might bring me something substantial to eat. My wife showed up around eleven PM, having made the twenty-mile drive from Hugo with a very nice steak dinner wrapped in foil. Even though I'd been nibbling though a box- lunch with peanut butter sandwich, fruit and cookies, I was pretty well famished, not having eaten much since noon. After finishing my late-night supper, and with the fire so quiet, it was a good time to personally check the fire from different viewpoints. I took my wife along with me during this mid-shift inspection in my pickup.

We drove up to an access road going to a rock pit about halfway up the mountain. There was a good view of the whole fire with the late nightlights of the city of Grants Pass in the distance to the right, and the lights from the city of Rogue River to the center and left side.

I've always preferred to personally see what a fire was doing, but this time there was not much to see. The night crews were placed where likely problems would occur, and were on the lookout for any spot fires or movement anywhere on the line. Instructions to all crews were to quickly and aggressively attack if the fire made a run at our newer line. There was no wind, no unusual incidents and all the lines were holding.

Without wind the slow-burning fire produced only thin smoke. It was rising straight up so visibility was very good. The places that were actively burning looked like thin glow-worms creeping here and there across the face of the hillsides. The gold threads against black mountainside were quite beautiful when silhouetted by city lights. Through the years there were times such as that night, when the mysticism of the burning hillside, with the twinkling of the lights or sometimes stars in the background could become almost hypnotic.

What needs to be remembered, though, is that the darkness was hiding much of what had already happened on the fire. The daylight appearance and land conditions on this hillside had already been tremendously altered in the few hours since the fire began. It was possible that a management team would soon come and make an assessment for rehab. The landscape would be shades of black and gray. Although once in awhile land that is burned over derives more benefits than losses, usually wildland fire causes more destruction than can be easily calculated. For this piece, some kind of management plan would be designed. Several years of hard work would be dedicated to make the hill something more than just scattered brush and sparse grass – which would just as likely burn again in a few years, given the history of lightning strikes and repeated burns.

In SWO the level of the success of the management effort would probably depend upon on agency ownership or stewardship philosophy of the landowner. Industrial owned lands or those under the management of a government agency would most likely receive extensive rehab work. On small private ownerships, not so much.

Even with accelerated scientific management, the length of time to grow anything but weeds would require years, perhaps centuries. If left to nature, the necessary duration for re-growth could be indefinite. In spite of what some critics say, Forest Management is not tree farming. It is an attempt to accelerate the natural sequence for forest growth under optimum conditions to permit the forest to be the best it can be at that particular site. Naturally, commercial owners want to encourage growth moving toward a product for harvest. ODF management used a formula of percentages of stands with mixed ages, with multiple use being the goal. All the potential backward steps that every type of forest must face are always still there and always possible. Interventions may or may not be successful. Management is not a set list to be done and checked off.

The job is a team effort by strangers working together over time. No human lives long enough to be present for the job to be completed from seeding to tall spire. Each participant brings different skills (or the lack of) to the team effort. Conditions will change over time, so flexibility is part of the process.

For example, maybe the rehab work would be well done, then a hillside would just burn again in another few years. It's possible that the previous repeated burns on that hill had all ready altered the soil so much that it would not be productive again in a very, very long time no matter what happened.

Others who take forest stewardship seriously, like me, might ponder burned-over land with similar thoughts. Wildland fire brings serious waste and destruction. I dislike fire because it is so random in outcome and placement. It takes apart what required much effort and time to put into place – either by nature or by management.

The crews on that fire accomplished a lot that quiet night. We were able to hand over a very subdued fire to the day shift just after dawn. The following day's fight was not a long campaign for control.

Not all the necessary work involving a fire is particularly interesting. For the Meadows Road fire in Sam's Valley (official name – Hull Mountain Fire) the Fire Camp was located at the Valley of the Rogue State Park. It was another big one, unusually hot burning with several homes taken. The timing overlapped another out-of-district assignment for me, so that I was involved only after returning home when the fire was partially into the mop-up stage.

My assignment was related to fire investigation; in this case to follow-up on damage complaints and to file reports to recommend action (if any) depending on the apparent causes. The area of my assignment involved mostly dozer flattened fences. Not overly heroic or the most glamorous, but still necessary.

On that fire, an equipment operator lost his life. He was a local resident of the threatened area who was using his own dozer. The man who died had left his machine when a sudden wind shift caused the fire to make a strong run in his direction. It appeared that the man had attempted to clear out an emergency safety zone around his machine, but decided to escape on foot before he was finished. He made it less than 100 yards before he was over taken by the fire and killed.

Sufficient training is required for all hired manpower; this man was at work without being hired and had no training at all.

There is a lot of camaraderie between people that fight fires. Put two or three together almost anywhere and Fire Stories begin to take over the conversation very quickly. When lives are lost, or injuries (or even near-injuries) occur, there is always the sober feeling: "There but for the grace of God, go I." along with a silent inner "Thank You" for coming through unscathed.

My wife says she's noticed something a little different in these conversations; a little more than just the empathy for the human carnage – the landscape always suffers as well. Most firefighters express some level of sadness for the place that burned. It is very likely the burned-over area will never be the same again within the lifetimes of the people who knew it. To a point, I think maybe my wife is right.

The Meadows Fire (Hull Mountain Fire) was particularly hot burning in several places. Some of these were so damaged as to take on a moonscape appearance. Selected stands of timber burned with explosive crowning and even occasional brushy areas were really incinerated beyond normal. Many houses and out buildings were taken as well, and of course the lost life of the equipment operator.

Dozer burned over at Hull Mountain Fire in Sam's Valley. The operator was killed.
Courtesy of ODF Grants Pass Unit

Nearly two years after the Meadows Road/Hull Mt. Fire on a gloomy early spring day, I drove my wife through some of the ground burned during that fire. She was then working for the Oregon Extension Service and was doing some personal research for a series of presentations she was to give to groups of local classroom teachers in regard to forests and wildland fires. Eventually I came to assist her with these teacher enrichment classes. She was quite discouraged by the lack of factual information about wildland fires, and forestry in general, these educators had available.

As I said, that fire had burned very hot in some places as it traveled overland. My wife was no novice to the after-effects of wildland fire, but even she expressed a level of shock by the totally barren appearance and obvious long-term damage over so much ground. There were places where any vegetation was having serious problems regenerating, because the earth itself was burned and sterile. Some spots showed where winter rains had helped some with greening up, but the widespread lack of plant growth overall was striking, especially after two winters. Also, I don't believe my wife ever experienced the shock of discovery when stumbling over the burned corpse of a dead deer or elk (or even smaller animals) soon after or during a fire. This has happened to me a couple of times – it tends to make me sick to my stomach and reminds me why I hate wildland fires.

The day we toured the burn, we stopped in a couple of places to examine the ground closely. Fine ash with the quality and color of gray to black sand was evident. It was periodically dimpled by slight depressions about a foot in diameter here and there. I explained to my wife that each of these dips was where a manzanita bush or small tree had grown before the fire. The round depressions gave no other evidence of any plant either dead or alive. When we dug into the center of the circular dents, in some, a bit down a black charred root or stem might be discovered that continued into the ground. Other times there was nothing left but the coarse ash.

Even more surprising to my wife, was the remains of larger trees that had burned off. Or perhaps the lack of remains caused the amazement. Again, a deep layer of sandy ash covered the ground. Occasional burned spears looking almost like single blackened fingers poked upward here and there, pointing at the sky in a stark and spooky way. These long fingers also originated from the indentations on the surface. I explained to my wife each black pointy spear was the remains of a larger tree. The depressions in the ash were many, but very few of the ugly burned tree trunks were to be seen. The fire had been so inclusive that evidence of so much from before had been totally consumed. It literally had "all gone up in smoke".

The place had a melancholy air about it enhanced, I think by the cloudy day. It was very quiet. The extinction of this once living ground hung over us as we examined the almost colorless and empty landscape. What a waste. No trees, brush, grass. No squirrels, rabbits, deer. No roots. No worms. No insects. Not even mud, as the ashy sand wouldn't even hold water from the winter's rain.

The damage was thorough and dismal to experience. Until the organic particulates in the soil were replenished, what would grow for many years would be restricted to mostly things with a marginal need for nutriments or even water, such as seasonal grass and weeds. With that kind of damage to the earth itself, replanting trees for rehab would be a waste of time and money for a very long time.

I've not been back to that site to see how much recovery change has occurred since.

A certain section of land ODF managed, named Trappers Cabin, is located on the divide between the Rogue and Umpqua drainages. Common School lands are different than other state forestlands. By legal mandate, that land is managed for maximum income to go into a fund in direct support of public schools. The Fund's principle dollars are invested to increase the balance by earnings. Only the annual interest is distributed to the schools.

Trappers Cabin was one of the most remote parcels, a good distance from the Grants Pass HQ, but was not quite as far out as Raspberry Mountain or Slick Rock Creek. My crew had a sale planned for that piece and it was a fairly simple prep, as sales go. The ease of set-up would usually make for a couple of day's field-work. With the distance from the office, the extra travel time would add a lot of hours until we had this job completed.

It was in the fall a year after our other two successful campout excursions, I think in 1979 or so. My crew had spent a long day doing pre-sale fieldwork at Trappers, with almost half the day was spent in the truck either coming or going. We were maybe a third of the way to finishing, and soon bad weather and short daylight would be issues. A postponement of the work over winter was impractical.

At the end of that first day during the lengthy trip back to the office, everyone joined in discussing what would be the best schedule to adopt for finishing the job. The extra hours for travel would increase the days needed. It seemed only fair to get input from all involved.

Of the four of us in the truck, three had been on the other campout trips. Everyone felt that we didn't need another full-fledged campout taking several days. Instead, on our next trip out, if we brought just basic overnight supplies, worked an extra long day and slept over, we would easily be able to finish the second day in mid-afternoon. That way, we would not be burdened with a lot of planning or hauling a trailer. Each of us would pack enough food to keep ourselves fed for the extra meals. The weather was good, so we would just sleep out in sleeping bags and on pads or air mattresses. Within the week we were able to follow our basic plan.

The sale preparation was not unusual or in any way different from the routine, yet that overnight trip did give us some interesting things to talk about for a long time after the excursion was done.

After the first day's work, we made our respective dinners over a small campfire. It had been a long day, so we hit the hay not long after dark. As we lay in our sleeping bags talking before we went to sleep, we were naturally looking up at the clear starry sky overhead. Just like multitudes of stargazers before us, the wonder and beauty of the moment led to creative thoughts. I do not remember whom, but one of us noticed some lights moving from the north to the south through the velvet black night sky. Naturally we all fell to tracking the movement overhead.

At first it didn't seem unusual to any of us, as often aircraft marker lights are seen at night when the sky is clear. Soon, one by one we each noticed some things that were not normal, at least not in our collective experience. But then we were kind of a woodsy bunch, in spite of a few college degrees between us.

There were three lights in a perfect triangular pattern, but not too close to each other. None of us could hear any sound whatever from the moving lights. We all agreed that if these were aircraft, the absolute silence was an indication of high-altitude flight. But even very fast aircraft flying high enough to be silent, would appear to be moving much slower to us on the ground. The object in the air was moving way too fast for any high-flying aircraft such as supersonic liners or military planes. Last and most intriguing, just as the three lights approached the southern horizon, another group of three exactly like the first lights, reappeared from the north following the exact same route of travel as those seen before.

The four of us lay in our beds atop that mountain, tracking the lights for some time. There was some amazement felt about what we were seeing. Naturally a discussion came about between us, lasting perhaps an hour or two. A few possible explanations came up during our speculations. Had the Air Force developed high altitude aircraft that had hugely greater speeds than anything within our limited knowledge? Maybe a totally silent aircraft of some kind was up there flying about. Perhaps these were a series of unique satellites with an orbit within the stratosphere. Naturally the UFO/alien vehicle theory was tossed out there too.

The four of us who witnessed the strange lights in the sky that night determined no satisfactory answers to our questions. Still, the speculations were kind of creative. It does show that foresters are not just guys who wander around in the woods counting trees, or stomping out the occasional fire.

Actually, in my experience, most people who work regularly in the woods are pretty much a very realistic, tenacious group. Nature puts an immense number of potential difficulties into the life-span of every tree in any forest. By natural-means or by human hands, seeds and seedlings are planted and nurtured, only to have these objects of much care die of thirst, poor nutrition, and disease. They are eaten by insects and animals, crushed by rock and mudslides, shaded and choked out, burned, drowned and blown away by winds.

Still, both nature and foresters persist in their jobs to help the forests grow. Sometimes foresters even get kind of sentimental about certain plots, almost like the feelings of parents toward their children. But trees mature slowly in relation to the humans, who may never see a particular individual tree reach full mature size in their lifetime.

Once one of my technicians and I were conducting an inventory of an ODF stand of trees. We ran some plots through a stand about 40 acres in size that had been thinned down to a low number of trees per acre. Efforts to encourage new growth had been done, with the objective to make enough space for new seedlings to germinate and grow. Annual surveys were taken. Our inventory indicated that there were very few seedlings taking advantage of the extra growing space.

Back in the office, I consulted with the Salem staff Silviculturist about this site. Using our numbers from the inventory we determined that the stand density was just a little too high to encourage reproduction of seedlings underneath.

We decided to follow through with the original objective for this stand, which was to develop an over-story of a few large trees and a healthy under-story of seedlings. To do so, we set up an additional timber sale on that site, removing about ½ of the existing large trees.

The trees to be removed were selected to be lower quality or having some type of defect. By leaving the best behind to produce the next generation, we would be able to make use of natural reproduction to give the more mature trees time to reach an age and size suitable for future thinning. We also designated about two trees per acre to be made into snags (dead standing trees) or become snags in the future. This was to encourage cavity-nesting birds, like woodpeckers and other wildlife that utilize these types of trees. This type of multiple- use is desirable, but not always practical within the limitations of the site.

Today, this stand is showing some success toward the goals the management team selected. I live not too very far from the site, and have visited it a couple of times since I retired almost twenty years ago. So far, so good.

To take on the forest stewardship role, the reality will often be failure. There are so many factors and events that work against even the best plan. Those doing the job have to keep at it, survey and note changes, be flexible, trust the next forester to take on the job and be willing to wait a very long time to experience small success.

McCullough Shelterwood after harvest. Note that the wide spacing of "leave" trees and dead future "bird" trees.
Courtesy of CC Dickerson

CHAPTER 40

*I*t's interesting that today (2018) so many people with limited experience want to grab onto the idea that Controlled Burns are the save-all solution to years of poor forest management that some claim is the cause behind the bigger fires that occur. Considering how often controlled types of fires take off – even in mid-winter with wetter fuels – this professional forester would strongly advise a closer look before adopting this (or any other wide-spread) treatment across the board.

To the well meaning but uninformed promoters of Controlled Burns, I say "Good luck with that, but use a good share of caution." Sweeping forest management treatments seldom react as expected.

The Smokey the Bear people have given good advice – **Always be careful with fire.**

Fire has a way of surprising those who dabble with it. Even the most experienced are often caught off-guard and humbled by the actions of wildland fires. There are just too many variables involved. Goof-up's will likely cause long-term and wide-spread damage to the forest, plus people can lose their lives.

Forestry is just too complex to think that one or two types of applications will fulfill the needs everywhere. Variables are the bottom-line in forest management. It is a science that must be applied in an on-going, site-specific way. The best choice of many options and treatments should be used – and selection of what is "best" usually is a tricky business. There are no quick and easy answers. Blanket rules are the work of the ignorant.

That pretty much means that for success, those with comprehensive education, on-site knowledge and A LOT of experience must make the decisions and plans. I doubt many politicians telling folks that more controlled burns and thinning are THE answer have such credentials.

If they want to play around with fire, buy a backyard fire pit.

The science of forestry is too important to air, water and environmental quality to have management practices decided by agenda driven politicians or well meaning but novice lay-persons. Sure, forests will grow without human intervention, but it is a slow process with many, many potential set-backs. In today's world do we have all that much time to allow all the natural false starts and problems that are a normal course of events as a forest grows? Also, like it or not, the presence of Humankind is a factor and cannot be excluded.

The mess out there now is powerful proof that stepping away from wild lands has not worked well. Over time, forests will repair themselves eventually, but it's anyone's guess how long the fix will require. There will be places where several centuries – maybe even more – will pass before renewal is complete.

THE ONES THAT GOT AWAY

On ODF lands under my supervision in Southwestern Oregon, prescribed burns were done late in the fall through very early spring. With my fire background in the area, I wasn't about to light up any kind of slash burn any other time of year. Usually the major problem during the colder months was calculation of the conditions to fit a careful timing requirement. Fuels needed to be dry enough to burn, but have enough moisture so as to be controllable. That is a difficult balance to achieve.

When there were management connected burns, my crew mostly handled the situations ourselves, not calling on the protection personnel. Partly this was because the majority of the summer initial attack people weren't on the job in the winter months anyhow. (Nowadays, experienced contract crews are available year-round.) Still, our winter burns had no lack of fire experience to call upon. Many of my management crew switched to middle-level protection Supervision during summer Fire Seasons; the total cumulation of wildland fire experience in the SWO Management Unit was notable.

As for controlled burns, they have their uses – and we employed them as a "tool" when it seemed to fit into the overall plan.

Most controlled burns are fairly boring affairs with a lot of waiting for a window of opportunity. Once the permit to burn is in-hand, there is almost always a pause. Too wet? Too dry? Weather is a big factor, as is the condition of the potential fuels. Sometimes the ideal conditions simply do not occur and the whole project has to be scrubbed after months of waiting.

Aside from the paperwork, the fieldwork in preparation for a controlled burn isn't terribly difficult. An area is designated, the moisture content of the fuel is determined and problem areas of the site are determined, then monitored, trailed or both. People who are very skilled with this type of burn can fairly accurately predict how hot the fire will be, plus what plants will burn, what will not and how the fire will probably travel overland – IF everything goes right. Sometimes predictions mean zilch.

Fire always has elements of unpredictability. There are burns that just don't follow the plan. Escapes have to be dealt with. The wind changes or the fuels are inconsistent. A rainsquall blows in and all you get is smoke (which can involve the Environmental Protection Agency with another paperwork and permit snafu to untangle). Sometimes those in charge are a bit too eager and push the envelop of safety when setting off the first flames. Hidden problem situations were missed at the start and/or human error pops up and twists a sound plan into a big pain in the rear!

I have some memories that weren't much fun dealing with Controlled Burns.

Climate plays a huge role in how and where forests grow, but it is weather that is the leading factor in the year-round story about wildland fires. The SWO district in late years of the 1970s enjoyed somewhat mild summers, although 1979 was a hot dry year. This led into the two very bad summers of 1980 and 1981.

The winter of 81-82 was very dry. A wet spring was about to bring relief, but of course we didn't know that as we worked under the gray winter skies. One of the escaped set-fires we experienced on State lands happened on a sale named Windy Creek Over-Story Removal. My crew got to know this particular area very well – we spent a whole lot of time there for a laundry list of reasons.

The site had been thinned once or twice over time and the remaining timber had gotten fairly large. Even so, regular monitoring showed evidence that the stand was having problems with mortality from several causes. I felt it was time to convert the site to a thrifty, young stand. For the sake of the whole site, some of the older, ailing trees had to go.

During sale preparation we had some problems with the cruise data. The site had such diversity in species types, ages and health that the sample plots produced information that produced a big paperwork issue. I should have had my crew do a 100% survey to get all the "I's" dotted and "T's" crossed. Instead, we made several trips into the stand, adding more samples every time, trying to meet the state guideline for statistical Standard Error (SE).

Our extra cruise efforts got to be a real pain, taking a lot more time and fieldwork for what was a pretty insignificant number of trees. After some thought, I wrote a report for the file stating that the variability of the stand (age and diverse species) just was too great to achieve the state's SE goal. The report did the trick.

Salem sent us the okay and the sale was sold by oral auction to Boise Cascade. Once the harvest was complete, Boise was required, under contract, to burn the slash remaining on the unit in order to reduce future fire hazard, and make a better planting site for reforestation. The requirement was pretty standard practice.

The unit is located in Douglas County just beyond the edge of the SWO District. To legally burn slash a burn permit would be required by the DFPA, rather than the GPHQ. A planning meeting and inspection was held on the site in late-fall to determine requirements for the permit. I was the rep for ODF, and Boise Cascade sent a person. Because of the location, we included a DFPA rep too.

Fire safety and urban smoke management issues must be met even with a winter burn. Since the terrain and the remote location would handle the smoke issues, the main concern in that case was only fire safety. The DFPA Forest Officer had tested the fuel moisture at several locations on the unit before our meeting. He said that he felt that it was still too dry to burn safely.

The Boise rep was experienced, but had recently changed jobs with a transfer to the SWO area. He felt that the larger part of the sale could be safely burned now. Three debris piles would be burned later in winter when it would be wetter and safer for all attending, but he convinced the DFPA rep and me that the remainder could be lit up within the week.

His reasoning seemed sound. He indicated that they would use a helicopter ignition for this slash burn. Fewer people on the ground by using a helicopter would give much more flexibility and control of safety issues than with slower hand ignition. He felt that by first lighting fuels inside and away from the perimeter lines, it would draft the fire inward giving even more safety.

Since the DFPA rep and I had no experience with helicopter ignition, we conceded to the Boise rep who had used the process before. Agreement was reached about the borders of the burn, with the exception that the main upper landing would be trailed out and hand lit before anything else along that line. The copter would ignite at the base of the unit only after the crew on the ground had completed the hand ignition.

With this agreed-upon plan, on the appointed day, some of my crew and I began to light up the lines next to the southeast landings as per the plan. The Boise crew went to work the north line near that landing.

Heli-torch lighting of logging slash and forest debris.
Courtesy of ODF Grants Pass Unit

I don't know why, but the Boise crew did not follow instructions in the plan. Instead of starting at the top of the slope and working downhill with the heli-torch as agreed, they first lit up the lowest parts along the line with the copter's big drip torch. This caused that part of fire to race uphill along the fire line. By the time it reached the top of the slope, the fire was going so vigorously that it simply blew across the trail. When it reached the top of the hill it continued on the other side, outside the unit. So much for a safe plan!

The BC rep ordered the helicopter to try and light more fuels inside the unit located next to the escape, trying to draw the escape fire back by draft. This might also give enough time to trail the slop-over. He called me as soon as the escape occurred, telling about what had happened and also to alert my guys to what he was trying to do.

It might have worked too, if the fuels had not been so dry and volatile. But his plan didn't do what was hoped. Add to the problem that the helicopter moved too fast. While trying to help by drawing the fire back with more fire, the swinging aerial torch accidentally slung more fire across the trailed line at another location on the north side. The rotor draft also sent burning debris in all directions.

So now we had a raging winter fire on our hands with minimal crew available on hand.

I called HQ for assistance, asking that the GP ODF send an engine and bring our D-6 dozer as soon as it might arrive. The DFPA people on hand also ordered their engines and another dozer. All these measures would have at least a thirty-mile plus drive time until arrival.

About this time the Boise guy shared over the radio that the BC 3,000-gallon water tender, its driver and an employee in a BC pickup had been positioned at the upper landing directly in the fire's path. They could not be contacted, and he feared they were trapped.

Oh Boy! This baby would be one for the books.

Since I was the closest, I headed up the access road in my pickup to the top road to see if I could locate the missing people. When I arrived at the top, a few of my guys were there, but they had not seen or heard from the missing Boise people. A Boise engine arrived, but the driver had no information about the other trucks and the two people.

There was a wall of flame to be seen on both sides of the ridgeline road leading out to the junction with the road where the Boise people had been stationed. We all felt the chill of doom realizing the missing would be on the other side of THAT.

Winter fires are crazy to work with. Sometimes they behave just like summer fires. Sometimes crews get lucky and the contours of the land make fuels so changeable that fires sometimes just die.

So far, this day had been very unlucky as far as the fire goes and I could only envision the worst possible scenario. Looking at the big flare-up on the ridge, my heart sank. This was one of those – "Oh please God!" moments.

I was the senior person on location. Something must be done. I decided that by using the road, I would drive through the face of the fire as soon as it cooled enough to be safe. The urge to act immediately was strong, but I had to wait a few minutes for the flames on the ridge to die down some.

Waiting is something I'm just not good at. I might have pushed the safety factor by a few moments, starting out as soon as I got all the windows on my rig rolled up. I drove as fast as I dared on the road, and the flame length was soon much lower on both right and left sides.

Once my rig crossed into the un-burned area over the ridge, things calmed down. I continued and turned at the junction to go down the access road to the south side of the ridge. If the trapped vehicles had made a run for it, this should have been the road they would have driven. My heart was in my mouth, fearing what I might find.

Coming around a blind turn, the first thing I saw was the water tender covered with ash sitting in the middle of the road with burned area all around it. My stomach lurched, but then I noticed two people climbing out from under the truck – BIG SIGH OF RELIEF!

It was the tender driver and he was helping the young BC woman to her feet. Both were covered with soot and ashes and the lady had streaks of tears running down her face, but they seemed all right. As I drove the short distance to where they were, I reported over my radio that they both were up and moving around. I climbed from my truck, next to the tender, and they told me their hair-raising experience.

They had heard the warning radio call about the escape. Immediately they took to the access road with the tender in front and pick-up following, trying for the exit route I had anticipated.

Abruptly big flames rose up from below the lip of the road. Hot embers were sucked into the tender's air cleaner, which then caught fire. This caused the tender engine to die and it would not restart. The tender driver did the right thing. As soon as he saw the fire coming over the cut bank and felt his engine die, he had radioed the smaller truck behind to back her still running pickup just a short distance down the road to a wider and hopefully safer spot, park and run to the tender. She followed his quick directions, and he had opened the valve on the water-tank totally soaking the ground and some blankets in his truck with water from the big tank.

The two had dived under the truck with no time to spare. With wet blankets pulled over them they huddled together with faces in the mud and waited out the fire that surrounded them.

The tender suffered little damage. Smart thinking and quick action, with more than a little bit of luck, for sure, was involved in the timing.

It seemed like just a few minutes passed when the equipment operator from Grants Pass drove up to us with the semi and the dozer on the lowboy trailer. I think he'd made record time from HQ, but then I'd been kind of busy for clock watching.

As soon as the D-6 was off the trailer, I climbed aboard with him. He and I took the dozer to the top of the ridge. From there we could see the head of the still moving fire below. The dozer started building trail down the east flank of the fire working across the side-hill. I was swamping for him and listening to my radio, covering his back. Soon we could hear the DFPA dozer working at the bottom coming up toward us. From the top, we turned down hill following the sound toward the second dozer.

About half the way down the steep hill our dozer drove onto some solid rock. The tracks had so little traction on the steep rocky incline that it began to slide downhill. With a crash of gears, our guy threw that big baby into reverse, but the dozer was still sliding and picking up speed as it slid, even with the tracks moving backward. From where I stood just a few feet away I could see that our operator was mostly holding on for dear life at that point. Thank goodness in a moment or so the dozer got some traction and the driver regained control further down-slope.

That guy had nerves of steel! After his brief wild ride, he brought the dozer back up the hill, skirting the rock face. Then he turned back downhill and completed the trail by meeting up with the DFPA dozer that was working the lower part.

The two big machines saved the day. It was fortunate that the fire had stayed inside the designated burn boundary on the west and south sides. The escape on the east and north had burned an extra forty acres of brush and young trees all on ODF ground (hooray for small gifts – no Trespass paperwork), bringing the total of the whole burn to 128 acres.

A month or two later that winter we still weren't done with that site. We had that new boss at HQ, replacing the fellow I'd liked and respected. The new Unit Forester was looking for ways to free up money to add to the summer fire budget. As a potential savings in cost he decided that we would use all ODF GP personnel on hand as the labor to plant the resulting burn area. When he announced this, I think my crew was beginning to consider that unit on Windy Creek as their home away from home.

With the tree-planting strategy, I am not sure any money was actually saved overall. Several of the in-office people, including a couple of clerical people, were not in very good shape. Tree planting was hard physical work that they were not used to.

To their credit, they rose to the job. There were several minor injuries within the ranks, partly due to the lack of conditioning. It was rough ground even for those of us whose daily work was on that very same site.

When the young trees were in the ground, the unit now was regularly monitored. My crew gathered data on the reforestation as per our directive. Over the next few years, the planting itself was a surprising success and the young plantation there did very well indeed. Even inexperienced office workers and old, plump foresters can plant trees properly. It is a very basic part of the job, as long as the roots are going down; not tangled in a bunch.

The last I saw of the site was in about 2014. I had a chance to tour some of the sites my crew and I had worked twenty-some years before, and made a point of checking that unit. The saplings were doing just fine, with plenty of surviving trees per acre and most of them about 30 feet tall.

I think it should be noted that several of the office people who were involved with this planting have visited the unit once or twice over the years – they have expressed real pride in this small, but tangible legacy to their work in forestry – even though most of their time was in clerical or other support roles.

One of the oddest winter fires that I was ever involved with was one that started in December a few years later. The previous summer had been unusually dry and the normal fall rains just didn't happen.

There were two origins for the fire that somehow joined up to result in about 400 acres burned altogether. One ignition site was from a holdover USFS slash burn that escaped and the other from a warming fire within an active State timber sale and logging site. The location was high up on the slopes above Yale Creek, south of Ruch in the Applegate River Valley (a tributary of the Rogue River).

A cooking fire lit by a logging crew caused the burn that started on the State sale site. The choker setters had a routine of starting a warming fire first thing in the morning. While they worked, they would leave cans of soup or stew next to the fire with a small opening in the top to release steam. When it was time to break for lunch, hot food was available without any waiting for it to heat up. On that day a strong east wind came up fanning the flames of the loggers' small fire. The blow-up moved into the nearby dry slash left from the area already yarded.

On that same day and up the hill, the same ill-wind also kicked up a few remaining embers from inside a USFS slash burn conducted a few days before and left unattended to burn out. Under normal conditions, neither site would have caused any problems.

Known variables, predicted by experienced field people would have indicated that both the warming fire and the slash burn re-ignition should have stayed small within their respective units, as fuel was limited and mostly quite damp. The terrain also should have limited the direction that both fires moved. The telling factor that overcame all the positive variables was the wind. Its direction, intensity and dry nature overcame all the telling factors.

Everyone involved with this little fire was well experienced – and everyone was caught off-guard. It took most of the day for ODF, USFS personnel and the logging crew to control the fires that burned together and with uncommon vigor, especially for the time of year.

Losses from this fire were almost nil for the USFS, except for their costs of fighting the fire. For the State and the sale purchaser, about ½ of the original timber volume was damaged, but still usable, with some volume deductions for charring and burned wood where tree trunks were in contact with each other. The charring also precluded any use of this wood for paper production. The operator had two heavy losses aside from the cost of his workers fighting the fire; a large shovel loader and a skyline yarder were both burned with extensive damage. I am not sure if they were able to do expensive repairs to make the machines usable again or if they had to be replaced. The value of the machines was likely between $250,000 and $500,000. I hope they had adequate insurance.

View of Yale Creek Sale, Unit 1 following operator fire and escaped USFS slash burn.
Courtesy of ODF Grants Pass Unit

Since the operator was primarily to blame on the state land, I directed the Scaling Bureau to add back any deductions for fire damage on the logs coming out of our unit. This was to prevent monetary loss to the state as a result of the fire.

Of note was an unusual after-fire agreement. With the fire's origin split between the USFS and loggers working on ODF lands, it was agreed that everyone would assume their own costs for putting the fire down. This was an important cooperative action that should be used as a frequent model.

CHAPTER 41

*B*eginning in the mid-1980s a major drought settled in the Pacific Northwest states. For several years the weather was unusually dry. Warm summer temperatures came earlier in the spring and lasted later into the fall. Some of the longest Fire Seasons on record were declared in Southwestern Oregon during this time.

Bigger, more destructive fires filled summer skies with smoke. Area residents were warned time and again to be especially careful with fire. Logging operations were shut down for long periods of time. Then a series of late summer lightning storms hit the area.

PROPERTY LINES AND PHILOSOPHIES

Being the Unit Management Forester (not protection) automatically put me into the very small group of in-district Overhead people. Local Overhead were called upon when any fire grew beyond a certain size, but didn't grow large enough to bring in a Fire Team from outside the district.

With my management assignment, my name was last on the fire call-out list. This was the only concession to my dual work assignment. Sometimes I was called out to fires because things cropped up late in the day, and everyone in protection was out already. That circumstance put me in as Overhead on nightshift. Other times the need for personnel was so obvious from the get-go that when the protection people took on the initial response, my crew was given some forewarning around mid-day. When that happened, it allowed me and anyone left of my crew a little afternoon time to tie up loose ends with whatever we were doing. Either way, the nightshift wasn't an uncommon assignment for those of us with mixed duties.

I still enjoyed the challenge of wildland fire fighting. The complex problems, the strategic decisions and the urgency always were a personal challenge, just as they had been for the previous twenty-some years.

The worst thing about being called out on nightshift would come about a day or two after the original call-out. I didn't sleep well during the day, ever, and certainly did not sleep while on the job. The result was that a nightshift call-out coming near the end of a day's work, pretty well led to at least one completely sleepless night. Even if it was only for one night, this was then followed by a few days of exhaustion when trying to switch back again to pick up the daytime schedule of my regular management responsibilities. For many of these years I was also changing irrigation pipe on the farm twice daily. In combination, summers came to mean that my body was running near empty a lot of the time.

If there were several fires in the district during the same time period, those reported and manned later in the day pretty well were handled with whatever resources that were still available. I became somewhat resigned to needed manpower and equipment already being assigned elsewhere.

I learned to be very creative with attack strategies, and also diligent in checking for possible terrain advantages. The old habit of monitoring the fire lines myself instead of relying on reports from others helped with problem solving choices under less than ideal circumstances. I also liked to hear the input from those working the lines – lots of good info was available from that source.

Yet, the needs of the Management Unit were always there. There are things in forest management that are done in a certain sequence. These can only be put off for a while, even during fire season. Since most of my crew did double-time on summer fires plus management, it wasn't unusual for me, with only perhaps one technician (or less) trying to complete a must-do project while everyone else in the district was dashing about on 24/7 fire action.

Angel Camp is located on the divide between the Rogue and Umpqua River drainages. An 80-acre timber sale to remove scattered over-mature timber that was deteriorating and dying, had just been completed on this full section (640 acres) of Common School land. A 160-acre tract about 2 miles south also had a small unit as part of this sale. The sale contract had required many snags be left to be more eco-friendly – the two plots had many dead and dying trees available to meet the need for more habitat for birds and smaller animals.

In late August, a lightning storm went though this area starting two fires from strikes hitting the snags. One fire was on the 80-acre state sale unit, the other started on USFS land about 1 mile to the northwest of the state land.

I was notified about the fires at home in the early evening. At this point I was concerned about the ODF forest at the site, but I hadn't been called to work the fire. I went to investigate.

Upon arrival in the area, coming in from the north, I found two USFS employees parked along the road just watching the fire burning mostly to the western side of the road.

As the fire was burning quite near the roadway and about to cross, I talked with them with more than a little concern for the state land on the other side. I was informed that they were monitoring the fire and waiting for crews and equipment to arrive. This "watch and wait" was pretty standard USFS attack strategy, but not for ODF crews.

I was extremely uncomfortable with their lack of worry, but couldn't really do much about it. I said that I was going on over to the state side of the property line to see what was going on there and drove on down the road.

The fire from the Forest Service land had crossed the road further on. At that location it was spreading down the edge of the roadway along the boarder of state land on fairly flat ground.

Going further east, on a secondary road branching off from the north-south road, I found a second fire on the higher ground near the south end of the state property inside the boundary of our Unit 1 sale. It appeared to have also started from a lightning struck snag and was spreading mostly to the north.

I went back toward where I had seen the USFS people and on the way found a medium-sized USFS dozer, without support help, heading north along the road toward the fires. I talked a moment with the operator, and I shared what I'd seen. I suggested that the skinner start where the fire had originally crossed the road and build trail along the south flank of the fire heading east. I said that I would try to get some re-enforcements for him as helpers (as per ODF practice) – thinking of the USFS people I'd seen observing.

As I headed back north toward the original USFS truck, I passed two BLM engines and crews also just sitting along the road watching the fire to the north of them. When I arrived back where the first USFS people were still parked, I asked if they might put one of their engines and its crew to work assisting the dozer and watching his back? They agreed.

Next, I returned to the two BLM engine crews, and actually relocated one of them where the dozer trail turned to the east. I instructed that crew of two to use hose lays to attack the fire line to the west, (which was not trailed) and to support the dozer operator to the west to prevent the fire from crossing the trail behind him. This was pretty basic fire attack strategy (at least with State crews) to protect the dozers as much as possible. The operators had a lot to do and needed the extra eyes on the ground for safety sake.

I had reported my actions and the situation as I observed it to ODF HQ via radio, indicating that we had about eighty acres on fire at that time. Since it appeared that I was the first ODF personnel on the fire, I indicated what resources I felt were needed in the way of crews and equipment.

For about an hour or two I scouted around some. When I returned to the dozer trail I found the BLM engine and crew missing, leaving the USFS dozer on his own. By now the fire had crossed the dozer trail behind the operator, which that crew was supposed to prevent or at least report to the operator. For the safety of the dozer, I left my rig and on foot followed the dozer trail to find and warn the operator. He needed to go back up his trail to hopefully catch the escape across the road and trail it in.

I do not recall much more of that night, but eventually in the early morning I drove back to the Grants Pass HQ. This incident, the Angel Camp Fire, was obviously going to involve several agencies due to mixed ownership responsibility.

I've never much liked the different attack strategies of the USFS, so felt pretty well disgusted by the actions of their crews that I'd observed. Also, up until then I'd mostly had a better opinion of BLM crews. It seemed that these particular crews had no intention of following any kind of cross-agency attack directives.

An Overhead Fire Team had been called. At HQ I discovered a fellow I had met on a fire incident at the Wildcat Fire (Wallowa) in Northeastern Oregon a few years before. On that fire we'd shared a position as Division Superintendent – he was on dayshift and I was nightshift. He had been sent to this Angel Camp Fire to act as the State rep on the Overhead Team.

My Management work at the site and overnight fire recon meant I had up-to-date information to share with the Overhead Team through the rep. There was also my lack of success with unofficial interagency fire attack to report. The boss at HQ directed me to take the Fire Team rep up to the site, fill him in on what I knew and get him situated with the team that had just arrived on the fire. When I had completed that job, this fire was no longer my problem – at least not until it was out.

Because of my split duties, I did not have any other direct contact with this fire again until it was in the final stages of mop-up. Being in and out of the office, I heard through the HQ scuttlebutt that the ODF rep I'd delivered to the fire that first night, was really good at grabbing what he needed for resources.

I returned to the site of the fire near the end, doing some specific tasks, and ran into the rep again out on the line. We talked a bit and he told me that the USFS were starting to send crews home but was "still building movie houses and hotdog stands" in their Fire Camp. (That is – going through set-up motions with a fire that was now in mop-up mode.) When he had questioned their unnecessary late-fire constructions, he was told that they had not yet spent their entire budget allocated to this fire and were going to finish the initial plan before they quit. I guess I wasn't the only ODF person who was confounded by USFS actions.

In regard to my Management responsibilities with this incident, I asked the rep how our forested sites had faired through the fire. I learned from him that it was his observation that not only had most of the vegetation and trees on our full section of ODF land been consumed, but the other 160-acre tract to the southwest had also been burned over.

As the rep described the condition of our forest, and since I was in the general area and had time that afternoon, I decided to drive out and look over the damage that day. This seemed like a good idea, because I could get a jump on what might need to be done about our pending sale. A written report wouldn't be available for a while.

I asked the rep if he'd like to accompany me on my look-see. It wasn't a long drive to the second unit, so off we went together.

We were out of the truck looking at the southern piece of the sale when a number of USFS high mucky-mucks drove up in a station wagon. Seeing us there and learning I was looking at the burned-over ODF land, one of the Forest Service guys said that they were trying to determine which of the various land owners affected by the fire might want to partner in an immediate aerial seeding with grass mixtures to keep down erosion from fall storms.

Without hesitation, I told the USFS group that the state land we were inspecting would definitely NOT be seeded with grass. The group of feds all seemed surprised by my decisive comment. The fellow who'd made the proposal became very condescending, acting like this was very unwise.

I tried to explain that my crew and I were very familiar with the two burned ODF sites. Grass planted now on these two parcels would have to be sprayed for control before or immediately after tree planting in late winter. Fall seeding of grass at this place was a waste of resources, time and money.

Showing more than a little attitude, the guy responded with "Who would make the final decision on this?"

I replied just as coolly, "You're looking at him".

That pretty much ended the conversation. They loaded up in their car and left.

True to their plan, within days after that fire the USFS people aerial seeded their land, taking real care to avoid getting any seed across the property line they shared with ODF. (For which I was quite pleased.)

I'm not sure when they planted their trees or what method they used, as I had more than enough on my management plate than to worry about Forest Service activities. Truth be told, actually I did decide to put down some grass seed on a very small portion of the site. It was just along the main stream running through the full section of state ground that had suffered badly in the fire. This was to help protect the burned over stream banks from erosion as the water level rose with winter rain before snowfall. We covered a strip about 50 feet wide on each bank. But, as I had told the USFS men that day we inspected the site, no seed went onto the main body of the site.

I guess I'd offended somebody who'd been with the feds that day, as it seemed someone in their management office wanted to prove something. The USFS was taking more than a casual interest in what was happening on the ODF side of the property line.

There was some noise about the State Land not being grass-seeded and how this "fool-hardy lack of action" was going to lead to excessive erosion with the fall rain.

Later I also was told that water samples were taken throughout the fall and winter in an effort to show the difference between the amounts of silt in the stream water as it came from state land verses that coming off the USFS land. Data was being gathered.

I don't remember how, but copies of the USFS reports showed up on my desk. I reviewed these mysterious copies. There was no significant difference comparing water samples. I knew the reason why too - grass seed would need sufficient moisture and time PLUS some warmth before it would be stimulated to germination and growth. That particular site would not provide the needed elements for grass germination to occur until mid-spring, after the erosion threat was essentially past. This information came out of the FIR study from the OSU School of Forestry research, and was available to all Management Foresters through professional publications.

I didn't know when the USFS land was planted to trees (and didn't much care). We had our tree planting crews on the burned-over ODF land in February. Also, we had been able to acquire Doug fir seed from an acceptable origin similar to the Angel site. Because we would not have enough two-year-old seedlings to plant all the burned-over State land that first winter, we broadcast the extra tree seed by helicopter in areas that were to be delayed until tree starts were available in a year or two. When that time came, the tree planters would have to watch for and allow room for the resulting seedlings that emerged. The seeded sites there were where very dense pole-sized stands had been growing. The standing skeletons after the fire gave needed shade protection for the newly germinating seedlings until they were established.

(Interesting side note: Because of the drought, so much forestland in the Pacific Northwest burned that year, that demand for young trees to replant the following spring exceeded the supply of seedling starts. In fact, during the height of the fire season of 1987, every Fire Protection Agency in the county was completely over burdened. This directly led to the explosive expansion in the use of private contract Fire Crews on fires in the region.)

True to our directive to carefully monitor our reforested units, the result of our surveys over the four years following the fire showed a good stand of young trees with little competition from grass on the state property. During that time, total growth was at about three to four feet in height.

By comparison after four years on the abutting USFS side of the property line, lush grass was about three feet tall. The tree seedlings were almost impossible to see from a distance. All the young trees were very difficult to find even when hiking through the area. The competing grass was choking out the seedlings. The tallest young trees were only at about 12 to 16 inches tall, few in number, scrawny and with poor color. I know because I went looking.

Knowing your growth site thoroughly, including every factor, is a pretty important part of forest management, most especially in SWO where almost every site is unique. There certainly are general rules, but more limited success should be expected when universal applications are in place.

With a little research and asking for local input, in reforestation it is possible to avoid a waste of manpower, time and money. A written report that some kind of action was performed may look good in the file, but doesn't mean it provided any kind of a remedy at the site. The detailed surveys and careful analysis of the site data used in our program really advanced our successes.

Silly interagency clashes showed up way too often for my taste over the years of my career. They weren't restricted to the Forest Management part of our job either. I was sent to a big fire near Mehama, east of Cottage Grove that became very disagreeable for the ODF people assigned.

The fire was on both USFS and private lands, which meant that by law ODF had a goodly share of the responsibility – or at least we were supposed to have. I think there were four of us dispatched from Grants Pass.

The State crews would control one side of the fire and the USFS the other. I was to be a Division Supervisor, a role I'd successfully worked many, many times before.

Upon arrival at the fire I was told that it was now to be a Unified Command. This was a term and type of operation I was unfamiliar with. It didn't take long to discover that the meaning (to the USFS Overhead people at least) was that Forest Service would call all the shots and everyone else kowtows. How correct the command decisions were or weren't was not part of the dialog

The first clue to me that showed this "Big Footing" of fire Overhead by USFS was when I was reassigned as a Sector Boss immediately following check-in. In a short while I learned I was working on a team under USFS Division Supervisor (DS) who was a woman. I'd held just about every position in this chain of command, so wasn't much concerned about who was doing what. It was a team-situation.

There were several women holding ODF state-level resource positions. I'd worked with many in various professional roles in Forestry, Fish and Wildlife, specialists in Entomology and Biology for example. Over many years I'd never had any problems ever with my female cohorts, and didn't even consider there might even be issues at all in this case either.

At our first team meeting the new DS shared with everyone that this was her first time in the role, and that she had little experience fighting fire except a "bit in the Midwest". Big fires were, in my years of experience, very much a team effort with a whole lot of sharing information and ideas. No one thought less of anyone asking questions or wanting input with no regard to what position they currently held. The central goal was to control the fire. The chain of command wasn't used to assert authority, it was in place to avoid confusion and facilitate the defeat of the fire.

On this fire everything seemed okay in the early team meetings. Our DC said she knew we were an experienced group and she was counting on this Overhead staff to help out by filling the gaps for her. If we had anything we felt should be done differently, to let her know. Once more this confirmed that we were working well within the norm.

But then, immediately after this the lady boss announced that due to "the rough ground and extremely dangerous conditions", all ground forces would be taken off our fire lines at 5 PM each afternoon. Only a few select engines would patrol accessible roads at night. This meant that no one would see the hand lines for easily twelve hours (from 5 PM until 5 AM) each day.

Hearing this statement was a lot like driving suddenly into a big pot-hole on what was thought to be a flat road. This type of conclusive directive was an Overhead Fire Team decision, and not hers or for anyone else at a Division Supervisor level to make.

Experienced team members kind of looked at one another, digesting this rather unusual announcement with long and deafening silence that expressed more than a little astonishment, and likely disapproval as well.

Well okay, for the time being. Trying to figure through the difference in attack philosophies, we knew there were some pretty spectacular rock formations in the area. Much of the fire was burning on ground much less difficult, especially when compared to SWO and the Coast Range. The ODF people present accepted the edict with shrugs. We knew what was normal terrain for us, often shocked others. We would probably work within this rule for now. In the long run – well things change. The boss was just learning.

And so, each of the next few days the SWO ODF people that were on this fire, walked away late each afternoon. We weren't overly surprised when we would return to the fire lines again each morning, to find as much as 70% of the hand line our crews constructed the previous day, with much sweat and effort required, was gone. Frustration began to grow.

Anyone with even the most minimal fire experience could see the loss of the line was not due to any hazardous conditions where the work was done. The loss of fire line was caused by minor slop-over events that were allowed to grow for twelve hours. They could have been easily controlled with a timely shovel full of dirt or a few swipes of a Hazel hoe as soon as it happened. But, of course, for half the time everyday no one was there with a tool in hand to get the job done.

Seeing this repeated escape problem, but trying to respect the chain of command and rule set by our DS, I offered an idea at the next Division meeting. I suggested that we try burning out our hand line as we constructed it. That way little unburned fuels would be left at 5 PM.

This time I unfortunately came to discover that, except for the Boss Lady, the rest of us weren't really part of any Overhead Team at all. Our novice leader said she needed to check with "her higher ups" about my "innovative idea". That she couldn't give an immediate yes or no, revealed a lot.

So much for relying on "her team" and for us to "just tell her." It was now obvious that our division on this fire was being micro-managed by some un-seen individual or group, whose accessibility, whereabouts and experience was to be kept a mystery to us.

Later, when the boss came back to me with her answer - which was "No burn-outs" - she said the un-named felt burnouts could not be safely controlled. At that moment I realized there was no trust by her (or by whomever she consulted) for our skills, our knowledge or the very large number of accumulative years of experience fighting fires in our own state.

I kind of lost it here, with an outburst, telling her, "Lady if you can't control your burn out, then you sure as heck can't control the main fire either!"

I didn't regret my heated comment at all, feeling she was in sore need of a blunt lesson in how things were done. Fiddling around with a big fire was dumb and dangerous. She had no response at all to my strongly voiced statement. I walked away, greatly frustrated.

When I went back to the line and since I am a stubborn type, I started to direct my crews to burn out as much of the ODF hand line areas as possible. Lo and behold, our lines held through the unguarded twelve-hour period from that night on.

It's very hard to feel respect for faceless directives when a person has personal knowledge that the rules are from a bogus source. On one hand I felt kind of like a naughty kid, but was pretty disgusted with the whole thing. Thankfully the circumstances showed the ODF personnel were about to be replaced and released from that fire.

Those from ODF that were traveling with me compared notes as we were driving home. All were in agreement in their frustration and shared disapproval about the situation they'd just left.

When I went back to work in the GP office, I told my supervisor that I did not want to be sent to a USFS administered fire in the near future. I felt their general fire fighting ideas were going the wrong direction and I wasn't going to help them do it.

I've known many well-qualified and able federal wildland fire fighters who have labored on the lines with me, and shared excellent advice back and forth while serving together as Overhead. My concern is not with any of these people. I do know that except for the smallest of fires, effective attack strategy must always be a team effort. The bigger and more difficult the fires the more important the team resolve. The accumulative years of experience is a tremendous asset that prompted the creation of the Fire Team concept in the first place.

Was the Mehama incident a fluke? From my own experience and from the tales I've heard from others who have worked multi-agency fires, I fear similar situations have happened way too many times.

Fires are tricky. No one can envision all possible scenarios. Over many decades, my many experiences with the USFS Overhead has shown that too often ranking USFS employees – often those from out of the area - feel that only others from their own agency are considered worthy team members. Maybe I've just been unlucky, and run afoul of the lemons and twits by unfortunate coincidence. I've dealt with the inappropriate arrogance of many of the federal Overhead people in project and complex Fire Camps – and sometimes with science driven Forest Management applications as well.

In Oregon more than half of the state has some kind of federal land administration, so there is no practical means to avoid contact with those organizations (except maybe by moving to Texas). So many of these encounters have followed a disturbing pattern. Not only was the basic philosophy so completely counter to that of my agency, the general attitude toward state and local people was highly disrespectful. This attitude problem has too often marginalized agency cooperative efforts. At best, good and very well-informed people have been slightly snubbed – at worst, they've been totally ignored.

It would be wonderful if I am the only person who has had this experience.

The newest and most current Oregon Department of Forestry uniform arm patch. (No more half tree!)
Courtesy of CC Dickerson

CHAPTER 42

The drought of the late 1980s kept the West Coast section of the county in a state of emergency for several years. The forests were so explosive that back-to-back fire seasons were record in length, (twice at 6 months each) with ignition of large fires in mid-winter. The two counties that made up the majority of the SWO District suffered twenty-eight larger fires over back-to-back summers, with over 158,000 acres of wildland (nearly 250 square miles) being charred.

During these very bad fire seasons, some methods of wildland firefighting rapidly evolved. A try-out of infrared tracking began to be used, as well as computer projections to try to predict potential fire behavior. Neither was a rousing success, but every little thing helped somewhat. Other technology advances in dispatch, detection, machinery and safety equipment were also introduced. The price tag on all these changes sky-rocketed.

One of the most noticeable changes, besides escalating costs and the use of more sophisticated and specific Fire Camp support materials, was the universal adoption of flame-resistant fire shirts and pants. Another innovation on large fires was the availability of pre-packed equipment kits and the storage of complete Fire Camp supply trailers available upon request.

Earlier during this trying time, an auxiliary workforce was available from privately owned lumber mills and logging companies that had trained their employees in the basics of wild fire fighting. A recession in timber industries left gaps in the traditional base of manpower available when large fires hit the region. An upsurge of the wildland fire crew-for- hire business occurred at nearly the same time. Trained crews began to travel great distances, even from thousands of miles away, to fight fires in the Pacific Northwest.

On the heels of these changes, the timber industry took a second massive blow. Repeated and tenacious litigation sponsored by the environmental community came close to total shut-down of the industry. The eventual outgrowth of the legal battles was that multiple-use forest management across hundreds of thousands of acres slowed to a crawl, and effectively stopped in several places. Capable professionals, trying to comply with restrictions that grew out of the Threatened and Endangered Species laws, struggled with rules applied with a broad brush when dealing with a site-specific science.

The predictable result has been that forest health in the Pacific Northwest has suffered greatly – much more than most lay-people can know.

SENT ALL OVER

During the very damaging fire seasons of the late 1980s that plagued the West Coast states, each of our kids had, in turn, worked for ODF, but in different ways. The older girl manned Lookout Towers in SWO four summers in a row. After the first two years on one particular mountain, she rotated as the relief for several different towers, with also a few days a month in the HQ Dispatch Center.

Our son spent one summer working on a Hotshot crew, with some time also on an engine at the remote Cold Springs guard station on the county line shared between Josephine and Douglas Counties. Our younger girl pulled a couple of weeks at one of the Project Fire Camps at Valley of the Rogue Park while holding down two other part-time jobs in town, earning money for college. Even my wife took on a role in the Dispatch Center. She manned the phones one nightshift when they were shorthanded during a lightning storm.

Peavine Mountain Lookout Tower, about forty feet from ground level. The author's daughter manned this tower and others similar to it, during summer fire seasons from 1987 through 1991.
Courtesy of ODF Grants Pass Unit

A fire that I attended during that time was located outside Bonanza, a small town in Klamath County. This was the first fire I worked as the Resource Unit Leader. As I recall, our Command Center was at the local high school, a very common location when large fires occur near rural towns.

I do not remember any unusual happenings on the fire except that I learned that the Resource Unit Leader job requires lots and lots of hours, especially in the first day or two. The daylight hours immediately after the Resource team people arrived at a Fire Camp were spent trying to get everything up-to-date. This was because many people and assets came on a fire before the Overhead Team, and were not recorded properly. Eventually the bills must be paid, so accurate records are necessary. There was a lot of catch-up necessary.

Action that continues through the duration of a project fire generates a lot of paperwork. The Fire Camp Overhead people have to be up and going extra early each day to check all resources (equipment and personnel) before anything goes onto the line or comes off as well. There are fueling needs and restocking of other equipment and supplies. This is repeated in reverse at the evening shift-change too. Medical and mechanical issues need to be addressed as well.

The extremely long hours are also used to track down additional equipment and personnel as needed and requested by the Operations group after their needs are reassessed at planning sessions. Resource personnel must be creative and tenacious in tracking down what is requested by the Planning group. There are few things that demoralize wildland Overhead as much as dealing with a growing fire when they must make-do with a lack of resources. Oh boy, do I know that feeling of both frustration and fear when no dozers or crews are available!

ODF fire commanders maintain very aggressive fire attack strategies, meaning there is an expectation that resources and assets are available and functioning on the line within the very shortest time possible. There is a lot of pride within the agency that fires handled by ODF are smaller, safer, of shorter duration, and less expensive than those of most other government agencies. ODF gets the job done.

One thing that was totally new for me on the Bonanza fire was witnessing the use of a big military type of ATV that had been adapted especially for firefighting. It supposedly would go almost anywhere and carried a supply of water with hoses and tools also aboard. It looked kind of like a cross between a tender with tracks and a snow-cat with a blade on the front. I heard that it performed well on the Bonanza Fire.

I never again saw the machine on a fire, so there may have been problems that were not widely known, or maybe it was just too expensive for whatever benefits it brought to the line. I saw one in a photograph about twenty years later.

Several succeeding summer fire seasons were particularly volatile in SWO. The Valley of the Rogue State Park was used for Fire Camp each of those years as lightning caused fires raged in SWO and became problems for several agencies far into the fall months. The initial Project Fires evolved into Complex Fires requiring inter-agency cooperation as the huge demand for virtually everything created shortages for everyone.

These fires spawned some of the first artfully done silk-screen T-shirts seen around Oregon fire camps. Nowadays such shirts are very common and even expected by crews working on bigger fires. The people doing the silk-screen work would sometimes bring a portable set-up to the fire camps and do their work on site. I know some protection people who have amassed a large collection of fire Tees, regarding them kind of like battle medals. I've proudly worn several to rag-bag condition myself.

There was a large fire north of Goldendale, a small town located in south central Washington state. Access from Oregon was by driving up the Columbia Gorge, crossing the river at The Dalles and then up the Washington side of the Columbia River to Goldendale. This rather nasty fire was giving the Washington Department of Natural Resources (WDNR) and the Bureau of Indian Affairs (BIA) some problems, and they contacted ODF for added personnel.

For me it was another opportunity to practice Resources Unit Leader skills on a multiple agency fire. There was a real effort on this fire to make use of equipment of a certain type to avoid damaging the site more than necessary. The agencies supplying Overhead personnel included very specific requests that added a level of difficulty to the Resources Unit to fulfill requests to support the fire attack plan.

In many ways the fire was much the same as Bonanza. From the beginning the Resource team was very much involved in trying to seek out specific machinery. At this fire, several dozers of a certain size were in short supply. It seems that there was a lot of large, dense timber involved in the fire, and the BIA (landowner) wanted to avoid unnecessary damage. Smaller sized dozers were having difficulty getting lines built, as they did not have the power to push the mid-sized trees over to get to bare earth for a viable fire line. On the other hand, large dozers were often too big, unable to move safely between trees, causing scaring and damage. Finding dozers that were big enough, but not too big was the very difficult goal.

On the Goldendale fire the first day was the worst. We worked twenty or even twenty-four hours continuously with very little downtime for rest or even meals. As things became more organized on the following days, things got a little better, but still involved long shifts, often sixteen hours or more. The usual was that team people would get to bed at or after mid-night, then have to be up at about 4 AM to get everything ready to present the Day Shift Operations Plan at 5 AM.

There usually was time for a quick meal after the day shift people went onto the fire lines. Then the orders from the Division Bosses would begin to arrive around 9 AM, and everybody would start on the Night Shift Operations Plan. After presenting the Night Shift plan at 5 PM, we would get some dinner and then start to receive the Orders for the next Day Shift and start preparing for the Day Shift Operations Plan.

There were debriefings and multiple meetings after each shift to discuss problems and needs or changes. In general, every waking hour was filled, and until the fire settled down. The only additional time available came out of what was set aside for sleeping – so we didn't sleep very much.

For a guy like me who worries over everything, sleep is one of the first things I consider unnecessary anyhow. I'd learned long before how to function pretty well even when sleep deprived, as long as the actual physical demand wasn't too bad. I function okay for quite a while on three or four hours of sleep. The only real fall-out was usually after I'd arrive back home, very tired and growl-ly with my wife, who didn't deserve my short-temper. She usually took it well, leaving me to sleep it off in a day or so.

The attempt at the Goldendale fire with ordering very specific equipment for a fire, foreshadowed an interesting situation I heard about that happened on a fire near Selma, Oregon a few years later.

Just building fire line wasn't good enough – even though it may have been effective in stopping the fire. The fine-tuning was more about exactly where a fire line was to be built than what kind of dozer would do the work. And I do mean Exactly.

Southwestern Oregon is awash with mini-environments. Most are diverse from the surrounding area, but not particularly unique. Others have somehow developed into true botanical and/or zoological wonders, complete with one-of-a-kind plants or insects. Not all of these are known or shown on any map. Some "ologists" get pretty dramatic about preserving such sites, and this is a good thing, but there are limitations.

At the incident I am referring to, a large fire was threatening such a location. Someone – I do not know what agency – sent a scientific specialist with the line fighters to guide the line building away from such sites during a big fire. This person's job was to direct dozers building fire line around fragile areas to prevent damage. Although that seems simple enough, the problem was that the conditions were so volatile on that fire, that the flames were not to be denied.

The whole operation was a dismal failure. The specialist was totally un-trained about fire-line placement or basic safety, and not very smart about keeping a watch-out for the big machines working nearby. They put themselves in danger, as well as the dozers and their operators. Despite all efforts, which were many, in the long run, much of the unique site was lost.

I heard of this incident from a dozer operator that was very seasoned and fire savvy. It is my opinion that the ball was dropped several times with this scenario. The agency with responsibility should have known the details about their property a lot better. These kinds of sites don't pop into place out of thin air. By the time the fire was threatening, it didn't matter much if the place was disturbed by dozers - with a possible, though slim chance of later recovery - or if the site was over-run by a hot and very destructive fire, so that regeneration was much more remote. Either way, what made the particular spot special - was gone. If they really wanted to protect it, long before the fire approached, measures should have been taken.

What I am referring to is called "defensible space". It doesn't always prevent destruction by a fire, but it's better than yelling at dozer operators when flames are just a few feet away.

The real choice should have been whether any location and construction of the fire line could stop the fire a safe distance away. Having fire line construction directed on the spot by a novice whose credentials included only an alphabet of letters behind their PhD simply is not acceptable. When the wild fire is approaching is not the time to start waving around the Endangered Species Act. Do things right before hand, and concede that sometimes things cannot be saved – even very special things.

It also seems likely that if fire-savvy people familiar with an area are helping design fire attack strategy on the Planning team, there will be input about sensitive areas to Overhead well in advance. If not, that fire is at a stage that super-human efforts will likely put crews into an unnecessarily dangerous situation. Defensive measures taken early in the game at the Overhead level will have more likelihood of success.

In regard to the Endangered Species rulings and comprehensive forest management; …. the very mixed ownership of forested land in SWO causes some regulatory problems in ODF Management. The Spotted Owl controversy may never have affected ODF lands. ODF parcels were few in acres, widely spaced and surrounded on all sides by USFS, BLM and sometimes lands in private ownership. I knew the ODF lands well. I was fairly sure there were no nesting sites on our lands, but large circles drawn around known nests on other ownerships swept ODF lands within the borders of the supposed range of the elusive raptors as well. Suddenly our properties we no longer ours to manage. Almost over-night, dictates from courtrooms and legislative offices replaced carefully designed science-based forest management plans. I have a problem with this.

One particularly hot June, SWO was suffering through a very uncomfortable heat wave. After several days of temperatures over 100 degrees, I invited my wife to accompany me for a night-time drive high into the Siskiyou Mountains to "call owls". It would give her a chance to get out of the hot valley for a few hours, and we would stop for dinner in the cooler evening on the way home.

We were armed with a pre-recorded audiotape of Spotted Owls calling to one another, and a portable tape player that plugged into the truck for power, equipped with a loud speaker. The idea was to go to several locations within a parcel of State land, play the tape for a while at a time in the evening that might be appropriate for owls to be out and about, then listen carefully if there were any answering calls to be heard.

We followed the protocol. From half-dozen or more sites we sent out the repeated unique call "hoo - - - hoo - - - hoo-hoo" through tall trees into the night. Never an answer was heard.

My wife was not very impressed by the practice for calling owls. As she freely admitted, she was just a lowly schoolteacher. Still, she did teach scientific method to her pupils. The lack of success, she said, was not surprising, and she didn't think it proved a thing about whether the owls were or weren't present.

As we discussed the scientific veracity in the process, the darkening sky quite suddenly and violently exploded into an "A-Number One" lightning bust. It liked to blow us both out of the truck!

That pretty well ended the owl hunt for the evening. We drove through a vicious downpour to the valley floor. The heavy rain continued until we were somewhere between Gold Hill and the City of Rogue River. I don't recall where or even if we stopped for dinner. My wife made the observation that if a down-strike started a fire in the vicinity of our owl-hunt, and the habitat was wiped out, would we replant? Wasn't that forest management? Her conclusion was that it appeared that decimation of the forest through forest fire was okay, but logging was not – even though logging was specific and controllable, but fire was general and unpredictable. An interesting outlook.

Later, more sophistication was applied to the owl locating activities. Over time a company offered its services to go into the woods, and both locate and tag the owls. Seems like everything gets privatized eventually.

Private enterprise really began to take hold on the numerous big project and complex fires during those years. As the big fires each summer were summarily contained, the centrally located Fire Camps at the state park near Rogue River were split up, turning the park back to I-5 travelers. One year I was assigned to a smaller part of one camp that was moved to be closer to the fire as crews moved into mop-up duties. The new site was a few miles east to a ranch property in the Sardine Creek drainage near Gold Hill.

Even with the fire in mop-up, at least 200 line-personnel were necessary to be on hand and close by. The site was large enough, mostly flat, but almost treeless. The late summer weather that year was brutal; very hot with dry winds every day. The blowing dust and lack of shade made the location less than ideal.

I was again handling Logistics for this camp as top boss. We had a great contract caterer for meals. That crew did a wonderful job of putting together delicious foods, mostly of the barbeque variety that the firefighters loved. A very large contract company also provided most of the mop-up hand crews and brought in a newly built shower-trailer for general camp use.

The hellish weather had many continuous days with temperatures well over 100 degrees. The crews were having a lot of heat related problems with blisters on feet and hands, heat exhaustion and muscle cramps. I worked closely with EMTs to make sure the firefighters had enough supplies to help the crews through the heat issues as much as possible.

We brought in a couple of presenters to talk about dealing with the heat problems at morning and evening crew briefings before the shift change. A lady EMT told the crews to make sure to make use of clean dry socks, even changing during the day if needed and to drink plenty of water. She told them if their urine was yellow and not almost clear that they were not getting enough water. I made special effort to get plenty of water out to the lines where it was easily accessible for everyone. It wasn't always cold, but it was wet.

The big contract company also brought in some nice looking, freestanding tents for their crews to get some shade. These were set up in an open field next to the other camp facilities. The tents had a rounded shape that reminded me of Geodesic Dome designs that were popular for a while for some houses being built then. The bright colors of the tents gave the camp an undeserved festive look of a big party.

When the afternoon strong winds came up it was always a mixed blessing. In the heat, the air movement felt good on sweaty skin, but everyone in the camp knew the wind brought extra problems to the fire line. The hot dry wind one day blew in stronger gusts and the shade tents were not well staked in the very hard ground. One by one off they went, rolling over and over across the open field like big bright beach balls. Several of them started casting off pieces and were wrecked. Later those that could be cobbled back together were reset, but somewhat sorry in appearance.

I believe it was the same season, though maybe the next year, that another fire assignment came to me, this time located again in far northeast Oregon. Four ODF folks, one from Coos, two guys from Medford and myself were picked up by airplane and flown to LaGrande.

There had been a doozey of a lightning bust that had worn down most of the local district crews around LaGrande. We were sent to help with mop-up on several lightning fires across their District, giving the local people a chance to rest, and if needed, respond to new fire starts.

Our group split into pairs, each assigned a different fire located far apart in the high elevation desert of Eastern Oregon. A fellow from Coos Bay, who had served on my Coos Reforestation team, was assigned with me to supervise mop up on one of the fires near Unity, a small town just past a signpost community of Hereford. Hereford wasn't much more than a wide-spot in the road.

When we arrived, our medium sized fire was only contained, and manned by a crew of about twenty. There were a few women in the group. Since mixed crews were still pretty unusual then, it is something that stands out in my memory.

Language was a bit of an issue with the crew. Only the foreman spoke any English. With his broken English and my nearly forgotten high school Spanish we barely made ourselves understood to one another. It was probably fun to watch us in conversation using impromptu sign language, miming and creative charades, each trying to be understood by the other.

Our group was assigned a local ODF employee to serve as our Logistics Officer (LO). The job is just about the same as a Resource person. Our guy was to get whatever was needed to successfully finish the assigned job. Generally, a mop-up situation like this would be pretty insignificant for a LO to be assigned, but in this case, there were some problems that were unusual.

First, in that part of Eastern Oregon water is very scarce. To address this, our LO set up an agreement with one of the landowners at the edge of the fire (also very near to our Command Center) to use water from a well on their ranch property.

I thought the water had an off and strong metallic taste like iron, and a notable sulfur smell. Under the circumstances, one can't look a gift horse in the mouth – the well was pretty much all there was available. At that time bottled water was not so easily available as now. I'm fairy sure the decision to use that well for drinking water came back to haunt me a day or two later.

Another serious problem was that we had to both feed and find over-night housing for the crew and ourselves. These are not problems that an IC usually deals with, but until our arrival, the fire was in local hands so there was no Fire Camp or any other support systems in place.

At that time, the tiny community had one café and one motel. The small, old-fashioned motel had several tiny cabins. It had just enough beds for all of us if we doubled, and sometimes tripled up with rollaway beds in the cabins. At the time I believed that we had taken up the entire motel.

We could all manage with sack lunches for mid-day, but something more substantial would be needed for an evening meal. A hearty breakfast for the next morning was also necessary. With meager basic resources available, some negotiation with local people brought about a creative solution – we would bring in unprepared food, and the little crossroads cafe would get the meals put together.

The café not only didn't have enough food, there weren't even enough cooks or servers to handle a group such as ours. The café owner called in friends and relatives to come to cook and serve. Our trusty logistics guy took off for a larger town several miles down the road in search of adequate groceries to feed 20-30 people.

Our guy eventually had to go all the way into Baker City to buy whatever groceries were needed, then deliver the goods back to the local cafe for preparation. There would be no individual choices on the menu – but that seemed okay, as everyone would be tired and hungry at the end of the shift. I don't remember what they served for dinner, but no one turned down the food.

It was agreed by our whole group at dinner that I would give everyone a morning wake-up call to all cabins at 5 AM. The plan was that we'd go back to the café for breakfast, then work the day through carrying sack lunches also provided by the café. Knowing about how long it would take to finish the mop-up with the manpower we had, we'd likely be releasing the crew in the late afternoon.

The next early morning, as planned, I went from cabin to cabin banging on doors and calling out that it was time to get up and get going.

At one of the first cabins I got a kind of odd response, something like - "Whadda ya want?" Without really thinking about it, I delivered my refrain of "It's time to get up and get going," quickly moving on to the next door.

I'd finished alerting all cabins in the line and was returning back to my own to gather my gear, when I saw a man, a stranger to me, come out of the cabin door where the wake-up call brought the strange answer. The guy coming out the door wore a loaded backpack. He climbed onto a bicycle he unchained from the wall and rode away in the pale early morning light. It appeared he wasn't part of our crew.

I felt deeply embarrassed, but it was too late to apologize. I figured he was probably thinking that this hick place sure had a really early Check Out Time. Oopps.

We had correctly calculated. Our mop up was finished that afternoon. We were able to release the crew as planned. Our early evening drive back north to LaGrande was uneventful. We met up with the other extra out-of-district ODF folks coming in from their assignment, gathering at a motel near the airport for the night. All were tired and hit the hay right after dinner.

The following morning all our people were loaded up and ready at the local airport for the flight home. Medford was our first destination taking us over Crater Lake on the way. Air turbulence was pretty bad as we flew southwest over the Cascades. Only my tightened seat belt kept me from hitting my head on the low fuselage ceiling. At times I wondered that the wings didn't rip off the little plane. It was one of the roughest flights I'd ever experienced.

At last somewhere past Crater Lake the air smoothed out and the rest of the flight seemed relatively easy… except my stomach was still jumping around. This was strange, as flying had never bothered me in the past.

The plane landed at Medford and dropped off two of our passengers. Just a few minutes were spent on the ground. Then we headed for the Grants Pass airport only about twenty minutes away.

It was about then that I realized my stomach was in more trouble than I first thought. It no longer would be ignored. The churning had gotten worse over the past half-hour or so, and was now sending out some pretty urgent distress signals. I was worried if I could hold everything together until we landed.

At the small Grants Pass Airport I thankfully stepped out on firm ground. It was a great relief to find my wife awaiting our arrival, ready to taxi me the five-mile drive home. The plane immediately took off going on to Coos Bay with the last ODF person aboard.

In the car I was increasingly uncomfortable. I just barely made it in the kitchen door at home when I was struck down with one of the worst cases of stomach cramps and a later onset of diarrhea that I can ever remember. I think it was from the water with the foul taste, but no ill reports were heard from the rest of our bunch. Maybe I was the only unlucky one. After that, bottled water seemed like a wise choice.

I do recall that earlier in my firefighting career the chance of food poisoning was a real threat for guys on the lines. There was a big run on the small coolers that came out in the early 1970s, to be used as individual lunch boxes – the boxes included re-freezable ice packs.

There was a time that eating the prepared sack lunches that were sometimes provided to fire crews back then was done with great caution. Almost everybody would poke through the usual contents, only choking down things we knew were safe – a dry peanut butter sandwich, a bag of potato chips and a couple of cookies with maybe an apple or orange for liquid relief. Cured meat sandwiches were considered risky, and anything with mayonnaise was a no-no. A personal canteen on the hip was used to wash it all down. Extra canteens were (and still are) common on most everybody's belt. None of this food was particularly appetizing, but it beat the very unpleasant alternatives of possibly passing out from lack of food, or food poisoning from tainted lunch meat.

In those days of my youth it seemed I was always slightly hungry. Being ravenously starved after every fire shift was the norm. Stopping at local eateries when released from a fire was a wonderful treat, even though we were always filthy and exhausted. We usually ate as a crew. Huge double orders were the norm for all – meals were paid with script or a chit carried by the crew boss. We never seemed to get indigestion or heart-burn, regardless of what or how much we ate. Mealtimes were great for team building – Overhead, mid-tier supervisors and guys from the line often mixed together. It was a perfect time for telling tall tales, perhaps minor pranks and just relaxing after a hard and exhausting work shift.

CHAPTER 43

By the end of the 1980s the ODF Management Unit in SWO gave me a feeling of great pride.
Useful reforestation and rehab information was regularly surveyed within an excellent system, and was proof that young tree survival was improving. Every year those trees grew older and stronger. Management problems that arose were being identified and addressed using factual evaluation instead of guesswork. Timber sales were at or near a sustainable level on every unit, while also meeting SWO Operations Plan requirements and providing an adequate operations budget for the Management section.

Fires had always been part of the management picture. As always, they involved lots of dirt, ash and hard physical work, even though I seldom worked the actual fire line any more. The urgency and potential danger that was always present was part of the over-all job of forest stewardship.

During the last decade of the century, changes in the points of emphasis in the world of humans reached far into the forest world.

A CHANGING WORLD

I am well aware that most things change over time. If I went to a Project or Complex Fire Camp today, I would see some big changes from my own experiences not so long ago. On the other hand, a lot would be the same. Some differences I experienced before I retired happened at a northern California fire. I was brought face to face with some social issues that had never been a part of my world.

The Command Center for the fire was located near the small town of Happy Camp. The Overhead Team was a mixed group called the Cal/Or Team. It was made up of ODF, CDF, BLM, and USFS personnel. The IC was our newest Grants Pass ODF headman. We had a real mixture of firefighters as well as Overhead, including USFS hand crews, CDF inmate crews, and private contract crews from all over the United States.

I'd had only occasional contact with the inmate crews on Oregon fires. They were very common in California. The excellent training of volunteer prison inmates as firefighters was a practice coming into its own. They were turning out well-trained, highly motivated and very effective crews available as line personnel across the state. The pride and camaraderie development through work on the fire line was excellent rehabilitation for the inmates.

On this assignment, I encountered two of the most unusual problems I had ever come across on a fire. One of these incidents was a jurisdictional confrontation between the CDF Inmate Guards and the USFS Law Enforcement that provided security in the Command Center and restricted public access into the fire camp.

The bottom line of this conflict seemed pretty simple - the USFS Law enforcement folks carried side arms at all times, but the CDF inmate crew guards did not carry firearms. They worked under very strict regulations that the inmate crews would not be in the vicinity of anyone that was armed.

The CDF rule was intended to prevent the inmates from being tempted to acquire any firearms while under a pretty loose supervision situation. The problem-causing issue on this fire was that the inmates going to and from their jobs on the fire line, would march in and out of the camp passing within a few feet of the Forest Service law enforcement people. CDF was not pleased.

The Overhead team had considerable discussion about this dilemma, as each agency refused to discuss any compromise. Finally, the ranking CDF rep went nose-to-nose with the USFS. A blunt statement was made, that if the Forest Service Law Enforcement folks could not stay out of the vicinity of the inmates, the CDF guards had no alternative but to take their inmate crews home. A deadline for an answer was named.

This seemed to rattle the USFS upper echelon. As the clock approached the deadline, an answer was given. USFS agreed to remove their enforcement people away from the inmates' route of travel when shift changes occurred. The crews coming and going from the camp would be avoided by the armed USFS officers.

Wow! Someone had finally stared down the biggest dog around.

A second unusual event at this fire fell directly onto me, to solve. I'm still unclear about how I was selected for the job. I was on the Overhead Team, handling an upper-level job in Planning – likely Resources Leader, though I'm not positive.

I'm not a very sophisticated guy. My one and only urban living experience was residing in the downtown area of Corvallis, Oregon while attending college during the early 1960s. The problem in question most certainly fell into the "cultural shock" category that this back-woods Oregonian had little urban contact up to that time.

A USFS crew leader was a very tall and muscular person with long blonde hair. This husky individual did not want to shower with the men, but instead requested to make use of the women's facility. The reason, the individual proudly shared, was a transgender status, which included the taking of hormone treatments and recently undergoing reconstruction surgery to acquire female gender. This was long before the military had even mentioned the "Don't Ask, Don't Tell" with cross-gender personnel issues.

There were several women in the fire camp. Fire Camp support personnel had always incorporated women, but by that time fire line crew workers also included hardworking females. Every one of the ladies objected strongly to sharing their bathing facilities with the person afore mentioned. I know this, because I had long sit-down talks with the women and heard all their comments and complaints. Their reasons were well stated and emphatic. There was absolutely no hint of any possible compromise. The single-word response to the request made was a universally stated "No."

Next, I had an equally long talk with the individual making the request. Reasons were again well stated, and I was informed of full female surgical conversion. Even an invitation to conduct a physical inspection to confirm the claim was included. I declined the offered disclosure with personal discomfort.

At that time, I was in the vicinity of my fiftieth birthday and still kind of a back-woodsy in my ways. To say I was naïve would be an understatement. I have light blonde hair and a fair complexion and often glow like a stop sign when perplexed. Throughout these discussions my face probably radiated my embarrassment in bright red. At least it felt that way. Even as a fully-grown man, such intimate conversations simply were not common in my life-time experiences. Hopefully everyone thought I had a sunburn. I was way out of my comfort zone.

After the meetings concluded, I put my personal discomforts aside. The only solution that I could figure was to have a separate shower installed for that one person. When I took this idea to the Overhead team, no one was particularly happy, but those personally on each side of the problem were accepting.

I traveled over to Eastern Oregon again, but it was a few years later. I was again Planning Section Chief on an ODF Fire Team this time. The whole existence of the Fire Camp was unusual.

I do not remember the name of this fire, but it was near Ukiah, Oregon (not to be confused with Ukiah, California). The Fire Camp was set in one of the most scenically beautiful locations I can ever recall. It was in the Blue Mountains in the central far-eastern part of Oregon beyond the high desert.

This was a very odd situation. The fire was not located in ODF jurisdiction, but was in the Umatilla National Forest several miles away. A number of the ranchers and other local residents were unhappy with the efforts being made by the federal government to protect their property, homes and rangeland.

The locals had all gotten together and made a group decision about what they wanted to be done. Their worry involved experiences they'd had in the past with USFS, and projections of what they anticipated might happen with this fire. A plea had been made to the ODF to step in and develop backup fire lines ahead of the possible USFS fire advance. The actual fire was visible in the distance, but direct contact by us was not made until fairly late into the incident.

This was a kind of touchy situation where manpower and equipment were being called in to be in readiness to assume control efforts if and when the fire crossed out of USFS ownership, thus coming under the ODF authority.

Talk about possible bureaucratic fall-out. The situation was a potential hot-potato! Somehow a major blow-up between agencies didn't happen. Remarkable.

Another reason I remember this fire very well is because I came close to freezing my rear-end every morning and night, only to sweat through the superheated mid-daylight hours.

One would expect that with more than thirty-some years experience traveling to similar call-outs all over the Pacific Northwest that I'd have known enough to bring appropriate clothing.

Well, I blew it – but I was in good company. Most of my Fire Team peers messed up too.

When I left home in the normal August hot spell for SWO, I failed to pack a heavy jacket. I'd been on several eastside fires before and never needed a thick jacket during summer months. Live and learn!

I think my traveling companion was a Forest Practices Officer from the Grants Pass ODF, but really don't remember clearly. Initially, we went to LaGrande and after meeting with the District Forester, we were redirected to the vicinity of Ukiah about seventy miles to the southwest.

We arrived at the fire camp late at night. The camp was just in the set-up stage when we were shown where we could bed down, but only for one night. We'd been advised to bring our own camp-out gear, but decided to forgo setting up our tents until the next day. It was pretty late and we'd be up and working in a few hours. Since we'd have to move to another sleeping area in the morning anyway, just using sleeping bags seemed okay for the time being.

Wrong again!

Four AM in the morning is the usual wake-up time for Overhead in a fire camp. I was groggy after only four or five hours of sleep, but roused immediately with gasps of shock. As I tossed my warm sleeping bag aside I was thoroughly bathed in a shower of frost. When I hustled to the portable toilet in flopping un-laced boots, pants and t-shirt (but no jacket), the air temperature completely disposed of any lingering sleepiness.

Returning to my belongings, I dressed in record time in my heaviest clothing. Everything had the feel of coming straight out of deep-freeze storage. The frigid morning air and no coat led to me grabbing my extra uniform shirt and shrugging it on too.

First thing on the morning agenda was the early morning briefing and hopefully some hot breakfast soon after. Some large tents were set up nearby, with propane heaters inside. Soon there was quite a group of us crowding around as close to the heaters as possible. This became the routine every morning we were there.

After the first day, and once the fire crossed onto ODF protected lands, all down-time disappeared. Since I was assigned to the Planning Section, my nighttime sleep became less each day. After that first night with ice-cold experience upon awakening, I most surely employed my tent for sleeping. I'd only brought the smaller single-man tent, so I had to sleep corner to corner. On the positive side, the very small tent at night let my body temperature and respiration pretty well heat up the limited inside space. Each following morning, I learned to slap the tent sides from the inside to knock the frost off before I tried to exit. If I forgot this little ritual, there was an uncomfortable lesson relearned, as frost would tumble down the back of my neck when I would unzip the door.

God bless those Tee shirt vendors. Using every dollar and nearly all my loose change, I put together enough money to buy a fire logo hoodie, which was a full size too small for me. It was all that was available.

That poor sweatshirt didn't come even close to my needs, stretched as it was across my shoulders and inches short at the cuffs, but when layered with all my other clothing it almost kept the frostbite at bay.

I still shivered a good-bit, but found myself just one more half-frozen Overhead person in the crowd. Just about everybody in the Fire Camp was in the same boat.

Each day would warm quickly as the sun rose. By noon it was uncomfortably warm and everyone began to peel off extra clothes. The day continued to heat up – causing most of us to develop a good sweat as we went about our demanding tasks - until the sun went down in the afternoon. Then suddenly we were all scrambling for more layers of clothes to put back on.

One of the humorous things with this fire was how everyone was trying to keep track of their extra clothes. Since most of us were wearing similar uniforms, there was an on-going shirt-shuffle depending on the time of day.

I had little time to worry about these inconveniences though, as the Planning Section is a vital and high-action part of Fire Camp. We were always busy. First after the early briefing and breakfast – mostly on the run - we were under a tight schedule to get out the Night Shift Plan ready for presentation. The afternoon briefing at 5 PM seemed to arrive immediately after breakfast. As we worked, we'd stuff some lunch in our mouths, often without even sitting down.

The team tried to be extra fast and efficient, but there was always the next morning's Day Shift Plan to be in readiness for 5 AM tomorrow. Finding time for dinner and a couple hours of sleep was hard. The exacting routine went on for 6 or 7 days before we were released to go home.

I was fifty-four that summer. By the time I arrived back home, I was pretty well wiped out. I'm not sure, but I think this was my last out-of-district fire. At that time, I was still playing slow-pitch softball and city league basketball. In fact, I even played in an Over 50/Three-On-Three team that won the regional and state-wide tournament to qualify to play an exhibition game during half-time at a Portland Oregon Trail Blazers NBA Basketball game. I was still in pretty good shape for an old guy – or so I thought.

North of I-5 between Grants Pass and Rogue River is an area that saw numerous fires during my 38 years with ODF. One hill had been the site of a good-sized fire (2591 acres) I'd worked on in 1981. Over the next twelve years scrub brush and poison oak so common to the area had filled in a lot of the burned-over land. True to the fire history of SWO, Tin Pan Peak lit up again in the early 1990s.

This fire scared the daylights out of me. The fright was perhaps even worse than that first burn-over when I was seventeen with my dad on the Merlin Hill Fire.

This time I was alone and very conscious of the grave danger I was in that day.

The fire started not too long after lunch on a really nice mid-summer day. I believe it was of human origin, but do not remember the details… something about a welding spark?

The fire had taken off from somewhere around the Rogue River Highway and ran quickly up the nearby steep slope. Even though that summer was a fairly mild fire year, the fuels were ripe and ready to go just like every year I fought on the line.

The blaze was beyond initial attack when the first crews arrived. Not long after ignition it was sending up a smoke plume visible well out Redwood Hwy all the way beyond the Rogue Community College. I know this because my wife was out that way, and later reported the impressive brown-white plume of smoke that she had seen high in the pristine blue sky as she drove toward Grants Pass from Cave Junction.

District personnel managed to handle this fire without calling for help across the state. The total size this time was bigger than 600 acres, perhaps more.

When called out, I was asked to go help with this fire not knowing what role I would be filling when I got there. When I checked in, the first duty assigned to me was to go do some ground recon – that is, go look things over and report on the fuels, potential terrain issues and what the fire was doing and might do in the next few hours.

Sizing up the burning hillside, I grabbed my radio and a water bottle from my management rig and headed off up the east flank (City of Rogue River side) of the fire. I tried to stay close enough to see what was happening but stay far enough away, I thought, to be safe. The hillside there is steep but not horrible.

As I was nearing the head of the fire, I came to a good-sized ravine descending from my left to my right. The upper part of the fire above me was nearing this crease in the terrain, so I quickly crossed to the other side. I didn't realize a ruffling of air was building into a breeze.

I had just turned to start up the other side of the ravine when I saw something that put the Fear of God in me. The fire had spotted ahead of me, both above and below my new position. This wasn't uncommon in this slot that the Rogue River passed through near these hills – something I knew too well. The spot fires were about 200 yards ahead of the main fire.

Immediately I realized I could not get between the two spots on the far side of the ravine. Each was spreading very fast. They would soon join up, forming a dead-end blocking my proposed route in that direction. The terrain and wind were controlling the fire's movement. Usually my assessment of what a fire might do was accurate, but I'd misjudged this time. Unless I got myself out of this location PDQ, my long, safe career in fire protection would come to an abrupt and unhappy end.

I quickly did a scan in all directions. I could not retreat back downhill because the main fire and the lower spot fire were nearing each other there. I was in a bad place with few choices left.

My brain was firing on all cylinders, both gathering information and working through the problem of getting off this hillside without personal damage. I kept moving the whole time. I do not believe I ever paused or delayed my movements during all my considerations.

I saw the ground fuels were mostly fallen madrone leaves, pine tree needles, and low grass with a few native shrubs here and there. The larger stuff was mid-sized and smaller oaks and Madrones, spread out, with some very thick brushy areas here and there. The small stuff burned fast, but not so hot. The bigger fuels were slower, but burned with much more heat.

I felt that if necessary, I could put on a burst of speed and run through the main fire edge where the fuels were low and thinner. If I safely got into the inside of the burned perimeter, where most low fuels would be nearly consumed, I might be okay. This was a risky, but possible choice on a very short list.

A fast-moving fire in local fuels.
Courtesy ODF Grants Pass Unit

I took a moment to radio the command center, telling them my situation and stating that I might be trapped.

My brain devised a plan as I spoke. I would stay in the ravine or near its edge and race as quickly as I could to the top of the ridge. If I could beat the head of the fire to the top, I would probably be okay.

On the other side of the hill there should be other additional escape choices offered – hopefully safer and better for me.

If I saw that I could not get to the top ahead of the fire, I would try to go through the burning front and into the burned area, but only as a last resort.

My words to the CC weren't even totally out of my mouth as I increased my pace and length of stride. I watched the fire moving on both sides of me with great focus as I still processed information.

I scanned everything in all directions. Were the fuels changing? How about the wind direction? Was the slope getting steeper, or easing up? Were there any other spot fires in my chosen path to safety? How were my legs doing?

If I had a bout of leg cramps hit me now, I was done. If any other variables changed, I wanted to know where and when to change plans.

In some places I moved to the lip of the draw to avoid more volatile fuels, but tried to keep to as direct a route uphill as possible.

For a guy my age, my legs were still strong. Almost everyday for about thirty plus years my management job required hiking wildland slopes and hillsides. Many were quite steep and unforgiving. During Fire Season, I was still able to sling dirt while building an effective fire line. I did my share during tree-planting season in the winter months. The leg cramps were the wild-card.

On this day I urgently called on this lifetime of physical conditioning and stamina, mixed with more than a little bit of respectful fear of that fire. Together, these assets helped me maintain a very brisk speed, almost trotting up the steep ground.

That I kept the pace all the way to the top is remarkable. I beat the moving fire to the ridge-top with time to spare. As I moved into the clear, leaving the fire behind and on the other side of the ridge, huffing and puffing, I didn't pause to catch my breath. I intended to get the heck out of Dodge!

Once over the top, I turned to the west and still kept moving. I called to the Command Center again, breathless, but still moving. I gave my quick report on the fire – and (thankfully) shared that I was in the clear. As if the spoken words confirmed the validity of my safety, I had to stifle a wry grin.

The danger was over. I wasn't even dirty – though sweaty, probably more from fear than exertion. Continuing to the west until I had totally cleared the head of the fire, I turned back downhill on the west flank and returned to the Command Center. When I arrived, my recon report described what I had observed - the terrain, the fuels and the movement of the fire.

I've always been super careful, and that, combined with a probably undeserved helping of good luck, had allowed me to escape significant injuries during a long career in a sometimes very dangerous job.

Still I was getting kind of old for this super-human stuff. A guy can only tempt fate so many times.

Over the next few years Forest Management work filled most of my time. I put energy into trying to consolidate the ODF parcels in the Southwestern District, and into educational efforts promoting sound Forest Management concepts. The general work done was pretty routine, including the occasional fire calls. I had a lot of experience and training with fires, but my body was on the wrong side of fifty years in age. I knew I was slowing down and respected that an ending was not far into the future.

I officially retired as of February 27, 1999. I continued working by contract for another six months, training my Management replacement and filling the ever-present gaps among the ranks of the Forest Practices enforcement personnel. My final "last day" was August 31, 1999.

I went home to the now quiet house my wife and I had built on the far west 10 acres of the old farm where I grew up near Hugo. My wife retired from her Extension Service job a couple of years later to join me full time.

Mostly I don't miss the long hours, the many problems, or the bureaucratic and political squabbling that has invaded the forested workplace. I do miss the great people I had the privilege of working with every day. My daily life became slower and the problems less complex than when I was with the Oregon Department of Forestry – but I don't regret any of it even a little bit.

Still in decent shape and health at retirement, I had a really good run – better than many.

POSTSCRIPT - RETIREMENT

A year or so following the death of my mother in 2001, we sold our Hugo holdings. The rest of the original farm was sold about a year later. On the property there are now two pot grows. One on part of my dad's old hay field and the other on a part of the property near the house we built. My parents would not have been pleased.

My wife and I bought just over 144 acres of badly run-down ranchland twenty-some miles to the north where we could run our cattle. The property is near some of the forested State Lands I managed.

The purchase gave us a lot to do for several years. We built about four miles of fence, a metal shop building, did considerable repair and improvement to the 1927 farmhouse, built a new barn (since the old barn was not salvageable), built a new house, and a pole type out-building we use as a garage. With some help, I built four small ponds and established a buried pipeline to provide irrigation to our fields from the nearby creek.

The Author and one of his younger granddaughters explore our Quines Creek ranch.
Photo courtesy of CC Dickerson

Our oldest daughter and her family moved into the old house to be near and help with the farm. My wife and I moved into the new smaller house when it was completed.

After a few years we were able to slow our pace a bit and became more involved in local community activities. I became a member of the Board of Directors for the local rural volunteer fire department and served as the Chairperson for 2 years. My wife served on the local School Board for about 6 years. We both worked to get an FFA (Future Framers of America) Chapter established at Glendale High School and I served on that advisory committee for several years.

In 2012, I designed and established an Outdoor Education Day for Glendale 6th graders and those from other nearby elementary schools. Generally, somewhere around eighty to one hundred students attend this annual event. Small groups of students attend personalized presentations in rotation by natural resources professionals covering several topics. The lunchtime has been a special presentation by Wildlife Images Rehabilitation Center staff along with live raptors and other birds.

For the two tree-planting seasons following the Douglas Complex Fire that burned very near the City of Glendale in 2013, I arranged for high school students to assist with replanting part of the burned-over ground under ODF instruction.

The author makes a presentation for school children at the local annual
Sixth Grade Outdoor Education Day – 2015.
Courtesy of CC Dickerson

During the years my nearby grandchildren attended school, I ran the scoreboard for all home softball games and coached high school Girls Varsity Basketball for two seasons. Now that our local grandchildren have graduated from high school, we have become more casual spectators at area youth sports events. We've sold the cattle and are taking on quieter pursuits.

This time we expect to really behave like retirees.

THE END

(Maybe)

PHOTOGRAPHS PROVIDED BY THE AUTHOR

Clay Dickerson - Following title page, Pic #2 - Oregon map; Chap. 1 - Pic #44 – Mount Sexton as seen from Hugo farmland belonging to the author's family 1945-2003; Chap. 3 - Pic #5 - Author's father with Merlin/Hugo patrol engine; Chap. 3 – Pic #6 - Merlin/Hugo patrol engine & crew; Chap. 5 – Pic #12 - Author at age 18 years, just arrived at home after first all-night fire; Chap. 11 – Pic #18 - ODF uniform arm patch circa 1966; Chap. 20 – Pic #48 - Author and wife, July 1966; Chap. 23 – Pic #21 - Author next to patrol engine with wife and newborn daughter; Chap. 28 – Pic #23 - Roosevelt Elk; Chap. 32 – Pic #26 - Helicopter working a management spray project; Pic #27 - ODF uniform arm patch circa 1971; Chap. 33 – Pic #28 - Author working a fire on night shift; Chap. 34 – Pic #29 - Author mowing hay about 1976; Chap. 41 – Pic #41 - ODF uniform arm patch circa mid-1990s; Chap. 43 - Pic #47 - Author and one of his young grandchildren exploring a new fall day; Pic #45 - school children at 6th Grade Outdoor Day presentation.

OTHER PHOTO AND GRAPHICS ACKNOWLEDGEMENTS

A special Thanks to the people below who went out of their way to produce or find photographs for this publication.

Elizabeth Whitaker – Chap. 35 – Pic #30 - ODF Grants Pass Unit HQ after 1980.

Travis Moore of The Grants Pass Daily Courier – Back cover - Author at retirement.

Alan Maul of ODF Fire History Museum, Salem, Oregon – Chap. 1 – Pic #3 - ODF Grants Pass Unit HQ circa 1950; Chap. 9 – Pic #16 - Hand trail crew building fire line; Chap. 25 – Pic #22 - ODF Astoria District Office taken several years after author moved from the area; Chap. 31 – Pic #25 - Coos FPA Office where space was shared with ODF Elliott Management staff; Chap. 35 – Pic #32 - Medium sized helicopter making a water drop on a fire; Chap. 39 – Pic #37 - Burned-over dozer, Meadows Fire.

Personnel of ODF Southwestern District Grants Pass and Medford Units Chap. 2- Pic #4 - ODF Grants Unit HQ circa 1961; Chap. 4 – Pic #7 - ODF Grants Pass Unit crew house, Pic #8 - A newer patrol engine & crew at HQ, Pic #9 - GP Unit Forester John Langrell; Chap 5 – Pic #10 - Fire blowing over a roadway, Pic #11 - Dozer attacking a fire; Chap. 6 – Pic #13 - WWII vintage bomber dropping fire retardant; Chap. 7 – Pic #14 - A fire in mixed brush and trees; Chap. 8 – Pic #15 - Sexton Mt. Lookout; Chap. 10 – Pic #17 - Ground and ladder fuels feeding a fire; Chap. 11 – Pic #19 - Brushy fuels burning; Chap. 12 – Pic #20 - A crown fire; Chap. 28 – Pic #24 - A Bald Eagle; Chap. 35 – Pic #31 - Smokey the Bear at a school visit, Pic #33 - Training a Heli-tack crew; Chap. 36 – Pic #34 - A patrol engine about 1978; Chap. 37 – Pic #35 - The Underside of Slick Rock Bridge; Chap. 38 – Pic #36 - A patrol engine about 1983; Chap. 39 – Pic #38 - McCollough Shelterwood management project; Chap. 40 – Pic# 39 - Heli-torch ignition; Chap. 40 – Pic #40 - Yale Creek sale after an escape fire; Chap. 42 – Pic #42 - Peavine Mt. Lookout Tower; Chap. 43 – Pic #43 - A wildland fire.

Trevor O'Hare of Trevor O'Hare Photography, Bend, Oregon – Front Cover photo - A wildland fire near Crater Lake, Oregon.

Also, warm appreciation to all the members of my family and friends that helped with the search for photographs, proof reading, sharing recollections, creative ideas, and in so many other ways through the years.

ABOUT THE AUTHOR

CLAY DICKERSON's childhood was on a small farm in Southwestern Oregon. His daily chores were those common to farm-life, and his outdoor lifestyle included hunting and fishing, with much free time in the woods. After high school he began a lifetime of hard forest work including fighting wildfire, at first earning money to finance college and later to support his family. A college degree led to supervision of reforestation activities of State Forest lands in the rugged Oregon Coast Range Mountains for nine years, while summers required continued suppression work on wildland fires.

A job transfer allowed his family to return to the family farm, where his children might have similar experiences as in his own youth. The family raised hay and beef cattle. He became the Forester Management Unit Forester for the Oregon Department of Forestry Southwest Oregon District in 1978, and held that position until his retirement in 1999.

Over the years at one time or another, his father, brother, all three children, his wife, brother-in-law, and two oldest grandchildren have worked fire lines or in support rolls on fires in Oregon. Dickerson's long career as a Professional Forester involved comprehensive, well-balanced multiple use Forest Management applications, including work on wildland fires in various on-the-line and overhead capacities all over the State of Oregon, as well as in northern California and eastern Washington.

His very active retirement has combined raising cattle, playing and coaching youth and adult team sports, volunteer opportunities on a variety of governing boards, teaching children and adults about forest science, and occasional consulting roles.

CPSIA information can be obtained
at www.ICGtesting.com
Printed in the USA
LVHW052041060219
606663LV00001B/1/P

9 781532 063350